Praise for *Smile When You're Lying*

. . .

"Impassioned, funny, and uniquely honest." —*Esquire*

"A rare victim's-eye view into the world of travel marketing and the nervous, unmoored corporate weenies who populate it . . . fascinating reading." —*The Washington Post*

"Thompson is the real thing, a travel writer in the sense that Mark Twain or Hunter S. Thompson was, and Redmond O'Hanlon is. He's a travel writer like Anthony Bourdain is a food writer. He's a travel writer for people who don't much like travel writing." —*The Oregonian*

"*Smile When You're Lying* could do for the travel industry what *The Tipping Point* did for the tipping point industry." —Joe Queenan

"(Thompson's) prose is quick and witty; it's like sitting down over a beer with the most experienced traveler you'll ever meet." —*Aspen Times Weekly*

"My three favorite travel writers of all time are Robert Louis Stevenson, Graham Greene, and Chuck Thompson. *Smile When You're Lying* not only tells the truth about the travel-writing racket, it gets to the heart of some of the travel industry's best-kept secrets." —Kinky Friedman

"More than confessions of a veteran gallivanter . . . an indictment of those who would prettify the world . . . full of trenchant truisms." —*Los Angeles Times*

ALSO BY CHUCK THOMPSON

Smile When You're Lying

The 25 Best World War II Sites: European Theater

The 25 Best World War II Sites: Pacific Theater

to hellholes and back

to hellholes and back

bribes, lies, and the art of extreme tourism

• • •

CHUCK THOMPSON

A HOLT PAPERBACK

HENRY HOLT AND COMPANY • NEW YORK

Holt Paperbacks
Henry Holt and Company, LLC
Publishers since 1866
175 Fifth Avenue
New York, New York 10010
www.henryholt.com

A Holt Paperback® and ® are registered trademarks of
Henry Holt and Company, LLC.

Portions of chapter 7, "Sex, Rain, and 100 Percent Cotton," were
previously published in a different form in *Outside* magazine.

Names and certain identifying characteristics of some people
described in this book have been changed.

Library of Congress Cataloging-in-Publication Data

Thompson, Chuck.
  To hellholes and back : bribes, lies, and the art of extreme
tourism / Chuck Thompson.—1st Holt paperbacks ed. 2009.
    p. cm.
  ISBN: 978-0-8050-8788-8
  1. Voyages and travels. 2. Developing countries—Description
and travel. 3. Adventure and adventurers. 4. Thompson,
Chuck—Travel. I. Title.
  G465.T593 2009
  910.4—dc22

                                                    2009014459

Henry Holt books are available for special promotions and
premiums. For details contact: Director, Special Markets.

First Holt Paperbacks Edition 2009

Designed by Kelly S. Too

Printed in the United States of America

1 3 5 7 9 10 8 6 4 2

Contents

• • •

to hellholes and back

. . .

Introduction:
The Four Horsemen of My Apocalypse

I thought Americans were supposed to be stupid about these things. Ignorant of foreign cultures. Disinterested in international affairs. This, I've always figured, was particularly true of Africa—Americans presumably have trouble distinguishing between the Kalahari, Sahara, and Luxor on Las Vegas Boulevard. Jay Leno hits the streets to prove what a bunch of insular jackasses we are, and even someone like me, who's never once laughed at that condescending bit, has to admit he's got a pretty deep reservoir of stars-and-stripes stupidity to trawl.

Which is why it surprises me that when I begin e-mailing friends and family about my upcoming trip to the Democratic Republic of the Congo, I receive in reply a storm of dire and frighteningly specific warnings. Americans, at least my Americans, appear to be quite impressively informed.

From buddy Dave Malley: "The current *Atlantic Monthly* has a thing about a British biologist who died in the Congo after contracting an illness from monkey feces. Thought you might want to know."

From sister Amy: "You're aware there's a civil war going on there, right?"

From Glasser in Japan, a man hardened to life's inequities first as a foot soldier in Vietnam, then as a jewelry salesman in South Central Los Angeles: "The Congo, and you may quote me, is Hell. Only without the interesting people. Pay for a week at the nearest rifle club. Train on an M16 or AK-47. Takes a monkey about two days on either one to begin shooting like Clint Eastwood. Your M16 tends to jam up if you don't keep it clean, but AK ammo weighs a ton, something to think about when you're humping through a croc-infested swamp with your mortally wounded local guide slung over one shoulder. But don't even think about bringing guns into the country. They're cheaper at the Kinshasa 7-Elevens."

From cousin Michelle, intrepid sufferer of Peace Corps and invasive-parasite abuse: "Do you know about guinea worms? They bore into your skin, then burst and release larvae and infecting cyclops, better known as 'water fleas.' If the worm is wrapped around a tendon or so deep that it's not possible to extract it surgically, you have to wait until 'normal emergence' occurs. This means waiting for the worm to burrow out on its own. When I was in Senegal I saw a woman with multiple worms in her leg, breast, and vagina."

From Dr. Bahr, a man I'd claim as my personal physician had I not personally witnessed his collegiate heyday. "In lieu of your latest effort to impress I don't know exactly who with your carefree spirit of misadventure, I'm pasting some information from the State Department's Web site: 'The Department of State again warns U.S. citizens against travel to the Democratic Republic of the Congo (DRC). Armed groups and demobilized Congolese troops in parts of the country, including Eastern Congo, are known to pillage, carjack, and steal vehicles, kill extra-judicially, rape, kidnap, and carry out military or paramilitary operations. Travelers are frequently detained and questioned by poorly disciplined security forces at numerous roadblocks throughout the country. Public Health concerns also pose a hazard to U.S. citizen travelers for outbreaks of deadly viruses and other diseases which can occur without warning and many times are not rapidly reported by local health authorities. During the months of August–October, lab confirmed cases of Ebola were found in the Luebo area of Kasai Occidental Province.'"

Perhaps because he wastes more on-the-job Internet time than anyone who doesn't have an addiction to fantasy football or two girls, one cup, my infamous Asia expat buddy Shanghai Bob began slamming me with daily e-mail warnings featuring links to archived *New York Times* stories bearing headlines such as "Rape Epidemic Raises Trauma of Congo War" and "African Crucible: Cast as Witches, Then Cast Out." The latter story dealt with a contagion of Congolese and Angolan children who were being persecuted as witches. One concerned father reportedly injected battery acid into his twelve-year-old son's stomach in an effort to encourage the boy's evil spirits to find a new home. Later, Bob would keep me informed of proceedings concerning a roundup of Congolese sorcerers accused of shrinking men's penises with special curses.

When I told him I couldn't possibly keep up with his force-feeding regimen of Dark Continent fearmongering, Shanghai Bob wrote me a note that summed up, if in less urbane terms, the prevailing attitude of everyone from my mother to my dental hygienist. (Even the relentlessly chipper Tete from Togo exclaimed, "Africa, it's all bribes!" while scraping my plaque.)

"I'm not trying to scare you, fuck with you, or be a wiseass in any way," Shanghai Bob declared, drawing upon his complete reservoir of personal empathy. "But I think you may want to be kept informed about these things as your trip nears. As Father O'Flaherty always counseled us, there's no shame in pulling out, even at the last minute."

This is the problem with having a lot of educated, liberal friends. Every one of them has an encyclopedic knowledge of injustices and outrages around the world—Congo, East Timor, charter schools—and jump at any chance they get to tell you how bad everything is out there.

More disconcertingly, my friends seemed to be right. Or at least consistent with expert opinion. A few weeks before going public with my plans for a Congo holiday, I'd sought the advice of a highly regarded BBC documentary filmmaker named Sam Kiley, himself on his way back to the Congo to shoot more footage in the North Kivu region, the place where that aforementioned civil war was raging.

I had no interest in being an eyewitness to war, but North Kivu had caught my attention for its mountain gorillas and position at the center of Africa's Great Lakes region. As a friend of a friend, I thought Kiley might be a good guy to tag along with for my first trip to Africa. He immediately rejected my plea to join his expedition, then did his best to discourage me from going it alone. From a twenty-minute phone conversation, here are a few of the more memorable moments:

"Congo's not the end of the world, but it's bloody close. As deep bongo as it can be."

"You can get eaten in the Congo."

"You mean by animals?"

"No, by humans. Try to stay off the menu, mate."

"You're kidding, of course."

"No, I'm quite fakking serious."

"Congo is very advanced fakking horror. Think Marlon Brando in the final scene of *Apocalypse Now* and then take some acid and you're close to it. I'm properly not kidding."*

"All Eastern Congo is a front line. A full-on war is going on."

"It's not at all rare to come across eight- and ten- and twelve-year-old boys with AK-47s using someone else's intestines to set up a roadblock."

I wanted to go to Africa because I didn't want to go to Africa. And I didn't want to go to Africa for many excellent reasons. Malaria. Cholera. Bilharzia. Yellow fever. Genocide. AIDS. War. Famine. Rebel attack. River blindness. Lions, hyenas, and other wild animals that occasionally maul and kill even dedicated pacifists. Eighteen hours in the coach cabin of an airplane. The aforementioned worms that nest in human sex organs. National dishes such as "foufou" that cousin Michelle reported on from her latest posting in western Africa as "gelatinous balls of yam or cassava with a thin sauce on top, often slimy okra."

---

* I love idiomatic British-English. Deep fakking bongo. Properly not kidding. Discussions with people who talk like this always make me feel about ten IQ points smarter. I easily would have been one of the hillbilly rustics suckered in by the Duke and King in *Huck Finn*.

All of which made me want to go. Not counting the eighteen hours.

Allow me to explain. While I'm admittedly a person who cowers instinctively from tests of individual resolve, I am at the same time strangely attracted to them. Like walking a little too far out onto a ledge or agreeing to speak at Rotary Club luncheons (where my little act goes down about as well as a hair in your throat), I often do things that I absolutely know I shouldn't. The Thompson coat of arms is, after all, a man being handed a beer while someone else twists his arm.

But beyond being an admitted contrarian—and, yes, part of the reason I'd chosen the Congo was because almost no one else would—I believe there's value in doing things the mind cautions against. Two episodes from my adolescent years come to mind. One winter, I agreed to play the part of the little drummer boy in a local Mormon Christmas pageant. (Juneau was small and apparently there were no Mormons in town who could keep 4/4 time.) Several years later, I took mushrooms with my reprobate friend Roger Sinclair and attended a midnight showing of *An American Werewolf in London*. Trusted advisers had counseled me against becoming involved with either mushrooms or Mormons, and upon making the decision to enter into both of these strange worlds, I was instantly consumed with anxiety and regret. Nevertheless, I plowed through both experiences, found one only slightly more bizarre than the other, and both, once the scarifying events were behind me, at least partially rewarding.

Challenging one's assumptions doesn't necessarily mean refuting them. I became neither a Latter Day Saint nor addicted to psilocybin. Sometimes it's just as valuable to reaffirm your belief system as it is to disprove it.

The larger point is that one should never let one's own

moral compass go unchecked for long. The world changes too fast. The worst thing is to become stagnant. Comfort is the enemy of creativity. Or, if you prefer your searching personal philosophy from Saul Bellow (who will appear again shortly in the unexpected role of traveler's aid in Africa), "Trouble, like physical pain, makes us actively aware that we are living."

We've done a lot to eliminate trouble and physical pain in this country. Like yours, my life is and largely has been too easy. I wouldn't have said or believed this at twenty-five, an age at which I believed high school geometry, female rejection, mean bosses, Ronald Raygun, and the inexplicable hot-rotation popularity of Duran Duran counted as legit personal traumas. In retrospect, I see that I've had far too little to complain about. Aside from the fourteen thousand exposures to "New Moon on Monday" and "The Reflex."

We've become soft. Like Jell-O. You. Me. Everyone. America. Americans. Too fragile to breath in someone else's cigarette smoke, ride a bike without a helmet, or play Texas hold 'em without a pair of wraparound sunglasses. We're turning into a nation of fearful twats, obsessed with supposedly tragic childhoods, lousy parents, career disappointments, social outrages, political grudges, and long lists of personal grievances that until recently were collectively known as the human fucking condition.

Our edges have been beaten away by trophies handed out just for showing up; schools that no longer make kids memorize multiplication tables; doctors who pass out brain meds like Skittles; and therapists who indulge the public's every impulse to whine and wallow in self-obsession. The pussification of America, promoted by corporate empires with an interest in keeping the nation locked in a state of suspended me-me-me childhood, is especially insulting to anyone with a memory that stretches back to a time when comic books and superheroes were cultural mainstays only for those under twelve years old and our national leaders didn't use words like "bad guys" to describe criminals, misfits, and every third unlikable foreigner.

Years ago in the Philippines, I hired a small catamaran to take me a few miles offshore to Hundred Islands National Park. The first mate was the captain's son. Eight years old. The kid ran around hauling jugs of fuel, dragging anchor chains, rigging fishing gear, and tying half hitches and bowlines like Vasco da Gama. I have no doubt that boy is running his own charter operation today; and that if his apprenticeship had taken place in the United States, social workers would have seized him from the abusive father before he'd had time to learn port from starboard.

If I sound angry it's because I'm no less culturally flabby than anyone else. My problem is that I can't afford to be. For travel writers, maintaining an intrepid reputation is vital in the never-ending quest for more work, and my biggest professional secret is an ugly one: much of the world scares me. Or worries me. Or, at the very least, repels me for no better reason than the extreme physical and social discomfort I'm certain a visit will require. There aren't supposed to be limits on "adventure travel," but until now I've privately kept a list of not-for-me destinations where beyond disease, crime, filth, intestinal viruses, and the possibility of rectal bleeding, I'm equally turned off by prejudices against pushy locals, monstrously bad food, paralyzing constipation, and hotel beds with only one pillow (I require two, minimum).

For several years I've been appearing periodically on a Canadian radio program hosted by an amiable iconoclast named Andrew Krystal. Like many others, Krystal reads my dispatches from places like Saipan and Kursk and assumes the best/worst of me. This has led him on occasion to introduce me to the "Krystal Nation" as "Indiana Jones's long-lost son." My limp protests to these pronouncements are meant to project an appealing, boyish humility—"Heh-heh, not really, Andy, but I'll admit that brush with the locals in Pago Pago was a close one." In fact, they mask the stuttering false modesty of a semifraud.

International competence is the stock in trade I've sold to editors and publishers for years, but like anyone else I'm given to wondering how one *does* manage to traverse the Congo, one of the largest countries in Africa, when it barely has a functioning government or infrastructure? More worrisome than my own wherewithal is the competence of others. Don't stories of airplanes crashing in remote jungles, tourist-laden buses plunging down ravines, and overloaded ferries sinking to the bottom of oceans come all too frequently from the more "exotic" parts of the world? Is it really wise to travel overland in places where car horns double as brake pedals?

And these are just the obvious concerns. Upon reflection, Africa proves to be the mere tip of a blade of personal paranoia that widens like a bloody cleaver on a butcher's block. Beyond the continent of Robert Mugabe and Idi Amin are dozens of places I've heretofore avoided even more assiduously than Dave Matthews albums.

I can probably be pardoned for not getting around to Yak Heritage Days in northern Mongolia or autumn leaf peeping in New Hampshire, but for a guy who's spent years passing himself off as a well-rounded traveler, three other locations stand out as the most shameful holes in an otherwise respectable resume. You wouldn't think that a man in my position could have managed to avoid not only Africa but also give the slip to India, Mexico City, and, perhaps most astonishing of all, Walt Disney World. Yet year after year I have. And happily.

Not only have I been to none of these traveler touchstones, I've diligently avoided them, and for mostly lame reasons. My fear of AIDS, for instance, is dwarfed by my fear of standing in line in the Florida sun next to rotund people from New Jersey and Texas who steadfastly refuse to discipline their little Jacobs, Justins, and Caitlins while they run off their Adderall highs in Frontierland.

And food. Being a picky eater is another of my more emasculating confessions. Few pretrip worries weigh on me like the prospect of being the haole guest of honor at some native banquet presented with a steaming bowl of goat ovaries and baked kittens while a klatch of locals watch in anticipation to see if I merely love the national cuisine, or really love it! Or, worse, figuring out what exactly the discerning palate falls back on in countries where chipotle flavoring has yet to make significant inroads.

But this unholy quartet of locations doesn't merely signify my personal hellhounds. Each of them, and for different reasons, are places many Americans spend their lives turning their backs on. Presumably for good reason. Of the dozens of people I've known who have survived India, for instance, not one, *not one*, has returned without some horror story involving a no-holds-barred bout with a gastrointestinal ailment that rendered them half-blind for days on a damp cot in some reeking backwater "hotel" praying for a merciful and speedy death.

"It's practically a given that a visiting gut is going to go south at some point on a trip to India." This is the lead sentence of the story that introduced me to India's most widespread reprisal to tourists, a piece in *Escape* magazine by a writer named Andrea Gappell whose Indian stomach cramps were so painful that she made an emergency visit to a doctor in Agra. The doctor informed her that her appendix was about to burst. After emergency surgery and eight days tethered to an IV drip—"Rows of Indian patients stared at me as they lay flat on sheetless mattresses in the dingy ward"—Gappell was released from the makeshift clinic, only to be informed by locals that the doctor who'd operated on her was notorious for running the old "Your appendix is about to burst; we must operate at once!" scam on panicked travelers felled by severe food poisoning.

Colorful anecdotes like this one are a big reason I've never applied for an Indian visa, despite being a big fan of any dish, movie, or stripper with "masala" in the name. No one wants to spend half his vacation laid out in Bangalore. Yet why go to India and not eat the food? Easier just to stay home.

Aside from being a digestively explosive travel destination (though *Condé Nast Traveler* runs stories about India all the time, so how bad can it be?), India is even more intimidating as a political and economic entity. The value of its stock market doubled in the mid-2000s. In 2007, the *Economic Times* reported an annual 14 percent rise in Indian manufacturing, the largest national growth on the planet. The country's stable, well-regulated banks largely escaped the global financial crisis of 2008–2009. *BusinessWeek* and *The Economist* routinely refer to India as a tech giant and predict the balance of power in the world's economy shifting from the United States to China and India in the coming decade.

On a pragmatic level, it's true that I'm worried mostly

about myself, but it does seem to me that now is an opportune time to get a close-in look at the challenges we as a nation are up against in the years to come: new diseases; new rivals; new enemies; entitlement seekers pouring across our borders; armies of hypermotivated, tech-savvy workers battling an anachronistic American labor pool whose most potent job-market skill is the self-esteem acquired in "fun" classrooms and on sports fields where everyone's a star and no one keeps score; an international up-from-the-gutter work ethic that trounces "follow your dreams" with "suck it up, get used to a little disappointment, and find a goddamned job that doesn't play to your dumb ambition to program video games and produce hip-hop records." If, as it certainly feels, the world is closing in around us, it seems worth the trouble to have a look at who and what is on the way.

All this is alarming enough and I haven't even factored in America's diminishing reputation abroad. During the week I began planning my daunting year of travel, the reigning Miss USA, a Tennessee stunner named Rachel Smith, was actually booed in a packed theater in Mexico City. Lustily. Not lustfully.

I don't care what side of the political divide you rattle your saber on or what you think of the wondrous Obama ascension, a moment like this demonstrates far more than any flag burning, effigy bashing, or orchestrated protest just how far America has plummeted in the world standings of likable countries (at the moment fighting for last place with North Korea). When one of the quantifiably hottest women out of a population of three hundred million from a country known for flashy displays of its most lurid perversions can parade her perfectly hard, twenty-two-year-old, multiethnic, beauty-queen, bikini-wrapped body in front of an arena filled with partying Mexicans and get booed, you can't help wondering what kind of reception *you're* going to get when you accidentally wander into the barrio at two in the morning with your head spinning with tequila and Los Lobos lyrics.

If you pay attention to media drumbeats, of course, you already know that testy pageant crowds are the least of Mexico travelers' concerns. The latest orgy of yanqui panic, fueled by more of those totally reliable State Department travel warnings and a blanket recommendation from university presidents around the country advising students to avoid Mexico during spring breaks, feels less like sober assessment and more like a concentrated effort to paint our next-door neighbor as a terrorist narco-state. Current conventional wisdom is that Mexico doesn't simply present the United States with a drug and illegal alien problem, but with a genuine security threat. From *Face the Nation*'s dyspeptic Bob Schieffer to *Rolling Stone* magazine—there's actually less of a difference between the two than you'd imagine, these days—there's been a tremendous effort to lump the land of margaritas and mariachi in with the likes of Iran, Pakistan, and Al-Qaeda.

Written by Guy Lawson, the *Rolling Stone* feature kicked off with an account of a violent drug raid in Mexico City carried out by a hundred federal agents wearing ski masks and armed with assault rifles. It claimed: "The real front in the War on Drugs is not in cities like Tijuana and Ciudad Juárez, or in the Sierra Madres, where drug kingpins hide out, but in the corridors of power in Mexico City." Typically, efforts to scare Americans away from Mexico have focused on crime around the U.S.-Mexico border. Now Lawson and plenty of others would have us believe that extreme toxicity also runs wild in the capital. And maybe it does.

"Extreme tourism" means different things to different travelers. It's often associated with billionaire space tourists and bombastic cable TV hosts who pit themselves, alone and ill-equipped, against the Tasmanian wilderness (save for whatever supplies are required to keep union television crews powered, fed, rested, and safe). For those who would complain that some of the places covered in this book might not meet a strict definition of "extreme," I maintain that anything that gets the traveler out of his or her comfort zone, or forces them to challenge their belief system, fits a fluid criterion.

To some, extreme travel might suggest living in a grass hut in Borneo for six weeks, but if you're the sort of person who enjoys spending time in grass huts, what's so extreme about that? No question, prowling the Russian steppe for wolf meat and potato vodka takes a certain amount of admirable grit. Far more frightening to me, though, is the prospect of exploring the comely mermaid fantasy of Ariel's Grotto inside the walls of a twenty-six-square-mile temple of consumerism dedicated to celebrating synthetic American culture at its overcrowded, fake-dreams, corndog-and-cotton-candy-inhaling worst, pushing a CEO-manufactured, ultraconformist mass "fantasy" presented fait accompli to American children. If it turns out there's more horror to shrink from in Disney World than in Africa, I for one won't be all that surprised.

While standing resolutely behind my newfound willingness to face down extreme challenges, I don't want to create unrealistic expectations. This isn't a book about dangling from the end of a rope off a nine-hundred-foot rock face along the south ridge of K2. You'll not find me dodging bullets and IEDs as I creep with my aide-de-camp Kareem over the border from Pakistan to Afghanistan.

I don't sleep well in the best of circumstances. I'm in

reasonably good cardiovascular condition, but I have the arm strength of a man half my weight. I'm leery of heights. I'm not interested in solidifying my reputation as a wise-cracking bon vivant by dying young (relatively) and leaving a good-looking (relatively) corpse. You can make your own fairly accurate assumptions about the mettle of a guy who includes Orlando on his primary list of scary places.

But if there's one lesson I've prized from my years of travel it's this: no place is ever as bad as they tell you it's going to be. Government bureaucrats are more concerned with covering their asses by issuing ludicrous "warnings" than with disseminating accurate situation reports. And our "news media"—if you want to call information largely regurgitated from self-interested corporate and government sources "news"—operates pretty much like your one crazy drunk friend, the guy who has a hysterical public reaction to even the smallest events, exaggerates all of his stories, and gets in a tizzy over every opinion whether he agrees with it or not.

I don't have to be reminded that the world collective is united in its dread of the Congo; that power vomiting on legless beggars is the national sport of India; that Mexico City is a sweltering hole of pollution, disease, cardboard shanties, and homicidal drug syndicates; and that I've got some personal issues to work through regarding Florida in general and Disney World in particular. It's just that for every warning I've ever gotten not to do something, someone has always been around to hand me a beer and twist my arm. And, of course, take my money for the privilege of showing me places and things that, while not always pleasant, usually end up leading to some surprising and enlightening discoveries.

PART I

CONTINENT
Africa

1

...

The Funniest Joke in Africa

Trouble starts as soon as I clear customs and meet Henri
in the parking lot of Kinshasa's N'Djili International Airport. Henri introduces himself, shakes my weary hand
with his damp one, pulls the cigarette from the side of his
mouth, exhales like the last survivor at Dien Bien Phu,
and says, "There are a few problems we need to discuss."

Five minutes in country and already things are going
to hell. Actually, things have been hell here for some
time. It's just me who's new to the game.

The problems concern the itinerary Henri and I have
spent the past month hammering out over phone and by
e-mail. My Congo plans revolve around a jungle town
called Mbandaka, a place whose name alone had radiated
sufficient exotic appeal to whip me into a state of blind
enthusiasm during my planning back in the States. I'm
the kind of chump who sees names like Chittagong or
Zamboanga on a map and says, "Only a fourteen-hour bus
ride out of our way? How come we haven't left yet?"

From Kinshasa we were scheduled to fly to Mbandaka,

where we'd buy supplies before striking out on a week-long canoe trip down a series of remote jungle rivers. These obscure waterways would lead us through pygmy villages and eventually to a hidden treasure of biodiversity called Lake Tumba. Henri has promised a once-in-a-lifetime adventure. I've been around enough to know that being stranded for two days in Blythe, California, with a busted radiator also constitutes a "once-in-a-lifetime adventure," but as I'm soon to learn, in the Congo you're forced to look past all manner of red flags when you place your well-being in the hands of guys to whom your only real connection is an e-mail address.

"The first problem is that the airline we were to fly to Mbandaka has gone out of business," Henri says. "This happened last week."

Henri speed walks ahead, keeping just beyond arm's reach of both me and the pack of child beggars who trail in our wake.

"The second problem is that the other airline with routes to Mbandaka has only one flight this week. And it is full. Same for next week."

Henri looks over his shoulder to gauge my level of disappointment. After a moment he nods as if to say, "OK, the quiet type, I get it," then continues.

"The third problem is that the destinations on this afternoon's schedule are closed due to the fact that it is Sunday."

For weeks, my visits to the Congolese art museum and bonobo reserve have been planned for the afternoon of my arrival. Had Henri been unaware until now that they'd be closed on Sunday?

"Will they be open tomorrow?" I ask.

"Probably not."

Much as I'd been looking forward to communing with

the freakishly humanlike bonobos, today's closures don't crush me. After the trip from Johannesburg, I'm happy for any excuse to trade sightseeing for a hotel bed and strategically placed fan blasting the layers of sweat off my face. For the entire flight from South Africa, the hairy Greek arms dealer in aviator shades beside me had maintained aggressive dominion over the armrest. Behind us, a man carried on for three straight hours in one of those amazing African languages in which it's impossible to tell if the speaker is winning big at the roulette table or merely preparing to hit his wife.

"What about the plane tickets?" I begin to pull out of my steerage-class stupor with the recollection that I'd prepaid both of our flights to Mbandaka. Nine hundred dollars. "Have you gotten a refund?"

"I am working on that."

Having built himself up on the phone and e-mail as a sort of postmodern buccaneer, Henri's appearance comes as something of a surprise. A white European in his mid-fifties, he's pale and a little paunchy. He wears faded slacks and a short-sleeved, white dress shirt with deeply entrenched sweat stains. His eyes are loose and watery and his gray hair has the look of a heavily teased Shredded Wheat biscuit. Despite my reluctance to employ any Congo material from the stupendously overemphasized Joseph Conrad, I'm compelled to borrow the *Heart of Darkness* author's description of Kurtz and apply it to the cagey, superior, and yet somehow endearingly irascible Henri: "All of Europe had contributed to the making of him."

We arrive at Henri's car, an ancient Mercedes sedan with dents in all four doors, its white paint job long since humbled into a mottle of rust and scrapes. The seats are torn to the stuffing. Rats appear to have been gnawing on the dashboard. Several instrument gauges have been removed, leaving gaping holes and naked wires dangling from the panel. Tomorrow during a thundershower I'll discover that the reason the passenger-side windows are always rolled down is because they were never replaced after being bashed out by thieves.

Loitering around the Mercedes are five or six African men I take for drug dealers. Or car thieves. Or loan collectors.

It turns out they work for Henri.

Henri introduces our driver D. B. (for Daniel Bertrand), a short, muscular guy with a prominent Cherokee nose and fixed expression about as cheery as an Armenian funeral. His smooth black head shines like it's been tumbled inside a rock polisher. He's fifty-four, but looks thirty-five.

During Joseph Mobutu's poisonous dictatorial regime (which lasted here from 1965 to 1997), D. B. was the personal chauffeur to one of Mobutu's brothers—a prestigious and occasionally dangerous gig. He'd won the job in part because of his exemplary military career, six-dan black belt in karate, and all-around "fucking with me would be a very bad idea" disposition.

"If action comes, I know the meaning of it," D. B. tells me in halting English while unhooking a pair of wires that keep the trunk closed.

Henri's man Friday is Gilles, a slim, handsome Congolese in his early thirties with the kind of Siamese eyes that leave you fairly certain Chinese merchants were landing up and down the African coast centuries before the white slavers.

"Unlike most Africans, Gilles does not wait to be told what to do," Henri informs me while his star employee stands next to us smoking and examining the clouds. "He anticipates problems and fixes them. This will make him invaluable to you. He will find a solution to the Mbandaka problem."

Gilles nods at me while I hoist my bag into the trunk. I've already been in Africa for nearly three weeks—mostly on safari in Botswana, Zambia, and Namibia, then in South Africa—and I've got Gilles pegged. Cool is in the African DNA. Two-thirds of the guys you meet here have the slow-breeze demeanor of 1930s jazz musicians. You almost respect guys like Gilles more for *not* helping a brother out with the luggage.

Henri, D. B., and Gilles form the core of Team Congo, my escort, eyes, and ears for much of the next fifteen days. Drinking buddies are one thing, but I've never had a genuine posse before, so even the lack of get-to-know-you chitchat and piece-of-shit Mercedes don't dim my white guy overenthusiasm for this one.

In addition to the principals, Team Congo will be supplemented by a taxi squad of sundry specialty types who'll move in and out of our orbit for the next two weeks without their official role or connection to the mission ever being formally declared. One such functionary is lounging on the hood of the car—a round, bald-headed, evil-looking dude named Jacques whose chunky baritone voice is the aural equivalent of wet cement. Henri tells me that Jacques maintains connections at every level of Congolese society—from shoeshine boys to government ministers—though over the next two weeks the man will fail at every single opportunity to distinguish himself as a results-oriented worker. If Gilles is worried about competition within the organization gunning for his gig, he's not sweating Jacques.

"How are the roads to Mbandaka?" I ask, beginning to stress over my crumbling itinerary. "Can't we just drive there?"

All the Africans laugh.

"There are no roads to Mbandaka," D. B. says. "This is Congo. Mbandaka is eight hundred kilometers from here. Between us only jungle."

"There's got to be another way," I say.

"Perhaps," Henri says, taking another meaningful huff on his cigarette. "Either way, it will be settled."

Planning a trip to the Democratic Republic of the Congo is like going through puberty. For all the mystery, antici- pation, and terrifying rumors, there's a startling lack of hard information about the whole experience. It seems to take forever for anything to happen, there's a troubling number of uncomfortable and unexpected procedures to deal with (buying a jock strap, getting a yellow fever shot, signing up for the selective service, finding a visa sponsor, etc.), and for a long time the more overeager the green- horn is for action, the more elusive action seems to be. A week into my largely gridlocked research back home, I'd figured out enough about the Congo to realize that land- ing there without contacts would put me roughly where I'd been at fifteen—anxiety prone, angry at my inability to be taken seriously, and jerking off alone somewhere wondering why I wasn't getting invited to any of the cool parties. Metaphorically speaking, of course.

I didn't want a tour guide in the Congo—few things ag- gravate me more than being prisoner to someone else's schedule so much as I needed a friend. Or at least some- one who knew the difference between deep bongo and survivable Congo. For two months I surfed the Net, called "We go everywhere in Africa" travel agencies, scanned guidebooks, followed bum steers in adventure magazines, wrote to the Congolese embassy in Washington, e-mailed

friends with Africa connections, attempted to worm my
way into the graces of religious and human aid agencies
with ongoing missions in Africa, and talked to guys like
Sam Kiley, all of whom gave me some version of the same
story: "Nobody goes to the Congo."

Finally, a guy who'd stopped running Congo tours
years ago—"Too bloody dangerous"—e-mailed me with
the name of a European expat living in Kinshasa known
to hire out his services to visitors. A "fixer" in the par-
lance of Africa freelancers, Henri wasn't just my first
break in the already extremely frustrating Operation
Congo, he was the first person I talked to about the DRC
who didn't scoff, hang up, or accuse me of having a death
wish. Instead he asked, "How much can you spend?"

"About two thousand dollars." This seemed like an extravagant sum for two weeks of insta-friend in one of the
world's poorest countries.

This is when Henri scoffed.

"How does five thousand sound?" he asked.

Even in the midst of the battle to chisel him down to
four thousand, I'd sensed that Henri was my kind of Euro,
nothing like the mismatched gang of bloodless Europeans
with whom I'd spent the preceding two weeks on safari, a
group so concerned with not offending anybody (at least
not to the Germans' faces) that they couldn't work up a
therapeutic session of America bashing even after I'd lied
and told them I was a Republican. Believe me, when it's
105 in the shade in Namibia and no one's spotted so much
as a dung beetle for three hours, you do what you can to
shake things up.

Traveling in poor countries, I've often found it useful to
carry small gifts to give as thanks to helpful strangers or

just to make friends with potential photo subjects. Candy bars or gum generally do the trick. To the Congo I've hauled a bag of Starburst singles, an assortment of individually wrapped DayGlo squares I'd picked up back home at day-after-Halloween prices.

Driving through Kinshasa—the congestion is so bad it takes two hours to get from airport to hotel—I realize what a sad and inadequate gesture a bag of candy is in the face of the city's desolate millions, many of whom, D. B. tells me while the Team Congo Mercedes slogs through traffic liked a drugged rhino, often go two or three days without eating. The moment I'd walked outside of the airport terminal child beggars had appeared and I'd known at once that breaking out the candy would set off a pint-sized riot of outstretched hands and open mouths. I'd walked through heartbreaking Third World poverty plenty of times, so it's startling to ponder the well-intentioned delusion I was operating under when I bought that bag of Starburst back home. It's true, I'm often as clueless about travel as many of the people I complain about.

Kinshasa is a reeking slum of heroic dimensions. Between the airport and city center stand relentless miles of street-to-street squalor. Hills of garbage spill into the banks of filthy drainage creeks. Shanties fall apart like bad alibis. People are everywhere. And children. God, the children. You've never seen so many. Children, children, children, children. Dressed in dish rags. Thin as sparrows.

"They are happy at this age of life," D. B. notes of a group of five- and six-year-olds laughing and running down the street playing tag, completely unsupervised, completely unaware of the broken glass, mongrel dogs, and Olympic filth that surrounds them.

There are 6.5 million people in the capital, most of whom will die before age fifty. My fear of walking into a French-speaking country with no greater familiarity with the language than a fleeting though personally rewarding Serge Gainsbourg period is ameliorated by the fact that about half of all Congolese receive no formal education and thus speak little more French than I do. This doesn't stop people from referring to Kinshasa as the second-largest French-speaking city in the world, after Paris. Judging by the way Gilles takes his nicotine, however, the locals do smoke cigarettes just as joylessly as the French.

According to the World Bank, the Congo is one of the top five countries in the world with the largest number of children out of school. At least 50 percent are completely outside of the school system. Henri tells me only about 15 percent advance beyond primary school; less than 1 percent attend university. Schooling at all levels is dominated by males. This means you'll probably never meet a Congolese woman with a college degree—and if you do you should regard her odds-beating with Powerball awe. You have a better chance of spotting a leopard or bonobo in the wild than chatting up a female Congolese high school graduate.

As for the DRC itself, it's a massive country bordering nine nations and encompassing as much land as the entire United States east of the Mississippi. Despite vast natural resources—copper, cobalt, diamonds, gold, rubber, oil, timber—mismanagement, corruption, and war have conspired to lock the country in perpetual poverty. Per capita annual income is ninety-eight dollars. Despite this, more than seven million people, even impoverished ones, carry cell phones.

Incidentally, I'll continue to let Catherine Zeta-Jones seduce me, but does the fact that my monthly cell phone bill nearly equals the annual personal income of a highly cellularized country suggest to anyone else that we may be paying criminally inflated prices for our technology? Or just that I need to finally break down and switch carriers? Just thinking out loud here.

The most fascinating Congo stat is that of the country's 58 million people, only 230,000 work in private-sector jobs or are enrolled in the national social security system. The most current figures available are from five years ago, but the situation scarcely appears to have changed. The black market and "informal" untracked economy overwhelmingly dominate every aspect of commerce.

As we drive through the city, I ask Henri how these millions survive with no salaries, no businesses, no goods to trade, no plots of land, no financial safety net. After a while he says, "The truth is, I don't know. I have no idea how so many of them manage." A decade and a half in the city and the mystery of Congolese survival is as complete to him as it is to me. In response to the same question D. B. and Gilles just shrug, then continue gazing blankly out the windows.

I've seen the worst of Manila, Bangkok, Baltimore, and Newark, and up to now these have stood as my personal standard for the kind of societal devastation that leaves you dumbstruck. In terms of communal wreckage, however, Kinshasa easily surpasses any city I've ever been to. A more desperate collection of humanity I never expect to encounter again. Of course, I still have India and Disney World in my sights.

"The UN guys walk around scared shitless." Henri says this as we pass a barbed-wire compound with machine-gun towers looming over the streets. "But the organization can be helpful at times, such as when we need to get somewhere."

There are eighteen thousand international peacekeepers stationed in the Congo, the largest UN force anywhere in the world. In fact, the organization is the first thing you notice when landing at N'Djili Airport, where a fleet of airplanes with the large UN logo in impotent blue (coincidentally, a Martha Stewart Colors shade) sits wingtip to wingtip on the tarmac. Henri raises the possibility of hopping a UN flight to Mbandaka. Jacques, the evil baldy from the airport, is supposedly on the case.

"Aren't UN flights reserved for official personnel?" I ask. It seems weird to be able to hop onto a UN jet with no credentials.

"Officially, yes." Henri lowers his eyelids in a Rick's Café way. "But if they have space, they will allow humanitarian workers to fly."

Henri explains that Jacques has contacts within the UN and that the pygmies whose villages we're scheduled to paddle through will unwittingly support a ruse that we're international relief workers.

"The pygmies are treated like slaves by the local Bantu population," D. B. says in an attempt to get me onboard with the plan.

I nod and say, "Just as long as nobody asks me to man a machine-gun nest." Nobody laughs. I can't tell if this is because they don't understand sarcasm or simply that, as at airport security, witty rejoinders about automatic weapons aren't what pass for humor in Kinshasa.

Henri was meant to be my insurance against the kinds of hassles I'd been fearing for the past three months—cancelled flights being a good example—but even from the States I could tell he represented the highest odds on the table in my Congo roll of the dice. Crafty, surly, offensive, unpredictable—these aren't qualities I normally look for in friends, but I'd already seen enough out the window of the Mercedes to appreciate that they might come in handy here.

By the end of the first day in the presence of his weird, chatty energy, I'd begun to compile the Gospel of the Congo according to Henri:

"The Congolese are far more afraid of Ebola than AIDS. It's why many have stopped eating monkey. No one has stopped having sex."

"Tourism in Kinshasa is a married man taking his girlfriend to a pool at a hotel on the weekend, having a swim, a meal, then back to the room for fucking. That is the extent of tourism here."

"When the husband goes off with his girlfriends, the wife is not jealous. She is angry because he is spending money on girlfriends that should be coming into the household to buy food and clothing for the children. The fucking is not the issue; it's the money that angers the wife."

"Married or not, African men are going to have a lot of partners. That is just how it works and it does not do any good to protest."

"If Africans could be paid for all the dancing and fucking they do, Africa would be the wealthiest continent on earth."

"I would never spend my holiday in Congo."

"The Congolese are a gentle people. There is no safety issue here at all. There is very little crime."

"I am not interested in the country itself. I am here because I love the daily fight. I need that adrenaline.

When I go back to Europe for a visit, I am bored without anything to fight over."

"The Congolese are begging for the Belgians to come back as rulers. With the Belgians at least there were schools and hospitals and government employees were paid."

Henri is proud of the fact that he's been able to keep his clients out of trouble: "So far, none of my clients have been arrested. Well, one guy, from the UK. He was found taking pictures of young boys and girls. But I had some discussions with the right people, and he was let go and sent home."

Henri himself was arrested several years back, he says, on false charges of stealing money from his company. "I have no investors. It is a company of one person. How can I be stealing from myself?" He spent eleven nights in jail before buying his way out with five thousand dollars.

So what's it like inside a Congolese prison?

"I had money, so it was no problem. I had my friends bring me food every day and also food for many of the others inside, so I was popular and allowed to sleep peacefully each night."

The subject of poverty finally stirs Henri's scant sense of public relations.

"Congo is one of the richest countries in the world," he insists. "Here you have oil, uranium, diamonds, gold, all in abundance."

"Well, potentially, one of the richest countries in the world," I interject.

"Yes, right, one of the richest."

Henri has been in the Congo fifteen years. Living in France in 1992, he tried to import tropical fish from the Congo to sell to aquarium owners around Europe. He found a supplier and set up a large order. Between the fish, shipping fees, insurance, customs bribes, dock and loading charges, taxes, agent commissions, and other costs associated with the maddening world of import/export, Henri sunk twenty-five thousand dollars' worth of francs into his first shipment.* All of his fish arrived on time. All were dead.

"My supplier had no idea how to pack fish for shipment," he tells me. "The insurance company refused to cover my loss because it turns out this guy had faked his paperwork. He was not even a licensed vendor."

Outraged and nearly broke, Henri flew to Kinshasa to confront his vendor and was quickly consumed by the country. He moved down for good a couple years later and has been here ever since running a variety of businesses, mostly exporting various goods including, for a while, tropical fish. Now he's a jack-of-all-trades who sees a future, of a sort, in tourism. Which is why he's agreed to act as my escort. Since 2002, I'm only the third American client he's had, but he remains bullish on his chances.

"I have been in jail, survived Mobutu, and two civil wars," he says. "I love this country. Every day is different. You cannot compare yesterday to today. In Europe and America, you already know what tomorrow will be like. You know what next year will be like. Here, you have no idea. We are now driving freely down the road. In one hundred meters we could be arrested for no reason. Probably not, but we would not be surprised if it happened.

---

* During our short-lived attempt to become import/export barons, the first meeting my brother and I conducted with our supplier of handcrafted Philippine carvings took place at an outdoor restaurant in Zambales on Good Friday. As we drank San Miguels and shook hands on our first big deal, a live Passion Play paraded by. Wearing a genuine crown of thorns and being whipped by mock Romans, the Filipino guy playing Jesus was literally gushing blood from his scalp and shoulders as he dragged his massive wooden cross through the streets. It turned out to be a powerful business auger.

"In Europe, I have never been arrested. I need this country. You want some company for the night? With a condom it's no problem."

I can't tell if this is a rhetorical question or not. Just to be on the safe side I say, "No, thanks," and explain that even if I wasn't married I wouldn't have casual sex in a place known as the cradle of AIDS with a triple wrapping of latex, aluminum foil, and burlap with a sealant of waterproof caulk around my dick and a coating of marine-grade polyurethane over my nut sack for safekeeping. Henri looks at my crotch and says, "I am married also; I was just asking for you. If you change your mind, it's not a problem to arrange."

There were available to me, of course, options beyond hooking on with a group of strangers for an ad hoc tour of the Congo's more desolate corners. The classic outing in this part of the world is the barge expedition up the Congo River past Mbandaka and into Joseph Conrad's mythic "heart of darkness." Since it's impossible to come to the Congo and not confront the gloomy shadow Conrad still casts over the place, I'll dispense with the subject up front.

Most writers who visit the Congo, and just about everyone else, invariably get sucked into the "Conrad's footsteps" deal and, worse, feel obliged to mimic not simply the man's century-old journey but his mournfully obtuse style: *In the pilot house the helmsman, filled with drink, eyes the color of smoke, stoically matriculated our solemn passage with an oppressive oath as the damp vessel snaked through a greasy waterway into the green-black forest bruised with a noxious fog of sorrow, hunger, desperation, abandonment . . . death like a widow's shroud assembled its proxies with hungry*

certitude at each moaning bend, the enveloping presence of
unspeakable secrets an intolerable weight hovering above the
sepulchral gloaming that stalked like sluggish murmurs this
apiary of malignant pilgrims. Etc.

There's no disputing Conrad's rank as a master, but
every time I read him I find myself wishing that just once
he'd pull out of his mood, walk into the equatorial sun,
wipe the sweat from his brow, and break up his consti-
pated labor with something like "It was hotter than two
rats fucking inside a wool sock."

I have no interest in traversing a well-worn literary rut,
and not just for what should be the writer's obligatory aversion to exhaustively covered ground. *Harper's, Travelers'*
Tales, and other high-minded publishers are credible institutions, but I've always disliked that "following in Hemingway's footsteps" or "retracing the Silk Road" gimmick
publishers like to keep alive out of some half-noble duty
to posterity. What's the point of these self-indulgent exer-
cises? To demonstrate how some things have changed over
time and some haven't? Well, no shit.

I mention *Harper's* because just before I left the States,
the magazine ran a very good, thoughtful piece called
"The River Is a Road" by a writer named Bryan Mealer
describing his Congo River journey and inevitable encounters with the merchants, fishermen, vegetable traders, soldiers, and everyday river folk who ride the slow-moving
barges not out of a sense of adventure but out of economic
necessity. It all came across colorful as hell, but if you
have any experience on Old World ferries and can read
between the lines a little, it becomes obvious that the
main problem with seven days on a slow boat is that almost nothing interesting ever happens on them. That's
why you end up acting like quotes from the guy with four
teeth and two coops of chickens amount to the type of

wizened pronouncements that "It takes a village" bozos
back home eat up like mashed cassava.

By the way, if you really think villages are so great, spend a year in an African one and see how you like starving, washing in a river the guys upstream dump their shit in, and having your neighbors up your ass seven days a week. For more on why "Let's bring the lessons of the Third World back to the States" is pure idiocy, see page 154.

The *Harper's* story included the observation that Conrad saw so much hell in the Congo "that he was inspired to write *Heart of Darkness*, a description the country has yet to live down." My immediate reaction to this was, "Absolutely right and to hell with Conrad and his septic analysis of everything Africa put in front of him." Old Joe pinned the tail on that donkey in 1902. Sure, the country has its horrors—admittedly more than most—but it's not like the natives are attacking up and down the river and ivory is being hauled out of the jungle by the Kurtzload. It's a great book, but perhaps one reason the Congo can't shake its gruesome reputation is that no one is willing to let it. Would it be too much to ask to allow the Congo to get on with the twenty-first century already?

Conrad himself had a monstrous time in the Congo. He saw more than his fill of death. He fell ill with fever and dysentery and was further hindered by what modern cubicle culture would call a "personality conflict" with his boss, a turf-guarding dickhead who denied Conrad the steamboat captaincy he'd come to the Congo to assume. Conrad left Africa broken and defeated. And then wrote his nasty little piece of revenge filled with hate, misery, fear, madness, massacre, and party starters like, "Droll thing life is—that mysterious arrangement of merciless logic for a futile purpose."

Ruminations such as this one went on to inform a century of Africa travel writing, but they also inspired an international allegory I don't care to perpetuate. Flat as the Kinshasa investment market and brown as a turd, that river belongs to others and I'm happy to let them keep it. I've come to the Congo to confront fear, not create it.

There are hundreds of great books and travelogues that recap historical horrors in Africa, and I prepped for my trip by reading a handful of them. I found most to be excellent and exceedingly dour, tinged with the inevitable influence of Conrad, as though written by people who, the minute they set foot in the place, tightened their jaws and became good and goddamned determined to approach their subject (and not coincidentally themselves) with immeasurable gravity and battle-hardened seriousness. One of the requirements of visiting Africa seems to be casting off your sense of humor somewhere over the Atlantic.

I get that in the face of disease, famine, and war the last thing you want as a visitor is to come off as an insensitive, hooting bonehead. In addition to being personally unattractive, this seems like a fast way to get on shit lists of organizations like the Congo's Hutu militia, the Interahamwe, whose name literally means "Those who stand together," but which has also been interpreted as "Those who kill together."

Even so, I'm a guy who likes a laugh now and then and I don't see why Africa or, more specifically, people reading about Africa should be deprived of a little levity. Maybe one reason we're so intimidated by Africa is that every image we get from the place involves hospital misery, rural starvation, angry mobs, and eight-, ten-, and twelve-year-old boys with AK-47s. After a few weeks in Africa I'd seen far more laughing and joking than shooting and stabbing, and I began wondering why Westerners so often come away from the continent with such long faces.

The more I thought about it, the more I began blaming Conrad for the anxiety I felt about Africa. I didn't come here as an aid worker, diplomat, anthropologist, epidemiologist, peacekeeper, election observer, war correspondent, or colonial river pilot. I'm a tourist. Why should that obligate me to confront the worst parts of the place? Without close contact with societal ills have I not experienced the "real" Africa, as opposed to the sensational continent exploited on CNN, BBC, and other bastions of global fearmongering? Weren't the friendly and trustworthy African guides I'd met on safari as bona fide as militia rebels in the field?

And if as a traveler with a social conscience I'm required by some invisible authentication board to amass what my friend Glasser calls "phantom university credits," are visitors to such "most livable" cities as Portland, Oregon, bound by the same requirements? Does experiencing the "real" Portland mean joining the army of homeless ghosts who line up each morning outside the city's most notorious shelters? Should they be shown the place where sewer lines pour filth into the once pristine Willamette River, making it unsafe for drinking, swimming, fishing, and just about anything else a river is useful for? Should tourists hoping to form a valid perspective of San Francisco line up at 5:30 a.m. in front of one of the city's methadone clinics—as I did with a junkie friend one deeply depressing morning years ago—to bear witness to the sad string of refugees from one of our country's many ill-defined wars? Do junkies represent the "real" America any more than the Grand Canyon or Yosemite; any more than Kinshasa's slum dwellers and AIDS clinics represent the "real" Africa vis-à-vis my organized safari or the thundering thrill of Victoria Falls?

Wherever you go in the world, most people are pretty nice. They're eager to show you the best parts of the places they live. What gives interlopers the right to riffle through their dirty laundry?

Having made the choice to shove sad Joe off the heights of Mt. Sacrilege, I proceed full bore into my Conradian antipathy by deciding to devote the rest of my trip to a search for the funniest joke in Africa. Had I stopped to consider the ill will I was likely to provoke by wading into such an impolitic swamp—"After slaughtering a village full of women and children, three Hutu Interahamwe walk into a bar and say . . ."—I might have aborted the plan to mine the Dark Continent for laughs before it had time to gestate. Luckily, D. B. happens to know two illuminating Congo jokes that he's happy to share.

"Two grasshoppers leave Egypt for a trip to the southern tip of Africa," D. B. begins, stone-faced as ever while I whip out my notebook with cub-reporter excitement.

"They are determined to see the entire continent. The grasshoppers have a good time sightseeing in places like Kenya and Uganda, but when they reach Congo they stop at the border. They discuss the matter and after a few minutes decide to end their journey and head back to Egypt."

Yep, that's the punch line, folks. And if you aren't choking with laughter it's presumably because you've never had a grasshopper wing stuck in your throat.

"This joke we tell on ourselves because people in Congo love to eat grasshoppers," D. B. says, clearly bummed by my tepid reaction. I pass along the best advice I ever got about jokes—"Never repeat 'em; never explain 'em"—and scribble in my notebook something earnest about the "Western concept of jokes juxtaposed with Congo's lack of ready hilarity."

Concerned that my brilliant "Funniest Joke in Africa" idea might be tougher to pull off than I thought, I nevertheless ask D. B. for his follow-up. Fortunately, his second joke turns out to be a little better than the first, proving yet again that the warm-up act is a reliable downer in any culture. D. B. squares his shoulders and says (believe me, this works better paraphrased):

When God was creating the world he reached into his pockets and began dispersing blessings around the planet—mountains and plentiful water to North America, abundant farmland to Asia, magnificent cities and culture to Europe, and so on. When he got to the Congo, however, he realized that he had too much left over, so that when he emptied his pockets the country received the most riches of all—a mighty river, endless forests, lush hills, magnificent wildlife, fertile plains, oil, gold, copper, and every mineral known to man. Noting this disparity of resources, one of his angels came to him and said, "God, it is unfair to the rest of the world. You have bestowed too much wealth upon the Congo."

To which God replied, "Ah, but you haven't seen the people I plan to put there."

Although everyone but me has heard it before, this one gets a pretty good laugh in the car. Even the aloof Gilles flashes me a catlike smile.

"This joke we tell on ourselves to explain Congo's poor condition in the world despite our great potential," D. B. explains, turning left onto another impossibly disorganized stretch of road and, not for the last time, ignoring the gift of my finely honed Western wisdom.

2

. . .

In This Way Children Are Fed
and Girlfriends Kept Happy

Before I can function as an adult in the DRC, I need my own stash of local money. This requires a visit to the money changers who do business in rows lining either side of a narrow dirt alley deep within the markets of downtown Kinshasa. Here, I'm told, I can get a fair rate turning dollars into Congolese francs, a currency worth less than a drunken promise outside the country.

After tossing and turning all night in a concrete bunker of a hotel that smells of embalming fluid, I meet Henri, Gilles, and D. B. in the lobby restaurant for the money errand. In that innocuous way of morning courtesy, I ask how everyone's getting along.

"Not so good," Henri says, and I can see he hasn't had much sleep, either. "Three armed militia men entered our neighborhood at one thirty this morning. They were in our courtyard, but entered another house. Even so, the commotion frightened my house girls."

"What were they after? Were they thieves?"

"By the time I grabbed my machete and looked outside, they had gone."

I'm normally skeptical of self-promoters who pepper their personal anecdotes with phrases like "By the time I grabbed my machete." And I'm skeptical of Henri, anyway. Even so, I ask him a few leading questions.

"It was a restless night," he continues. "There have been two armed assaults in my area recently. A girl of twelve was raped."

A rifle barrel had apparently been put in her vagina. Or else that was a story from a refugee who had recently arrived from Kivu. Either way.

During Henri's story about the armed hooligans, I'd been planning to throw in his face yesterday's assertions about the Congo being a mellow place with an excellent safety rating. But this business about the twelve-year-old girl and the gun barrel shuts all of us up while we crawl through traffic.

Our slow progress through the polluted streets further dampens the mood, but it provides an excellent opportunity for the city's policemen, one or two of whom are stationed at nearly every major corner, to put their sophisticated training and crime-fighting skills to use. When D. B. slows at a curb to let Gilles and me out of the car, a pudgy policewoman rushes up with a wild barrage of hand gestures and Lingala invective. In one hurried motion, she opens the passenger door, grabs Henri by the shoulder, jerks him out of the car, and deposits herself in his seat, all while berating D. B. like he's an insubordinate stepchild.

From the front seat, D. B. turns to me with an apologetic grin and says, "It may take time to fix this problem. You go now with Gilles." Then he resumes bellowing in Lingala at the policewoman in the seat next to him. Another cop arrives and shoves his baton through the open window. Gilles grabs me by the shoulder. Surprisingly,

neither cop bothers to look at us when we get out of the
car and take off down the street.

There's no pretense of procedure here. No one is asked
to produce ID or account for themself in any way. It's a
straightforward shakedown, a display of power and intimidation of the type that supposedly keeps Congolese
society in line and, more importantly, Congolese cops in
business.

Gilles and I snake through a maze of alleyways jammed
with people, garbage, and all manner of shanty shops—
radios, fabric, dried fish, electric fans, CDs. The usual
Third World bazaar, though this one is spaced at regular
intervals with clusters of mean-faced young men with
guns sitting behind rickety wooden tables piled high with
cash rubber-banded in bundles the size of bricks. Millions of francs, everywhere, sitting in the open just like
the pig shanks and untied sacks of rice teeming with
flies.

It's unsettling amid Kinshasa's ocean of destitution to
see the lifetime income of forty or fifty families stacked on
every corner like a Great Wall of Mammon. Imagine fifty
card tables at your local Saturday farmer's market, only
instead of shiny apples and bunches of asparagus, each
one leans under the weight of four hundred thousand or
five hundred thousand dollars in tens and twenties. When
I reach for my camera to take a photo, Gilles places a gentle hand on my wrist and lowers it to my side.

Gilles instructs me to keep one hand on my wallet and
to turn my daypack around so that it's pressed against my
chest. This makes me feel like a more obvious mark than
a guy walking into Tiffany's on Christmas Eve, but then I
notice Gilles and every other Congolese have assumed

the same defensive position as they dodge and shimmy through the relentless tide of human traffic. Gilles presses ahead, but wheels around every two or three seconds to confirm that I and my forest green JanSport pack are still behind him.

On safari in Botswana I spent several nights lying in my tent while hyenas and elephants sniffed around camp. One afternoon I awoke from a nap to find a large, male baboon sitting on its haunches three feet away calmly staring at me through the mesh window. But the money changers' alley is the first place in Africa I feel at risk. Still, what the hell, I haven't seen the inside of a gym in months and it's nice to get my heart rate into the fat-burning cardio zone with so little effort. I'm nothing if not a seeker of silver linings.

We stop in front of a money changer who looks exactly like the inmate that runs the entire prison black market and decides which guy will receive the evening's punitive ass rape. The money changer takes my ten fifty-dollar bills and looks at Gilles as though some eight-year-old just broke open his piggy bank and brought in a load of pennies and nickels to be changed. Gilles shrugs. The money changer grins at me—if you saw Forest Whitaker in *The Last King of Scotland* you know the smile—and grunts an order to one of his lieutenants.

The young guy begins stuffing bricks of francs into a plastic shopping bag. Carrying a king's ransom through Serfville will be nerve-racking enough, but unbeknownst to Gilles I'm holding an additional two thousand in unchanged dollars—as well-hidden on my person as possible without engaging a major orifice. This is emergency cash I'll be hauling as a hedge at all times in a country where credit cards, traveler's checks, and ATMs are largely theoretical outside the capital.

Meanwhile, Gilles makes a side transaction, handing the money changer about three thousand dollars in euros—Henri must be doing better than the piece-of-shit Mercedes suggests. He receives in return a quantity of bills that you'd normally strap to the back of a mule in saddlebags booby-trapped with scorpions and dynamite.

With the house take of Monte Carlo pressed against our chests, Gilles and I thread through the carnival of despair back to the car. We arrive to find the policewoman gone and two tall male cops smiling and chatting with Henri and D. B. Henri is lighting a cigarette for one of them. The other offers Gilles a friendly greeting as we roll up.

While Team Congo ties up the final details of our little traffic kerfuffle, four or five beggars approach me with pleading eyes and outstretched palms. In *The Third Man*, Graham Greene wrote, "Humanity is a duty." I love that line, but the situation here argues more for the street smarts of Bison Welles. With the cops still nearby, opening my plastic bag of cash seems like a very stupid idea. I ignore the beggars and turn back toward our group just as Henri slides one of the cops twenty-five hundred francs (about five dollars). Henri shoos the beggars and orders us all back in the Mercedes.

"That is how they do it here," Henri explains as we pull away. "They see you slowing down, they jump in your car, and invent an infraction."

"In this case, the lady officer said we are not allowed to exit the car at that particular corner," D. B. adds from the driver's seat. "This is nonsense, but police can make whatever rule they please."

"What was she saying when she got in the car?" I ask. "She seemed pretty angry."

"She demanded one hundred U.S. dollars to begin with, but you must always refuse their intimidation and threats to arrest you until they arrive at a reasonable price," D. B. says.

I ask if we were targeted for being white. Henri says no, police harassment is applied equally to everyone in Kinshasa. This appears to be true. I look around as we drive and see motorists stopped everywhere, cops sitting in front seats, haranguing like evangelists. But later I ask D. B. the same question and he says, "When the lady officer got in the car her first words to me were, 'You are with white people, so I know there is a lot of money in this car!'"

Traveling with white people in Africa is a burden I'm already well acquainted with. Before arriving in Kinshasa, I'd spent sixteen days circumnavigating the world-renowned Okavango Delta in a modern, open Land Rover truck with twelve docile European tourists, a German translator-assistant, a camp cook, and a freakishly competent African guide. Covering parts of Botswana, Zambia, and Namibia, most of the trip had lived up to the promised wildlife bonanza. A single afternoon along the vibrant Chobe River, for example, had included spiritual near brushes with hippo, giraffe, crocodile, impala, zebra, cape buffalo, antelope, fish eagles, vultures, and, the coup de grâce, eight lions feasting on a rotting elephant carcass. All in all, a triumphant orgy of *Planet Earth*–worthy encounters.

Nights were spent sitting around campfires in crude bush camps and "sleeping" while predator killing machines sniffed around just outside our tent flaps. "Under no circumstances are you to leave your tent during the night," warned our no-nonsense guide Tebo. "If you must urinate, cut the top off a water bottle and keep the contents in your tent until I give the 'all clear' order at dawn."

On safari the animals are the main attraction but, as with coworkers back home, it's your fellow camp mates you end up spending the most time with and consequently forming the deepest connections with. Signing on as a solo traveler with a safari outfit based in Maun, Botswana, I ended up thrown in with a random bag of mostly middle-aged Euros: six German, two Dutch, two Italian, and single Austrian and Belgian tourists. I generally get along well with Europeans, but this jumbled bunch was maddeningly bereft of social skills. Say what you will about Euros, they're usually not at a loss for opinions, a quality that tends to make them interesting conversationalists. For two weeks, though, the pinch-mouthed, taciturn, and communally stunted continentals in my midst were unable to produce anything more than the kind of cultured small talk exchanged by people who don't really like one another but who don't want to appear impolite.

Among the more mysterious personalities was Klein, a fiftyish German whom I often walked behind on single-file hikes through the bush. I couldn't help being impressed by his robotic stride—each pace was identical in form and measure, and his arms swung with the precision of a metronome. Taking a not-so-wild guess one afternoon I said, "Klein, you seem to have retained the march they taught you in the German army."

Without breaking stride, Klein swiveled his head, eyed me coldly, and declared, "*East* German army."

With his wind-burned face and arms turning as brown as sausages in a pan under the desert sun, it was easy to imagine Klein with the Afrika Korps, goggles pitched jauntily above his brow, squinting into the sun, scoffing at Monty's latest flaccid maneuver, and barking orders at his panzer division to keep pressing for the Kasserine Pass. An antiquated model of Eastern Bloc austerity, he was the only person on the trip who hadn't brought a camera. Indeed, he seemed almost disinterested in the animals.

By far the most interesting figure, however, was the Belgian woman in her midthirties whom I dubbed in my notebook the Tittering Belge Hermaphrodite, or TBH. Even through the dark Belgian winter, I suspected the sun shone every day on the TBH, a chronically hyperventilating giggler who quaked with unrestrained delight at everything from sightings of common birds to warnings that campers exercise extreme caution around baboons and hyenas. Her ceaseless tittering initially struck me and several others as some kind of rare medical condition.

Incessant laughter is incredibly annoying, particularly when you're with fifteen people trying not to scare off wild animals, but I soon came to appreciate the TBH's irrepressible demeanor. As my unkind nickname is meant to suggest, the TBH was not a woman to whom life had dealt a strong hand. Round and soft as a wheel of brie, she bordered on obese. Wild tufts of hair covered spotty patches of her cheeks, chin, and scalp. Spacious gaps between all of her pointy teeth gave her the appearance of a crocodile with irritable bowel syndrome. On hikes and in camp she moved like a garbage truck backing up around a tight corner. Upon meeting her, I'd spent several hours of surreptitious study before satisfying myself that she was in fact woman, not man.

Yet for all her physical disadvantages, the TBH was the only tourist on safari whose energy never flagged, not even on endless afternoons in the barren desert when temperatures soared well over a hundred and the air was as still as a dead animal. The TBH spoke the native lan-

guage of every white person in the truck and almost
never stopped smiling. She sweated like a melting candle,
but neither complained about the heat nor bothered fan-
ning herself with the heavy pieces of cardboard the Germans and Italians used to constantly and ostentatiously
cool themselves. She never failed to be excited by even
the smallest discovery: "Fresh onions in the tuna salad
sandwiches? *Mein Gott*, we are truly blessed!"

One night around the campfire, enjoying an impromptu
field dessert after a dinner of chewy kudu steaks, the
TBH made a rare ugly face and asked Kap, our African
camp cook, what the crunchy bits in the pudding were.

"There is only pudding in the pudding," Kap replied.

The TBH clicked on her headlamp and tilted the beam
into her bowl, illuminating a dozen or so large black ants
crawling though her chocolate. I would have flung the
bowl like a hot ember and "motherfuckered" for the next
three days. Elated by this matchless safari experience, the
TBH merely erupted with her trademark laughter.

"Don't worry," Kap said, laughing with her as he shined
his own light into the swarming mass. "It is good for the
nutrition."

If it was my bad fortune to be cast alongside a truckful
of Euro end pieces, it was twice my good luck to draw the
redoubtable Tebo as native guide. From a tiny village near
the Okavango Delta, the stocky, mustachioed Tebo had
grown up subsistence hunting for impala and kudu with
his uncle. Even as a child he'd been a superior tracker,
learning to find animals by copying their behavior. After
an eighteen-month stint in the Botswanan army and an
improbable year as a water-pump salesman, Tebo enrolled
in guide certification courses and aced every test. A professional guide for the past twenty-five years in Kenya,

South Africa, Zimbabwe, and Botswana, he was filled with safari lore.

"In South Africa, in places like Kruger National Park, many of the lions have radio collars," he told us one afternoon. "Before game drives, guides locate the positions of lions using electronic devices. Some of them drive around telling their clients, 'I can smell lions nearby.' A few minutes later the lions appear and the tourists believe their guide is so skilled that he can track by scent."

"Really? That's true?" I asked.

"Oh, yes. I can tell you this happens on a regular basis. This is why I prefer Botswana. There are no fences. The animals are completely wild. They can come and go as they please."

Tebo's witchlike ability to track game was a daily wonder, and no matter how monotonous their conduct the Euros were largely benign—in the presence of any animal large or small they uncharacteristically carried on like six-year-olds on a maiden voyage to Chuck E. Cheese's, but I'd gotten used to that. Near the end of the trip, however, the party's incompetence in the wild ruined what should have been the high point of the entire safari.

The event began with Tebo spotting a single hippo in the distance lumbering toward a small, unoccupied water hole just next to a larger lake. The sighting brought a jolt of excitement to the vehicle. On safari you see plenty of hippo heads poking out of the water, but it's a treat to see the whole of their vast, absurd bodies cavorting on dry land in broad daylight. By the time Tebo had maneuvered the Land Rover within easy viewing range, the hippo was just getting comfortable in the water hole—no easy feat for a thirty-six-hundred-pound creature. This effrontery, however, greatly displeased a second, until-then-unseen male hippo, who appeared with an emotional bellow from the center of the nearby lake, hauled the full girth of his own tremendous frame out of the water, and trundled toward the reclining intruder.

"The first hippo is a lone male who has entered the territory of a dominant male," Tebo explained quietly, as twelve of us jockeyed for photo position inside the truck and Klein sat passively, mentally reconstructing the Battle of El-Alamein. "You will now see the first hippo leave the water hole."

As predicted, the challenger hippo took stock of the dominant male, swung his head in an aggressive side-to-side show of resentment, then heaved himself out of the water hole and onto dry land, confirming the old African adage: never bet against Tebo.

"We are going to see a battle of hippos!" Tebo whispered, raising his binoculars to his eyes and continuing with a barely audible play-by-play. "The first hippo is signaling for a challenge. If we see him drop his dung nearby, it means he is attempting to mark this territory for himself. If he does this, the dominant male will become enraged and have no choice but to fight. A battle for dominance will occur."

Right on cue, the upstart hippo cranked out the mother of all "Take that!" dumps. Then he began kicking dirt over a dried pile of existing dung, the property of the dominant male, who took in the whole scene with an expression of supreme hippo mortification.

I don't know a lot about hippo behavior but I can say with a high degree of certainty that dominant male hippos protecting their turf do not appreciate having their territory-demarcating feces treated with such blatant disrespect by rogue males looking to stir up trouble. Like a purple volcano, the older male exploded at the impudent treatment of his no-shit zone, shaking his amazing bulk in a furious dither and bluff charging to within thirty feet of his rival. The rogue trespasser never flinched. Both mammoth creatures then began roaring like enraged Wookiees, opening their mighty jaws to display magnificent sets of ivory choppers capable of slashing through radial tires in seconds.

When you're sitting at home deciding how to spend your vacation dollars, deciding which country or even which safari outfit to put your faith in, these are the moments you're thinking about. This was the award-winning *National Geographic* photo op I'd been imagining since the words "African safari" had first formed in my mind: the privileged front-row view to a whisker-to-whisker hippo slaughterfest for the right to hump any three-thousand-pound cow in the lake while your pathetic rivals with their inadequate scat piles watched powerless from the bushes.

The dominant male advanced with plodding menace, closing the gap to ten feet. Seven thousand pounds of raging hippo were seconds from throwing down. Birds twenty miles across the delta suddenly felt the urge to get as far away as possible and didn't even know why.

Then, with a confused stutter, the dominant male hesitated. For a moment he stood as still as a statue. Then he began rapidly shaking his head and spinning in a turgid frenzy as though a swarm of invisible wasps had begun attacking him. Finally, in an utterly unexpected gesture of appeasement, he buried his snout in the dirt.

"Something is wrong!" Tebo called out. "The hippo smells something strange. What is that on the ground between them?"

Tebo peered through his binoculars.

"It's a hat!" he gasped. "A human hat!* The hippo is alarmed by the smell of a human! Who has lost a hat?"

I looked through my own binoculars. A floppy blue denim hat with big, shiny buttons—the sort of thing Paddington Bear might wear to the beach—lay on the ground between the two hippos.

Momentarily regaining the composure that had made him the swinging dick of the lake, the dominant hippo shot his young rival a look of desperate accusation. The challenger met this with a "Hey, bro, don't ask me what that thing is" shrug. The dominant male backpedaled into the lake. Completely freaked out himself, the challenger skulked warily into the cover of some nearby bushes, staring uncomprehendingly at the hat and plotting his next move. A move, alas, that no one in the Land Rover would ever see. The fight was off.

The explanation for this bizarre turn of events unfolded through a flood of Euro jabbering. In her haste to remove her camera from her bag and then from its case—God forbid you'd drive through a game reserve in Africa with your camera already out and ready—the TBH had knocked her floppy blue hat off of her head, out of the Land Rover, and onto the road, setting up one of the strangest and ultimately most anticlimactic episodes in the history of hippo blood sport. Too busy tittering and squawking over the impending face-off, the TBH hadn't realized that her hat was missing until it was too late.

Tebo jammed the Land Rover into gear and rolled over to retrieve the hat. It was coated with a layer of viscous white hippo snot. This naturally sent the TBH into a paroxysm of laughter. Without apology, she held

* As though there could be any other kind. Unfair, I know, but I'm endlessly entertained by foreign English.

the hat aloft while the Euros snapped photos, Klein stared into the distance, and I sulked in the back of the truck.

After dinner that night Tebo told me, "If not for the hat, we would have seen a great hippo battle." His tone was matter of fact, with no hint of disappointment or blame. He'd seen his share of hippo fights. He'd see a few more before his guiding days were over. I, on the other hand, had missed the only opportunity I'd ever have of bearing witness to the violent ritual that determines hippo hierarchy, thanks to one blithering idiot's inability to muster even a trace of outdoors protocol or put a damper on her natural obliviousness.

I stewed over the hat fiasco for the rest of the night, but it was impossible to stay mad at the TBH. Her high spirits were too infectious. The next day I sat beside her on a draining all-day drive to a new camp, sharing my stash of Starburst and, to help pass the time on the arduous haul across flat, roasting Botswana, passing her my camera when she asked if she could flip through my pictures. When she came across a shot of an elephant at a watering hole with his pachyderm penis dangling like a piece of industrial plumbing, her ensuing convulsion of magnum force tittering shook the entire vehicle.

Like the blasphemous three-foot-long shlong I'd inadvertently captured, there was something gigantically entertaining about the TBH. Even so, by this stage of my African journey I was dying to disengage from the supervised amateur scene and get on with a more independent adventure. Despite the warnings that Tebo, Kap, and every other African I'd met so far had heaped upon the mound of paranoia started by my friends back home, for the first time the Congo beckoned as a place where I might actually escape my troubles rather than find them.

One of Kinshasa's few alleged attractions is the mausoleum of President Laurent Kabila, who was shot dead in 2001 by one of his own bodyguards. The bodyguard did the deed in the presence of a gang of disloyal army generals Kabila had injudiciously attempted to fire moments earlier. Officials initially said that the killing did not amount to a coup attempt—that it was merely an argument that descended into violence—though twenty-six alleged conspirators were eventually given death sentences in a Congolese court.

Even so, the African and world press speculated that the murder had been carried out with authorization from the United States—our government was at the time backing Uganda in a war involving the DRC. Jesus Christ, if anyone would stop watching the ridiculous Hollywood portrayals, actually talk to run-of-the-mill field agents, and look at the CIA's record of incompetence overseas, that feared organization's reputation might eventually correspond with reality. Lucky or not for our national intelligence agencies, people all over the world are too busy believing in indestructible Bourne fantasies to check the scoreboard in places like Cuba, Vietnam, Laos, Central America, Afghanistan, and Iraq.

Kabila was succeeded by his son, Joseph, who ordered the construction of a mausoleum before proceeding to deal with dad's enemies—a familiar enough scenario for aficionados of political dynasties. The mausoleum had been conceived as a point of paternal tribute and expression of patriotism and solidarity. But I know my exalted poobah death cribs—Napoleon, Grant, Lenin, Elvis—and this one barely befits a beloved small-town mayor. A cracking concrete canopy looms fifteen feet above the ex-president's flower-covered casket, which is encased in glass ten feet below ground level. Four concrete fists at the base of the posts supporting the canopy represent the structure's primary artistic motif.

After changing money in the market, Team Congo arrives at the mausoleum's gated entrance, where three presidential guards sit on folding chairs. They're dressed in combat fatigues topped by bloodred berets with special forces insignias. They carry Chinese-made Kalashnikovs. They smoke cigarettes. They are exceedingly courteous. They want money to let us through the gate.

Gilles protests in Lingala. The president's tomb is free to all. The lead soldier, a young, well-built, Hollywood-handsome type, tells us with quiet gentility that this is a tricky day to see the tomb. This must be true since the large square surrounding the presumptive tourist gem is completely empty.

After fifteen minutes of negotiation, we hand the guards two dollars in francs and half a pack of smokes and are allowed to pass. When we approach the casket, another soldier appears and informs us that if we want to take pictures we must give him five dollars. I say, "That's OK. I don't need any pictures." He insists, however, that once back in the States I'll regret not having taken some photos at this historic spot. It's not clear whether this is a threat or not, but I give him five dollars and grab my camera.

Since our arrival, an older man in a torn yellow T-shirt has been trailing ten or twenty paces behind, shadowing our every step. The moment I lift my camera he rushes forward and introduces himself as the mausoleum's official photographer. He explains that I'm not allowed to take pictures. He'll take them for me, using my camera, and all the better since I can now appear in my own photographs. He will, of course, need to be paid.

The soldier nods at me as if to say, "I know, it sounds

crazy, but, seriously, it's actually the rule!" The old guy assures me that he can operate any camera on the planet, but when I hand him my little Canon PowerShot he backs up about ninety feet and becomes hypnotized by the zoom function.

At a traffic light not long after the mausoleum, a cop wearing a dirty blue uniform shirt and jeans sticks his head and nightstick in the passenger window and demands to see our fire extinguisher. It feels like another random shakedown until D. B. opens the locked glove box and produces a tiny red fire extinguisher.

The cop grunts like a fat man denied pie and stalks away. Amazingly, no bribes are demanded. I tell Henri I've never heard of a law requiring drivers to carry fire extinguishers.

"They created this law a few years ago," he says. "One of the cabinet members was friends with a Lebanese businessman who imported these small extinguishers. But no one was buying them and he was stuck with tens of thousands of them. So they passed a law—every vehicle owner must carry a fire extinguisher or face a severe fine. The Lebanese man has made millions. He's the nation's sole supplier."

The hell of it is, it actually sounds like a pretty good law, even if it did come into effect pretty much the way our enforced gambling, uh, mandatory car insurance, and most other laws do anymore.

Ten minutes later a livid policeman opens the door and jumps into the Mercedes as we make a right turn. Apparently, right turns are illegal on this street. At the moment, anyway.

We pile out of the car and stand on the sidewalk for

another round of a game that's becoming routine. A rictus of verbal abuse from the cop. Demands for an outrageous sum of money. Threats to haul us downtown. Protests from D. B., Gilles, and Henri of near though not quite equal intensity. Arrival of more cops. Calming period. Amiable personal discussion—what part of town you're from, what village your wife is from, the business of the tall white dude in the Seattle Mariners cap looking like he's carrying a fresh load in his boxer briefs.

Before long everyone is getting along and the cops begin moaning that the government hasn't issued paychecks in three months and now that we're friends, hey, brother, anything you can score me would be appreciated by me, my wife, seven kids, and two girlfriends. This last point always clinches the deal with knowing laughs and pretty soon two or three dollars in francs changes hands followed by more easy laughter and handshakes. The lesson? To quote Kevin Cronin, "If you really want to get through to somebody, you got to speak to them in their own language."*

It's not quite noon. We've been on the road two and a half hours, paid five bribes, and narrowly avoided a sixth. Henri's fragile PR nerve has been touched once too often.

"I can't believe it," he says with genuine disgust. "I have not had this much trouble in at least six months. Please do not get the wrong impression of Congo."

An hour outside Kinshasa at a boat harbor in the riverside village of Kinkole we board Henri's battered old twenty-

---

* Anybody who gets that Kevin Cronin reference without having to Google it can head down to 157 Riverside Avenue and become instant buddies with my good friend Brian Brink, who is feeling good right now with a beautiful lady by his side, a big ol' glass of his favorite wine in one hand, and a big ol' J in the other, to whom this long overdue joke is fondly dedicated.

foot wooden scow—the only thing missing is Kate Hepburn hectoring an emaciated Bogie—for a short cruise along the Congo River. On the north bank is Brazzaville, capital of the Republic of the Congo (much smaller than the DRC, it achieved independence from France in 1960), but we'll not be crossing into foreign territory. Nevertheless, we stop at the port's immigration office—a low-ceilinged hut with no electricity and stacks of boxes for chairs—to assure the pseudo-officials of our intention not to break any border laws. For some reason this requires us to hand them a few dollars before we can board our listing vessel.

The famed river is eighteen miles wide here, and it's pleasant to chug along the water away from the anarchy of Kinshasa, enjoy a light breeze, and check out the fishing boats and grass-hut villages that sit on the waterline. The highlight is a stop in a subsistence fishing village called Lokuta, where, as visiting whiteys, Henri and I get the royal treatment—a tour of the village from the chief, in an African-print shirt, and a plate of sliced bananas and dried fish.

An hour before sundown we're back tying up at the marina at Kinkole.

"What are you doing? You may not moor your boat here!" Another soldier, another red beret, another Kalashnikov charge toward us.

"Yes, we are allowed," Henri shouts back. "I paid the harbor office for this privilege."

The soldier stands in front of Henri and tells him that whatever deal he cut with the harbor office isn't applicable. Not today. Not while he's in the neighborhood.

And so a little more arguing, then a transition into cheerful banter about the wives, kids, and girlfriends. A couple of cigarettes. A few dollars. Handshakes. A twenty-minute delay. And we're off again.

Team Congo closes the day at an outdoor bar—more accurately four plastic chairs set up on the banks of the Congo River—with three warm beers and a Coke. (As a devout Christian and professional driver on call at all times, D. B. never drinks.) Below us swirl the infamous rapids that vexed colonial developers—steamships couldn't get past them, requiring a torturous portage through thick jungle—and still occasionally claim the lives of thrill seekers attempting to conquer them in rafts and kayaks.

An elderly man hustles out from his small house on the side of the river with another round of drinks. As a magnificent purple-red African sky takes form, I ask Henri how many bribes we paid on the day. Before we departed Kinkole I'd wandered around on my own for an hour and missed part of the action.

"I have no idea," he answers. "I lost count."

I remind him of my quest to find the funniest joke in Africa and ask if any good ones come to mind. He drops his head like an exhausted prizefighter and takes a massive hit off his lung dart.

"Not at the moment," he answers, blowing smoke and staring into the man-eating rapids.

Finding jokes in Africa isn't a cakewalk. Once I got the idea in my head, I sent off an e-mail soliciting jokes from my many Peace Corps friends and relatives who somehow remain friendly to me despite my occasional Peace Corps tirades. I figured it'd be a good idea to stockpile jokes from across the continent, but reaching out to my extended PC tree netted precisely zero replies with Africa jokes.

Two e-mails did come back bluntly stating that I was going to be rightly regarded by the reading public as an ignorant asshole for attempting to be funny about Africa. (Peace Corps volunteers are tragically unable to find the humor in anything that doesn't belittle American society; it's part of their training.) Fortunately, on the banks of the Congo, I recall a story told to our safari group by a native Mokoro poler on the Okavango Delta in Botswana:

After Creator made the world, all of the animals on Earth got together to throw a big party. Everyone was getting along well, but there was a mischievous rabbit in attendance who decided it would be funny to play a trick on the hippo. When no one was looking, the rabbit grabbed a burning stick from the fire and jabbed it into the hippo's rear end. The hippo immediately ran for the river to relieve his pain in the water. The water felt so good that he decided to make the river his home for the rest of his life.

This did not sit well with Creator who quickly appeared and sternly addressed the hippo.

"Hippo!" said Creator. "I thought I told you that you are not allowed in the river because you are so big that you will eat all of the fish."

"Yes, this is true," answered the hippo. "But I'm so heavy and it's so comfortable here that I'd like to stay. How about if you let me remain in the river on the condition that I promise not to eat any of the fish."

Creator thought about this and replied, "How can I trust you to keep your promise?"

"I'll tell you what," answered the hippo. "I'll stay in the water during daylight hours where you can easily keep an eye on me, then leave the river at night to feed on plants and grass. Before returning to the river each morning, I'll take a big dump and spread it all around. That way, you can look through my shit and see that there are no fish bones. The day you find fish remains in my stool is the day I'll abandon the river."

After considering this for a minute, Creator agreed to the deal. And that explains why, to this day, hippos live in the water, but don't eat fish, feed on land at night, and spread their scat wherever they go.

Now, that's a decent enough story, but in my experience it's what's more often known as an "origin myth," not a joke. The striking thing about hearing it told in the Okavango Delta, however, wasn't the story itself, but the reaction it received from those listening to it. When the "punch line" about scattering scat in the morning arrived, all the whiteys in attendance, including me, nodded in respectful, New Agey appreciation of this quasi-religious psalm from a wise and dignified (if ultimately assbackwards) ancient tribal font. Never mind that, like all vegetarians, hippos have an enormous cross to bear and that modern science tells us the reason they spread scat is to mark their turf. Our reaction indicated that we were all immensely honored to have this solemn piece of oral tradition passed down to us by such an authentic source.

Meanwhile, I'd noticed that as the story had been gaining momentum, the seven or eight Mokoro guys among us, obviously familiar with where it was going, had been smiling and shaking like kids about to wet their pants. At its conclusion, they broke into a chorus of locker-room laughter, a completely different reaction than their tourist counterparts. To them, the story clearly resonated with a humorous, absurdist value.

I'm no cultural anthropologist (as though this fact needs to be reiterated), but I have some experience with

Trickster Owls and Light-Giver Ravens, and it occurred to me that one thing Westerners often overlook in legends such as the one about the rabbit and the hippo is that one of their main purposes, aside from any ethereal explanations of life and nature, is entertainment. No matter what the point, a story doesn't survive a millennium or two of campfire retellings if it sucks. Whether you make a living bringing down impala with spears, poling tourists through the delta, or using a police badge and AK-47 to collect bribes from passing motorists, the last thing you want at the end of the day is to be preached to. This was as true a thousand years ago as it is today when I sit in my faux bistro chair, crack a frosty one, shout, "This dumb fucking ass-clown!" and quickly move on when I accidentally bump into Joel Osteen on my rounds through the dial. That's why *The Office* is on channel 2 and the Trinity Network is on 87.

Look at it from a less reverential perspective and you can see a lot to laugh at in the hippo story. The Stooges-esque slapstick of the rabbit jabbing the mighty beast in the ass with a burning stick. An all-powerful creator capable of putting together an entire planet and its inhabitants reduced to bargaining with a hippo, which, for all its other attributes isn't historically regarded as the craftiest of animals. And, of course, the scatological nature of the punch line—there isn't a culture in the world that doesn't love a good fart or shit joke. As Howard Stern will be happy to tell you.

It might not be the funniest joke I find in Africa, but on the banks of the Congo the hippo story feels important for shedding light on a disorienting day in which the flower of Kinshasa squalor has blossomed into a garden of hopeless dysfunction. In a society based largely on intimidation, success is based upon not backing down to bullies (God, cops, whomever), the ability to negotiate impromptu deals (scattering feces, francs, whatever), and at all other times partying hardy (with silly rabbits, mistresses, whomever).

When I mention this fascinating cultural connection to Henri, he fakes an appreciative snort and goes back to his cigarette. Gilles stares sullenly into the sky. However else they might be described, Team Congo cannot be accused of intellectual snobbery.

After a few minutes, Gilles calls the old man over from the house to settle our bill. D. B. finishes his Coke, walks to the car, and turns the key. Three, four, five, then six times the starter whines and whines, but doesn't catch. I hear him try a seventh time before he opens the creaky car door, gently closes it, and walks back toward us on the crunchy gravel.

Without turning around, still staring at the river, Henri blows a plume of smoke and says to me, "Now we have something to laugh about, don't you think?"

3

. . .

The Most Beautiful City in the Congo

Our story about being aid workers desperate to help the Pygmies hasn't been taken seriously. The UN has denied our request to fly to Mbandaka. So far the Congo has been a bigger letdown than *The Sopranos* finale.

True, Kinshasa is temporarily fascinating in an end-of-days kind of way, but so far my stay here has amounted to little more than an elaborate time killer. I've pretended to care about river rapids and presidential deathbeds, but the only reason anyone comes to Kinshasa is to get a flight out of Kinshasa. No planes, no boats, and no trains whittles the list of options. Thankfully, there's one solution guaranteed to haul even the saddest sack out of the doldrums and fix, temporarily at least, all problems: road trip.

Driving anywhere in Africa is a painfully slow process. Before you can even address the shitty roads, you have to deal with the Michelin map, the Central African edition of which is so enormous and unwieldy that it requires a surface roughly the size of a soccer field before it can be fully spread out. Making matters more difficult,

Henri and D. B. aren't wild about the idea of embarking on an impromptu roader—Jacques is waiting for a callback from a crop duster or helicopter pilot somewhere—but stagnating at the intersection of Congolese corruption and Team Congo's professional inadequacy has me in such a funk that they have no choice but to play along when I officially declare Mbandaka dead to me and begin pointing at roads leading to places I vaguely recall reading about in history books. As a result, discussions of plans B, C, and D go roughly like this:

"This place Kimvula looks promising," says I, pointing at the map with the get-up-and-go of an Eagle Scout. "What's out there?"

"The road to Kimvula is impassable at this time of year," answers D. B.

"At what time of year is it passable?"

"Most of the time it is difficult."

"Kikwit sounds interesting. Man could really lose himself in a place called Kikwit."

"The road to Kikwit is restricted by military checkpoints. Very difficult."

Resigned to the fact that, once aroused, my spirit of determination recognizes only victory—and that a four-thousand-dollar down payment counts for something, even in the Congo—Henri reluctantly enters the conversation. He begins pushing a drive west toward the coast to Boma, the first Belgian capital of the Congo, a rarely visited city steeped in history. Boma isn't anyone's idea of a prom date, but given our current paralysis, the idea of standing at the edge of the continent staring out at the vast Atlantic, the plains of human evolution at my back, holds a certain appeal.

"There must be a decent beach out there," I say.

"Due to the condition of the road, we cannot drive all

the way to the ocean," D. B. says. He's been pegging the buzzkill meter now for forty-eight straight hours. "But along the way is a waterfall and Matadi, which is the most beautiful city in Congo."

So, Matadi. Then Boma. Swapping Pygmies and Mbandaka for waterfalls and Boma feels like trading Lou Brock for Ernie Broglio and Bobby Shantz, but what the hell, it could be worse. Of course, it was supposed to have been much better.

"There is just one problem," Henri says. "The brakes in the car must be repaired."

"We've been driving around Kinshasa four days in a car with bad brakes?"

"It is only a small problem. At high speed if you must stop suddenly, they may not work. In the city it is OK because there is so much traffic."

"Yes, I can see how that makes it OK."

Henri acknowledges sarcasm only when he wants to.

"As you may have noticed," he says, "it is impossible to attain a dangerous speed while driving in Kinshasa."

I have no choice but to concede the point and marvel once again at Henri's incredible knack for winning arguments in which he's nearly always wrong.

Before we can leave, we have to pick up the Mercedes across town. Henri and Gilles meet me at the hotel in a rust-corroded 1980s Mazda driven by another Team Congo auxiliary member, a guy in his early twenties whom no one bothers to introduce. From the backseat I assess the Mazda's cracked dashboard—none of the gauges work. The interior is gilded in soot. The vehicle has clearly been engulfed in flames within the past few weeks.

Ninety minutes later the airport terminal appears in

the distance. Gilles explains that our mechanic is actually an airport security guard. He's got the Mercedes in an airplane hangar out of which he runs his side business using the shop's tools. It is unknown whether any of the major airlines serving Kinshasa have a problem with this arrangement.

Turning onto a service road leading to the airport, we immediately plunge into center stage of a terrifying show. Five young African men rush into the street, surround our car, and begin thumping on the windows and making surly demands in Lingala. Our driver wisely accelerates through the mob, but not before one assailant scrambles onto the hood and another hurls himself butt-first onto the trunk. Everything about the way this unfolds—the suddenness, the shouting, the beating on the car—feels exactly like a Hollywood re-creation of a Third World kidnapping.

"What the hell is going on?" I shout at Henri.

"Do not panic," he answers, not unlike the pilot fumbling for his rosary beads as the second engine catches fire and the nosedive begins.

With the car careening through traffic, the guy on the hood spreads his body across the windshield. It's an effective tactic. We're forced to slow down.

The car is surrounded again, this time by eight or ten men. A short guy in a black shirt jogs along next to me, actually smiles and says hello, then thrusts his hand through the open window. Money, passport, camera—everything important to me is in the backseat of the car. A reasonable lunge and the guy could have it all, a move I'd be forced to resist. Judging that a physical altercation here will greatly complicate matters and likely result in defeat for me, I begin cranking up the rear window. The driver wheels on me and shouts to leave the window down.

"If they really want to get inside, they'll break the windows!" he shouts. "I cannot afford such a repair!" Impressed with this flash of Congolese horse sense, I leave the window down and do what I can to push the guy away from the car.

Seconds later, a soldier with a bandolier of high-caliber shells strapped across his chest steps in front of the car. At the wave of his rifle our attackers disperse like roaches. The soldier directs us to the side of the road. After a brief negotiation we cough up five dollars and receive full military escort into a dirt parking lot. Here we find D. B. and the world's largest mechanic—six-eight, shoulders like shanks of beef, ass like a beer keg—waiting with the Mercedes.

With the soldiers and motley security types gathered a few feet away, the mechanic informs Henri that the difference between his original estimate and the actual cost of the repair differs by about 400 percent. This touches off one of those high-comedy French arguments in which all participants wave their arms in a blind fury and make faces that suggest the accidental intake of German wine. Between outbursts, Henri regards the mechanic with icy glares and sucks in soothing lungfuls of cigarette smoke. Eventually, he motions to Gilles, who reaches into his bag and hands the mechanic a wad of cash the size of a Jack Daniels bottle.

Once final details have been wrapped up and the mechanic departs, Henri turns to me and says, "I like that guy. He's the only honest mechanic in Kinshasa."

Two hours later, sailing down a smooth, Chinese-built highway, Kinshasa fading like a bad memory, a brilliant late-afternoon sun setting the jungle colors ablaze, Henri, D. B., Gilles, and I get into a discussion of colonialism.

Henri is a trip-hammer of opinions—worse than me, if that's possible—but this is the first time I've managed to draw out more than stunted conversation from the African contingent of Team Congo.

"The Congolese would love nothing more than for the Belgians to return to power." Henri repeats this for the third or fourth time in as many days, but this time I'm surprised by D. B.'s reaction.

"Life was easier with the Belgians in charge," he agrees. "There were good roads, hospitals, free public schools, government employees received their salaries on schedule."

Born during Belgian rule, which ended in 1960, D. B. is able to offer firsthand perspective on his country's five-decade decline. Like most Congolese, he blames the nation's woes on the disastrous Mobutu kleptocracy. "With Kabila now in office, things are getting better," he says.

Gilles, who's thirty-one, suggests that D. B.'s problem is that having been born during colonial times he's really Belgian-Congolese. Born after independence, Gilles himself can claim pure Congolese status. This is a bit of a joke and both men laugh, but I sense that it's also an important dividing line. Even so, Gilles agrees with most of what D. B. says.

"For several years I ran my own boat-repair company," Gilles says. "But there were always complications, and I had no one to turn to for help. Bribes and harassment from officials and difficult employees and theft. The situation became so bad that I had to give up my business. Without a network of support, the Congo is impossible. Now I work for Henri. I can turn to him if I have a problem."

D. B. and Gilles agree that the Congo would be better off if the Belgians returned as rulers, but they stop short of saying they actually want this. After several days of saying almost nothing to me, Gilles hits a nerve by thanking me for having the courage to come to the Congo. He asks me to spread a positive message about the safety and stability of his country, a prerequisite, he believes, for much-needed foreign investment.

I tell him I'll do what I can, but I feel a little sick to my stomach while making this promise. The whole conversation reminds me of the famous quote, not quite a joke, from Jomo Kenyatta, Kenya's first president: "When the missionaries arrived, the Africans had the land and the missionaries had the Bible. They taught us how to pray with our eyes closed. When we opened them, they had the land and we had the Bible."

As a rule, I'm bored with discussions of race relations. This isn't because I don't consider the topic to be an important and ultimately defining point in any review of U.S. history. It's just that in my view the problems always get framed in the most irrelevant terms imaginable—how a talk-show host defamed a certain ethnic group, why an offhand remark made by a politician betrays racial insensitivity. Such obvious red herrings. You want to fix racial inequity, focus 100 percent on education. Overhaul the school system, give all groups equal access to equally funded schools, and stop wasting time griping about racist jokes and the 10 percent of prejudiced Neanderthals who will always be with us, and you'll get to the mountaintop a lot faster.

I'm not a bullhead about this. I'm willing to admit, as with most issues, to a lot of gray territory and to the limitations of my typically reductive logic. I'm also willing to concede points to those more familiar with the tribulations of living in a racially divided world, particularly to any nonwhite person in the United States. Still, after a couple decades of discussion, debate, and spittle-filled shouting matches, this pretty much sums up my core position: it's all about education; if you want to change racial discrimination, discussion of any other point is a waste of time.

That said, it's pretty much impossible to tool around Africa and not reflect on the incredible history of African Americans. It sounds naïve, but it's startling to travel across the continent and see so many *American* faces. Judging strictly from appearances, D. B. and Gilles might have been raised in Mobile, St. Louis, Tucson, New York, or Los Angeles. Right down to Gilles's Brooklyn Dodgers baseball cap.

History really does come into clear and unsettling focus when you come face-to-face with the people whose ancestors we know primarily as terrible statistics from history texts and disturbing cinematic re-creations of the slave trade. All across Africa, I was consistently moved by the familiarity of the people and the instant "American" kinship we shared. In a weird way, this often made me feel at home in a very foreign place.

In Botswana, I came across a guy in a market who bore an absolutely uncanny resemblance to the late rapper Tupac Shakur. (Jay-Z and Kanye are amazing, but for me, hip-hop as art form begins with the Sugar Hill Gang and ends with Tupac, so I'm sort of partial to this story.) I was so taken with the similarity that I actually followed the guy around for a few minutes, trying to get in position to snap a surreptitious photo to show to friends back home. Seriously, you could start an entire "Tupac lives" cottage industry with a couple pictures of this dude. Alas, the guy never emerged from the crowd near the fresh goat section, and I felt too awkward to approach him with my bizarre request for a photo.

All of this felt a little impolitic; it's strange to wonder if a future rapper's people had been snatched from the very acre of earth you're vacationing on. Nevertheless, I mentioned the Tupac doppelgänger to Kap, the sometimes philosophical, twenty-six-year-old safari cook I'd accompanied on the market run. It turned out he was also a huge fan of the man he referred to in reverential tones as "the late, great legend."

"There was also a guy at my school, near here, who looked so much like the late, great legend that we only called him 'Tupac,'" Kap told me. "His real name was discarded. He became known as Tupac, even to his parents. So maybe those infamous genes can be traced to this place."

It's staggering to stand in a barren landscape still dotted with circular mud huts and grass roofs and ponder the historic calamity that led from an unfortunate bushman or woman taken away from southern Africa to the likeness of a martyr sanctified on T-shirts around the planet. Not to mention the immortal lyric, "Even as a crack fiend, mama, you always was a black queen, mama."

Because restaurants are few and literally far between in the countryside, we stop at an industrial complex where Henri has connections and have dinner in a workers' cafeteria decorated like a Hong Kong banquet room circa 1975—naked fluorescent lights, cheap paper lanterns, wall calendars with Oriental babes in silk dresses, and, naturally, an assortment of ceramic good luck kitties. With public works projects all over the continent, the Chinese have been buying goodwill and UN votes in Africa for decades, so, like the paved roads, this bizarre tableaux of midcentury Cathay in the deep countryside isn't as rare as you might think.

One thing I like about the Congo is that the steak always arrives well done. I'm no connoisseur and well done is the way I like my meat, even though most waiters back home treat me like a simpleton and nearly always defy me to send my steaks back by bringing them to me medium rare—as though they're the ones, not me, paying thirty-five dollars for the goddamn things. This is actually a big issue with me, so I mention my happiness with the well-done meat to Henri.

"It's done completely for hygienic purposes, not because they like steak prepared that way," he says. "All the beef you eat here has worms and other diseases. It's just local cattle that wanders all over the place exposing itself to the same parasites as everything else. They overcook the meat to kill those things. But don't worry, it's perfectly safe."

As I've noted to the dismay of many a self-styled barbecue expert, it's possible to cook a piece of meat thoroughly without destroying the flavor. Tonight's entrée, however, might as well be a flank of rhino. I struggle through five bites, leave four chunks of angry, half-chewed gray flesh on the plate, and wait for the trichinosis to set in.

Inspired by his earlier candor, I decide this might be a good time to draw some personal details out of D. B. On several occasions, Henri has bragged up our driver's ass-kicking skills and from time to time I've written for *WWE Magazine*, so I figure a discussion taking advantage of our mutual interest in knockin' skulls might loosen him up.

"So, a six-dan black belt in karate," I say. "That's pretty impressive."

D. B.'s face darkens, the way Bruce Lee's might in the vicinity of a winnable fight that a vow of nonviolence he's sworn to uphold over his mother's grave prevents him from entering.

"I still keep up my training, but not at the same level as in my youth," D. B. says, staring into his plate.

"How about a demonstration?"

D. B. laughs off the idea, but after five beers I'm pushier than usual.

"Let's say a drunk in a bar attacks you like this." I make a mock grab for his throat, no doubt emitting a poisonous fog of Primus beer breath in his face at the same time.

The moment my fingers graze D. B.'s neck, I realize my mistake. Responding with lightning reflexes honed through years of Mobutu-brother bodyguarding, D. B. whips both of his hands behind his head, latches onto my pinkie fingers, then rolls both of my hands over his head while twisting my digits like dried spaghetti. It's funny; you go through half a lifetime without thinking about how much pain can be focused in your little fingers until someone is about to turn them into a pair of mismatched chopsticks.

I howl like a badger in a trap—which is amazing, since at the moment it's almost impossible to breathe. D. B.'s eyes widen as though he's just been awakened from a nightmare. This is good because I actually am in the middle of a nightmare. In mine, I begin whimpering like a five-year-old. What's the safe word in a situation like this? Mobutu? Kabila? King Leopold's beard?

D. B. drops my hands and begins apologizing profusely, almost as embarrassed by his reaction as I am by mine.

Freed from his grip, I reach for my beer. D. B. buries his face in his iced tea. After a moment of penitential reflection, he says, "I reacted poorly. Grab my throat again. I will show you more ways of stopping an attacker."

"No, no, it's cool, really. I'm sorry, I just wanted to . . ."

"Please, I insist," he says. "Attack me again."

"No, seriously, I just thought . . ."

"I am serious also. Please. Attack me."

The edge is still on, but in a damned if you do, damned if you don't situation with a former presidential bodyguard trying to make amends, you do what the man tells you. Like an archaeologist handling a priceless Ming vase, I place my hands on D. B.'s neck. Lifting one arm up from his waist, D. B. snakes a hand between my arms and applies a twisting pressure on my elbow, then breaks my grip by gently wrenching my shoulder. Even in tender stages I can feel the devastating potential.

"Your instinct is to grab an attacker's wrists and try to pull them away, but if he is stronger than you that will not work," D. B. says. "It is better to apply leverage to the joint."

I simulate more assaults—bar drunk wielding bottle, bar drunk attempting blindside tackle, bar drunk attempting old-fashioned kick to the balls. I don't attack well, but I do "bar drunk" with impressive accuracy. D. B. demonstrates the most effective method of countering each attack while graciously not crushing my windpipe in his Gila monster grip, although he lets it be known that he could. I like D. B., his inability to smile notwithstanding, but he's got an annoying way of making you feel more dickless than the collected works of Air Supply.

Mindful of the dozens of broken promises that have already marred the trip, I've been silently dreading whatever accommodations might be scared up in Matadi. But the Hotel Metropole is an unexpected jewel—a five-story, dark-stone, Venetian-style palace of porticos, archways, ornamental palms, patios, and balconies overlooking an enclosed tiled courtyard. The hotel was built by the Belgians in the 1920s as a vacation spot for privileged whites; along with Chinese businessmen and government dignitaries, the same clientele keeps it in business today.

After our late check-in, Henri and I convene in the courtyard for a midnight closer. He has a Primus. I order Fanta. My inability to face alcohol at this point in the day is as good an indication as any of the bone-aching fatigue of car travel through rural Africa.

As soon as we sit down, four women barrel through the lobby door and beeline for our table. Standing in a circle around us, they smile and pitch massages and "girlfriend fucking," billed as a better and more convincing lay than normal professional fucking—which, while plausible, would depend on the girlfriend and what stage of the relationship you're talking about. The girls react to this observation with blank stares. Yet again my rapier wit goes unnoticed in Africa.

Two of the women could be grandmothers, which here means they're probably in their early thirties. There's a beer-goggle chance the tall one in the blonde wig is a tranny. The fourth, in baggy cargo pants and loose-fitting tank top, is good-looking in an aggressively conventional way—like the local weekend news chick who can't quite work her way onto the weeknight team.

The weekend coanchor motions to the empty chair next to me. I nod and say, "Sure, go ahead." She sits down and slides the chair over so that our shoulders touch.

"Now she thinks you are going to sleep with her, you know?" Henri says through a haze of freshly lit cigarette.

"What are you talking about?" I say.

"You asked her to sit down. That was your invitation to fuck her."

"I didn't ask her to sit down. She invited herself. I just said OK."

"Aren't you familiar with prostitutes?"

"It depends what you mean by familiar."

The woman asks me to buy her a beer.

"If you buy her a beer it really means you are going to fuck her," Henri says.

Even in the interest of journalistic research I'm too tired for this game. Rising and saying goodnight, I leave the bartender money for four beers, a round for the table on me.

Henri fills the elevator with smoke as we ascend to the fourth floor.

"Typical American, paying for something and getting nothing in return," he says. "This is Congo. You do not have to pay for anything here unless you get fucked."

Which strikes me as perhaps the most honest thing Henri has said since we've met.

Even for the devoutly hitched, sex in Africa cannot be ignored, but already, wow, this is more than I bargained for. African women are sensational. Blinding white smiles. Proud, graceful chins. Long, elegant necks. Thrusting breasts. Sir Mix-a-Lot asses. Calf muscles you could write entire sonnets about. A continent of track stars. And that's just the Atlanta airport!

I'm kidding here (sort of), but Africa's infamously free-wheeling attitudes about sex and its bottomless well of urgent, extroverted beauties pretty much demand attention. These days, of course, the ribaldry comes at the price of the worst of the world's four-letter words. Despite a continent-wide media barrage offering free advice on everything from condom use to abstinence, however, the problem does not appear to be abating. In the words of the director of a Kinshasa AIDS clinic, quoted in Alex Shoumatoff's *African Madness*, "Sex is a big part of Africa; take it away and there is nothing." Though his book was published in 1988, Shoumatoff's observation seems to be holding as true as anything Stanley or Livingstone discovered when they passed through the area.

In a society as open as the Congo's—most African countries maintain what anthropologists call a "sex-positive culture"—AIDS is the ultimate cosmic joke. A Congolese man told me the story of a village whose people believed in the sacred commingling of semen and vaginal fluids not just as a means of procreation, but for attaining divinity. So anxious were the villagers to please both their God and their government that they dutifully wore condoms during sex . . . but not before cutting off the tips.

Disease, however, is just one of several potentially fatal byproducts of unguarded relations in Africa. Henri tells the story of a Belgian who owned a bar in Kinshasa. During one of the recent civil wars—he didn't specify which one—there was no electricity in the capital. Because the Belgian owned one of the few large and reliable generators in the city, his bar had lights and, more importantly, cold beer.

"For a while he was making a lot of money and a lot of friends," Henri says.

Running low on fuel one afternoon, the Belgian gave his trusted Congolese assistant money to buy gas. Instead of going to the gas station, however, the assistant bought fuel at a reduced rate from a black-market dealer, then pocketed the leftover cash.

The gas turned out to be diluted—"Water, alcohol, beer, they put anything in it to make it go further," says Henri. The black-market fuel ruined the generator. It ran for twenty minutes, then stopped forever.

The Belgian's business quickly declined. He fell out of favor with the local cops and soldiers who had served as his protectors, and, worse, began fighting over money he no longer had with his Congolese girlfriend. Eventually tiring of the drama, the girlfriend attempted to resolve the entire matter by killing the Belgian with poison.

"It's not such an uncommon solution to problems here," Henri notes.

The Belgian survived the attempted poisoning—he'd been sick at the time and was throwing up daily, and this is probably what saved him—but he was understandably alarmed enough by the attempt on his life to cut things off with his girlfriend. A wise move, especially when compared with his next one—taking as his new girlfriend the ex-girlfriend's best friend, whom he'd been screwing on the side, anyway. Again, not so unusual a situation in the DRC.

Amazingly, further complications ensued. Some weeks later, when the Belgian was discovered back in bed with the ex-girlfriend (the one who'd poisoned him) in what can only be imagined as a breathtaking hate-fuck extravaganza, the new girlfriend tried to poison the Belgian anew.

This time the poison worked. Or almost worked. The Belgian spent two months in bed certain he was going to die. Finally, he regained the strength to fly home, never to be seen again.

"He lost everything," Henri says. "His business, his

money, his women, his reputation, almost his life. This is Congo."

"What is he doing today? Do you keep in touch with him?"

"When you leave Africa in such a way, you do not keep in touch with people. No one has any idea what became of him."

Henri plays the savvy foreigner routine a bit too convincingly for my taste. For example, instead of ignoring or handing small change to beggars, he prefers to antagonize them. A typical exchange, always in French:

> Beggar: *"Patron, patron,* I am so hungry. Nothing to eat for two days. How about a hundred francs? (This is about twenty cents.)
>
> Henri: How about you give me a kiss?
>
> Beggar: What!?!
>
> Henri: You can't expect me to give you something and get nothing in return. I'll give you a hundred francs and you can choose either to kiss me on the lips or kiss my ass."

This gets a few laughs from bystanders—you can't go anywhere in Africa without bystanders—and an embarrassed smile from the beggar.

> Beggar: Oh, *patron,* please. Just one hundred francs.
>
> Henri: Monsieur! What species of pigeon do you take me for? I'll tell you what. I'll give you one hundred francs if you will give me one hundred francs."

Beggar: But I haven't got one hundred francs. I need money only for food.

When the argument stalls, Henri's go-to move is to put a friendly arm around the beggar's shoulder, begin rubbing his belly, and address the laughing crowd.

Henri: It seems he has been eating well enough, no? I believe he wants my money to buy beer and cigarettes.

In the face of the jeering crowd, the beggar—playing along in the expectation that good humor will earn him a handout—is defused. Henri walks away and the beggar is frustrated.

Crudely tolerable as it might be once, the act becomes exceedingly obnoxious after you've seen it four or five times. But in Africa there's always a new audience and Henri is a born showoff who never tires of attention.

Once an important trading post filled with Belgian Beaux-Arts architecture, Matadi's city center today remains surprisingly functional and handsome. (On the Congo scale, anyway, which is like the scale for all-white track teams and Polish cuisine.) The dramatic old buildings have inspired a sense of community pride and suggest comparable affluence. After Kinshasa, Matadi's streets seem almost clean. Locals are polite and easygoing. Even small stores have shelves full of goods.

Anxious to escape Team Congo for a day—the guys have been harder to get rid of than a pizza box and I'm no good without my Chuck time—I wake up early and set off for a walk through the city. After exchanging heartfelt

"Bon jours" with a dozen or so strangers, I cross the street at a wide intersection. Bursting with good cheer, I step off the curb and feel on my shoulder the thinnest pretense of a tug. A vibration, really, as though a large insect has landed on my back.

One of those unaccountable instincts—like the inner voice that warns you to avoid coed baby showers and Dane Cook movies—tells me to check the knapsack slung over my shoulder. I turn and find to my all-consuming horror that the zipper on the front pouch has been pulled wide open. The words "Holy Fuck!" blast through both hemispheres of my brain. The sight of my valuables exposed to the entire African continent shoots a wave of nausea through me.

As quickly as I can choke back the rancid taste of fear, however, a miracle reveals itself. Nothing has been taken. My passport and enormous wad of francs are dangling half out of the bag—another tremor of weakness courses through my body as I riffle through the wreckage—but they remain in my tenuous possession. Nothing is missing. For the moment.

Yanking the zipper shut with trembling fingers, I spot a young guy—fifteen, sixteen tops—approaching purposefully from behind. Our eyes lock for a telling instant before he peels off in the opposite direction. In front of me, a kid in a blue T-shirt with "Wildcats" silk-screened in white script across the front whips around, looks at the kid, then at me, then back at the kid.

From Munich to Mumbai, here's how the scam works. Picking out a tourist rube with a knapsack in a congested street, a thief approaches from behind. With a single, nimble motion, he whips open the zipper of the pack and keeps moving in front of the mark. Trailing a few yards behind, an accomplice then sticks a hand into the open pouch and grabs whatever he can while making his pass. Oftentimes, a third confederate will make another pass-and-grab, walking off with whatever the second guy couldn't.

In Matadi, the heist doesn't go off as planned. Maybe the zipper whipper wasn't a pro. Maybe the thieves didn't count on the sturdy double-stitching of the Jansport.* Maybe I actually do have the superhuman powers of perception I've always suspected myself of having. Whatever the explanation, I duly praise the sweet and bleeding Jesus for his righteous intervention. A potentially devastating robbery has been averted.

Sensing trouble, the kid in the Wildcats shirt turns to me again. This time we share a millisecond of you-guilty-motherfucker eye contact. Plainly busted, he makes a theatrical check of his watch, then takes an abrupt U-turn through onrushing traffic, as though he's just remembered an urgent appointment or spotted an old friend directly behind him.

Pickpockets in the Congo are generally presumed to be in cahoots with local police, who get a generous cut of the take in exchange for leaving the thieves alone. Although I wouldn't necessarily be afraid of a wiry shit like Wildcats in a normal situation, I'm at an eye-of-the-tiger disadvantage in any altercation with someone of a desperate criminal mind-set. And Christ alone knows what friends he's got lurking nearby.

Despite all this, I make a U-turn in the middle of the street and follow the kid—unleashing car horns, shouts, the whole African ruckus—and begin closing the short distance between us. When Wildcats quickens his pace, I double-

---

* The workhorse of independent travelers since it came on the market in 1976, the classic, heavy-duty Jansport daypack deserves a hermetically sealed display case in the Smithsonian.

time mine. What I plan to do if I catch him I have no idea, but with my heart thrashing in my chest like a marlin in a boat and flush with confidence from my street-fightin' tutorial with D. B., pursuit feels like a viable option.

In the end, the adrenaline rush is all for nothing. The moment he sees me closing in, the kid breaks into a dead sprint down a crowded sidewalk, hairpins into an alley, and disappears forever.

In 1879, at the age of fifty-eight, African explorer and scholar Sir Richard Burton—easily among the top twenty stallions ever to trod the Earth—was set upon by thugs in Alexandria. Biographer Edward Rice wrote of the incident: "In the old days Burton would have knocked his assailants' heads together, or even better, killed them, but now he collapsed on the street and was left for dead. . . . If any lesson came out of the episode . . . it was that he was getting too old for excursions into dangerous and now-strange worlds."

Getting rolled by scofflaws was a disheartening turning point in Burton's career. The valiant participant in unspeakable sexual rituals of the African jungle; the mighty linguist who'd written dictionaries and translated ancient poetry; the first Englishman to pierce the secret world of Mecca; after Alexandria, an unshakable gloom descended that remained with him for the rest of his years, though being denied promotion by pissant bureaucrats back in Old Blighty and spending his golden years with a harpy Victorian wife bent on payback for years of neglect certainly didn't do anything to salvage the old wolf's pride.

Regrouping from my near miss in Matadi, I reflect on Burton's tragic denouement and consider our depressing parallels. True, at fifty-eight Burton had nearly two decades on me at the time of his encounter with African riffraff, and he endured a fairly severe beatdown. Still, in world's-most-virile-adventurer years, I figure fifty-eight is equal to nineteen or twenty mortal years.

Physically and intellectually, on my best days I couldn't approach Burton with both legs broken and half his brain tied behind his back. Even for the most intrepid, though, there comes a point when the impromptu let's-hop-in-a-brakeless-Mercedes-with-total-strangers-in-the-Congo vagabonding has to stop. After certain experiences—narrow brushes with thieves, hotel rooms that smell like wet dog—the meditative outrider has to wonder if, like Burton, he's simply getting too old for this shit—and whether this unspoken fear might have been at the root of his self-inflicted year of challenge travel all along.

Knapsack snatchers thwarted and composure more or less regained, I resolve not to let one negative experience color my opinion of the entire town. Pressing on, though with newfound caution, I find a mellow dude behind a table stacked with CDs. Needing souvenirs for friends back home, I ask, "What's new in Congolese music?"

After a debriefing on the contemporary Central African music scene—females in loincloths specializing in spiritual numbers are big this year—I settle on a pair of CDs by a chubby, middle-aged dude named Madilu System, a local legend who's recently passed away. The salesman pronounces my taste in music top-notch. My faith in African humanity takes a tiny step toward recovery.

The CD purchase draws a small crowd from which emerges a twenty-year-old named D'jino who wants to try out his English. Despite my general dislike of nonnative speakers looking for gratis conversation hours—I was once a professional in the ESL racket and can still get on my high horse about freeloaders—D'jino turns out to be a pleasant guy.

I agree to a guided walk through town. We start with a short climb to the top of a bluff overlooking a glorious stretch of the Congo River. Well-preserved colonial-era houses amid swatches of lush jungle dot both banks. There are so few postcards in the Congo that you appreciate views like this the way Detroit Lions fans appreciate touchdowns.

I didn't haul two Canon bodies and lenses all the way to Africa for nothing, but just as getting in the shower or sitting down on the john is guaranteed to make the phone ring, whipping out a camera in the Congo brings the cops running. The Congolese have a weird pathology about cameras, an almost Soviet suspicion of anyone taking a photograph of anything other than a crime scene. Sensing a shutter about to fall, a police officer awakens inside a building two blocks away and rushes toward us.

The cop jabs a finger in my chest and screeches, "Terroreest! Terroreest!" D'jino laughs the way you would at a crazy uncle. He explains that the two of us are friends from school. Given the two decades that separate us, perhaps I'm being portrayed as a kindly visiting professor. It's impossible to know. The drama ends with the cop smiling, shaking my hand, and shoving off without demanding a friendly payoff. D'jino is smooth. Henri could pick up a trick or two from this guy.

Back in the city center, we wind up in front of a heavyset, middle-aged woman selling beignets off the top of a wooden crate. I buy one for each of us, which, with D'jino handling the transaction, cost five cents apiece. Pressing the change into my hand, the woman tells me how much D'jino and I look alike. This is a patent load of caca, but the woman goes on to tell me that D'jino could be my son if only I was the type of man who went around screwing lonely black women and fathering bastard children. I wouldn't by any chance be that kind of man, would I? In the States this sort of cheek from strangers would be offensive, but in Africa it seems sort of normal, even charming, especially since the woman gives my leg a warm squeeze when she says it.

D'jino and I split up in front of the Hotel Metropole. I give him a five-dollar tip, a couple dollars more than I would have had he asked for one. Feeling good about myself—survived robbery attempt, hooked into local music, evaded bribe, made new friend, felt up by beignet lady—I walk into the lobby to find D. B. looking at me the way a dad looks at his teenage son sneaking in through the garage door at two in the morning.

"Henri is looking for you," he says. "There is a problem."

D. B. and I drive twenty minutes across town to the local office of provincial immigration. We pay two dollars to the soldiers guarding the main gate before we're allowed through. A woman in traditional African dress meets us in the lobby and walks us to the second-floor office of the director. Inside this august chamber, Henri is already sitting in a plastic chair. (If you haven't already clued in, "plastic chair" describes 99 percent of the furniture in the Congo.) Across from him, behind a large wooden desk, sits the living embodiment of the shady Third World official cliché.

Fat, self-important, and sweating profusely—despite

cooling himself nonstop with a plastic geisha fan—the director of provincial immigration clasps my hand like a church deacon and tells me he's privileged to welcome me to Matadi. A lackey fetches me bottled water. We stumble through a moment of niceties—"Enjoying your stay in Congo?" "Very much." "Excellent."—before the big man sucks a raspy breath between clenched teeth, the universal signal that official negotiations are about to begin. From the top drawer of the desk he produces my passport and begins thumbing through it.

"When did you enter the DRC?" he asks me in Ivy League English.

"November seventeenth," I say. "Five days ago."

"Where was your Congo visa issued?"

"The Congolese Embassy in Washington, D.C. I sent off my passport for the visa in October."

"At least one of your statements must be false."

I turn to Henri and ask, "How did this man get my passport?"

"In order for us to pass through the Inga Dam site, it is necessary to gain official permission," Henri replies.

"But we're not going to the Inga Dam. We're going to Boma."

"Inga Dam is a tourist attraction."

Leaving aside the issue of why I would want to pass through the site of Inga Dam, I turn back to the immigration director.

I already know what the "problem" is. On the day of my arrival, an immigration official at N'Djili Airport "inadvertently" stamped a September 15 arrival date into my passport. The date conflicts with the November start date on the visa issued to me by the DRC embassy, not to mention my actual arrival date. Though I hadn't noticed it at the time, the clerical "error" makes it appear as though I entered the country illegally, a federal offense that's seized upon by eagle-eyed officials all over the country. Several spot the inconsistency so quickly that it almost seems like they know it's coming. In Matadi, the director of immigration wants to know, like all the others, how I managed to enter the country without a valid visa and escape detection for two months.

"I have no idea why September 15 was stamped into my passport, but I've done nothing illegal," I say. "I was in the U.S. in September. It's a simple mistake. Obviously no official would have let me in the country in September if my visa wasn't valid until November."

"Where is your vaccination card?"

I hand over the International Certificate of Vaccination with my yellow-fever inoculation dated October 2, pointing out that it would have been impossible for me to enter the country without this vaccination—proof that I couldn't have been in the Congo in September. Over the top of his fan, the director regards me like a sink full of dirty dishes. Some people (public officials often as not) are simply born immune to reason.

I reach for my airline ticket and show the director my itinerary, still more evidence that I'm telling the truth. He reaches across the desk and the ticket disappears into his massive paw. Along with my passport and vaccination card, he stuffs it into his shirt pocket. All these years of travel and I continue to astonish myself with my own stupidity.

"I want to help you," the director says in a semibelievable way. "But I am compelled by law to prosecute anyone who has entered the DRC illegally. The only solution I can see to this problem is to invalidate your original visa and personally issue you a new visa and entry stamp, both bearing today's date."

"Sounds good to me."

"The cost for the new visa will be U.S. five hundred dollars."

For the duration of this petty drama, Henri has been brooding in uncharacteristic silence, but with this new demand his outrage boils over. Uncorking one of those extravagant, saliva-gushing Gallic dressing-downs normally reserved for poor table service and reviews of sub-par Gérard Depardieu movies, Henri rises to my defense with a pair of inspired albeit highly dubious arguments. In the first place, he informs the director, as he (Henri) is close, personal friends with the national minister of tourism, he (Henri) is on the verge of making a phone call to Kinshasa that will surely cost the director his job. If this insignificant parasite wishes to continue his sleazy charade any longer, he (the director) may rest assured that Henri will shortly have his head or balls (the director may choose which) in a pretty little guillotine. Second, as a government functionary, the director should be aware that he is harassing a citizen of the United States of America whose leader, the eminent George W. Bush, has recently made known his country's full financial and military support of the Congolese government in their fight against the well-armed rebel faction based in Kivu.

"Without the support of Mr. Thompson's president, you might not even have a job," Henri finishes in a crescendo of indignation worthy of the Taiwanese Parliament. "So do not go fucking with your country's strongest ally!"

This is the first time any kind of favorable alignment has been conceived between me and Kommandant Bush, and it feels pretty slimy.* But a sidebar with Henri just

---

* Criticize my hysterics if you like, but a president who pushes fascist vocabulary like "homeland," "axis of evil," and "enhanced interrogation techniques" on us deserves to be remembered accordingly.

now will get us nowhere, especially since the director seems to be taking the threat of international scandal seriously. After a moment of contemplation, he announces that this extremely tricky situation requires an out-of-office consultation.

"Please remain comfortable for a few minutes," he says, walking out of the office with my passport, vaccination card, and plane ticket.

For thirty minutes Henri and I sit side by side, barely speaking. Waiting like this is usually like waiting for a guy to finish in the gas station bathroom—the longer he takes in there, the worse it's going to be for you. When the director finally returns, however, he's a new man, a man who might well have been out sucking the kindest bud from the biggest bong on the entire African continent.

"I want you to know that I have reviewed this matter thoroughly and I do not believe there is any dishonesty on your part and that you are not a terrorist," the director assures me. "The mistake in your passport is the fault of a negligent official with airport immigration. I am happy to make a note of this and let you go. At no charge to you."

Henri beams, but we're far from done. Placing my passport on the desktop, but not exactly handing it over, the director pulls a sheet of paper from his desk. For my benefit, he begins breaking down the grim economics that force a nice guy like him to hassle a nice guy like me.

"Do you know what I make in salary each month?" the director asks me.

When I say I haven't the foggiest, he shakes his head plaintively, scribbles on the paper, and turns it around for me to read: Par roi 22,000 FRC=$45

"That's not much of a salary," I say.

"It is a crime that a man in a position as revered as

yours is not remunerated more fittingly," Henri chimes in. This isn't the first time I've seen him switch emotional gears with such disturbing ease. Henri would make a terrific game show host.

"I am forty-five years old," the official continues morosely. "Do you know how many children I have?"

I shake my head. Like a coroner filling out a death certificate, he scratches another line on the page: Pere de 10 enfant

"Ten kids? Wow!"

"It is a terrible burden," Henri adds. "Life is truly unfair to the Africans."

Next, the director jots down his monthly rent: $120. Then figures covering other expenses. School for the younger children. University for the older ones. Food. Electricity. Gasoline and car maintenance. All told, the guy needs about $250 a month just to keep his head above water.

"So," I ask, the guileless lamb being led into the room where they shoot the pneumatic bolt between its eyes, "how does a man in your position make up the difference between such a tiny salary and such massive monthly expenses?"

"My friend," the director replies, spreading his arms and grimacing in a way that suggests a recent viewing of Braveheart being stretched on the rack. No one sneers like the French, drinks vodka like the Russians, deceives like the Born Agains, or takes bribes like the Africans.

Ten dollars later, my passport comes back across the desk. That evening, Henri will say to me, "When guys who have nothing become important government officials with access to bribes and foreign aid, they go from fucking their girlfriends in ten-dollar hotels with two bottles of beer to fucking their girlfriends in three-hundred-dollar hotels with two bottles of champagne. That is the only difference between the government official and the guy on the street."

Like guests lingering after the party, Henri and I stick around for some polite parting conversation in the lobby. This is the now-we're-chums portion of the payoff process, and it feels like as good a time as any to mention my quest to find the funniest joke in Africa. The director seems honored to be asked for help and obliges with gusto.

"Yes, ha-ha, there is so much to laugh about in the Congo," he begins. "For instance, do you know that in the DRC it is against national policy for visitors to make cell phone calls from inside a government office?"

"I had no idea," I say.

"Yes, it is true," the director continues. "It is a punishable offense. No cell phone calls. Visitors are, however, allowed to smoke. This means that according to the government, ingesting cancer-causing cigarette smoke into your lungs is less dangerous to your health than calling your wife to check on the status of your dinner. For many husbands, this is quite literally true. Ha-ha-ha!"

Government buffoonery provides the mildly amusing setup, but it's the last line, the hint at marital difficulty, that's the real kicker. Henri coughs out an appreciative cloud of smoke. I force a laugh. The director's guffaw sounds like an extended fart and leaves him just as satisfied.

I'm not sure if the director has just made up this joke or if something's been lost in the retelling, but it reminds

me of one I heard in South Africa, also disparaging bu-
reaucratic inanity.

> As in many countries, South Africa maintains a "TV li-
> cense" system, a tax that requires every household with
> a television to cough up 250 rand (about $30) each year
> for a TV license. The South African government is un-
> usually efficient in enforcing the law, regularly sending
> inspectors to peoples' homes to check on licenses. The
> fine for being caught owning a television without a li-
> cense is 2,000 rand ($250). Meanwhile, with capital
> punishment having been abolished and a recent trend
> toward lenient prosecution of violent crimes, murder
> suspects are routinely released on bail of 500 rand.
> The moral of the story? If you have no license and the
> TV inspector comes around, your cheapest option is to
> shoot him.

Again, not exactly a knee-slapper, but if you lived in a
country with 40 percent unemployment, you might get a
laugh out of it.

On our way out of the most beautiful city in the Congo
we're required to stop at the state security office, a
plywood hut where we're told to wait outside until an official who can authorize our route to Boma—through the
sod-eating Inga Dam site—can be found. After a few minutes of horse-lather sweating in the midday heat, I move
to a cinder block that occupies the only bit of shade in the
yard. As soon as I sit, the receptionist, watching from a
plastic chair in the dirt outside the hut, asks me to please
go back to standing near the doorway.

"If my boss sees you sitting in the shade like an animal, he'll accuse me of mistreating you and it will bring trouble to me, so if you wouldn't mind," she says sweetly.

I leave the cinder block and reclaim my position in the baking heat so as not to give the impression that I'm being mistreated. It's two o'clock. Two hours past our planned departure. The sun bores into my forehead like a laser. I find a PowerBar in the bottom of my bag and lick melted chocolate off the wrapper. Back home it's November 22, Thanksgiving Day.

4

. . .

We Have a Winner

Congo towns are inarguably poisonous, but there are crooked cops, shifty expats, purse snatchers, felons, disease, filth, poverty, and pocket-lining bureaucrats in every big city in the world. To confront the white man's grave that Africa is truly renowned for being, you have to get into the countryside. By now it was past time to go see it.

In the States we have a collective understanding of "urban" and "rural" and the fundamental differences between places like Los Angeles and Wagontire, Kansas. Yet few Americans live more than an hour from the interstate and almost everyone has the means to get to a metropolis—or, going the opposite direction, to reasonably empty country— pretty much whenever they want. To our universal mobility, add the homogenization of print, broadcast, and Internet media and the strip-malling of America and you've got a country in which the steak quesadilla tower is as popular a menu item at the Applebee's in Mishawaka, Indiana, as it is at the one in Times Square.

No such consistency exists in Africa, where country means country, as in deep bongo, no electricity, no TV, haul your water out of the river, shit in the woods, life's about as cheery as a baby's coffin country. Just getting to rural Congo requires prodigious effort, so Henri is in an even more pessimistic state than usual on the morning after our Matadi misadventure.

"We have a small problem," he says between slurps of Corn Flakes and drags of cigarette. "It seems the road to Boma is in bad condition."

"How bad?" I ask. "Impassable bad? Or it'll-take-a-couple-extra-hours-to-get-there bad?"

"I don't know. Last night there were heavy rains. Our informant in Boma says only 'bad.'"

Our informant? So now we have informants? It's no wonder things keep going wrong around Henri. Counting every card in a five-deck Vegas shoe would be easier than keeping track of his payroll.

The first word you learn in the Congolese countryside is "mundele," which means "white man." Pass through any village and the word follows you like a shadow. "Mundele" is often accompanied by "mbongo," which means "money." If a stranger yells, "Mundele, mbongo!" it means they want you to give them some money. This happens more or less all the time.

In the beginning I found "Mundele, mbongo!" sort of charming. The people who shouted it always wore big smiles and it sounded to me a little like "Hakuna matata." Whenever I heard "Mundele, mbongo!" I grinned and waved like the big, friendly dork international travel so often turns us into. Then someone clued me into the meaning of the phrase, and I began to recognize the shouts only as whim dictated. Little kids usually got a wave.

Gangs of unemployed men squatting around bottles of wine, not so much.

This newfound selectivity put me in mind of the single Austrian member of my safari crew, a young, near silent, shaggy-haired blond named Rolf. At some point in our journey I noticed that in addition to nodding to villagers on roadsides, Rolf had discreetly begun waving at animals on game drives. I kept a watch on this curious behavior out of the corner of my eye, and the funny thing was that after a while I noticed Rolf waved only at the nice animals. Giraffes, turtles, and baby impalas became regular recipients of his affable alpine salutations, while baboons, crocodiles, and wild boar were passed without acknowledgment.

There are few animals left in the DRC, and centuries of hunting have left the ones that remain in deep hiding. Wilderness, however, is abundant. The highlight of our planned exploration of the Congolese sticks is a long hike through the "Luki Biosphere Reserve," a nature preserve established in 1937 by a group of farsighted Belgians familiar with the behavior of Europeans in virgin jungle. To help protect a piece of ancient forest where unique species of trees and plants grew, the Belgians laid out boundaries and constructed a handsome research center in the heart of the preserve. UNESCO and other international organizations ultimately lent support. When we arrive at the front gate, the line-art panda of the World Wildlife Fund is one of several familiar logos adorning the biosphere's peeling welcome sign.

We pass an abandoned guardhouse and broken fence and enter a world of steaming swamps, giant ferns, prehistoric vines, and soaring umbrella trees. Walking along the trail, we hear the rhythmic sound of chopping and encounter dozens of locals walking in the opposite direction with bundles of wood on their backs. Some drag large tree trunks over the dirt path.

"They need the wood for cooking," D. B. tells us. "No one can convince them of the importance of this place."

The Congolese are not impressive stewards of the wild. In the markets of Kinshasa it's still possible to find leopard pelts. A man trying to sell me one scoffed when I rebuffed his pitch by telling him I didn't want to encourage the killing of leopards by buying a skin.

"But this one is synthetic," he argued. "Fake fur."

"Then why does it cost eight hundred dollars?"

"It can be as you like," he replied enigmatically.

Our clothes already beginning to be eaten through by jungle rot and fanatical mosquitoes—for protection against bites I'm wearing more toxic chemicals than a Chinese river—we reach the vacant research center, now the focal point of a makeshift village. Locals have taken up residence in the dilapidated staff housing quarters, living with no electricity or running water. When I ask why the preserve is abandoned, Henri says that although some organizations continue to support the project, all funds are channeled through federal ministries in Kinshasa.

"Once the money is in Kinshasa, it goes no further," he says. "Officials in the capital pocket it. The aid groups begin to insist that they be allowed to give money directly to the center. When their request is denied, they stop giving money altogether."

We talk to a few villagers. We watch an older man and young apprentice making chairs and tables with handsaws and chisels. We meet a guy who sports what is surely Africa's most fully realized neck beard. We buy a bag of mangoes from a fourteen-year-old kid even though we could walk fifty feet in any direction and pick ripe ones for ourselves.

The most interesting character is an old man who strides out of the brush back near the main road and introduces himself as Phangu Albert. A traditional doctor specializing in herb remedies and spirit treatments, Albert tells me that he's eighty-two years old and that as a teenager he fought in World War II against the Italians in Abyssinia as part of the Belgians' Force Publique, the infamous organization of white officers and black conscripts with all the attendant suffering one imagines for the lower ranks in colonial Africa. Albert served as a radioman on the frontlines calling in enemy positions. For all sides in the war, forward radioman was as close to a death sentence as one could get outside the cockpit of a Japanese airplane in 1945. He says he later served in Egypt as part of the Allied forces.

On a continent where males often don't live past sixty, much less seventy or eighty, Albert is a find, and not just because he's the first African WWII vet I've ever come across. His answers to a few questions about the campaign in East Africa convince me of his authenticity—I'm a natural skeptic and I spent several years researching a pair of books about World War II sites, but Albert's story seems legit—and for the next hour we talk war exploits. His most enlightening story is from a comrade who somehow ended up serving for a brief time alongside the Russians after the war: "They liked only two things: drinking vodka and shooting guns. For them this was sex."

He strains credulity, however, when claiming that his father lived to be a hundred and thirty years old.

"You must mean a hundred and three," I say, giving the old man the benefit of the doubt by a wide margin.

"No, I mean one hundred and thirty." Albert is emphatic on the point and doesn't appear the least bit senile.

"A hundred and thirteen maybe?"

"One hundred and thirty years old."

The mileage shows on Albert's face, but otherwise he's sharp as a cat, none of that old man shambling or mumbling, so maybe he's not bullshitting. When he tells me he still walks five to ten miles each day, I ask the secret to his longevity.

"I always tell the truth," he says. "If you can speak the truth you are free, even if you have nothing. This is why I have always avoided politics and never took a leadership role in my village. Politics makes you hide your true feelings. Hiding your true self will cause you to suffer. Jesus Christ came and showed us the light in the darkness, and that is the way I live."

Albert is just one of many friendly people I encounter in the countryside. Eating lunch on the banks of a river, I watch a fisherman in a dugout canoe drift by, pulling in his net and singing a song to himself in the local dialect, one of those elegant falsetto hymns associated with Ladysmith Black Mambazo and post–midlife-crisis, pre–Edie Brickell-era Paul Simon. The fisherman's song adds a transcendent quality to an already beautiful scene—the sun illuminating thousands of beads of river water on the net, birds circling purposefully above, now and again folding back their wings and diving like darts into the water for fish. It's moments like these that justify the headaches of travel.

As the fisherman drifts closer, his singing becomes clearer. The handful of nearby locals begins laughing and staring at me. An older guy motions to me and says, "He is singing a song about you."

"Really? What's he singing?" I ask.

"His song says, 'There is a white man in our land. Why is the white man come to this place?'"

Not exactly "You're Beautiful" or "I Touch Myself," but, still, to my knowledge this is the first time anyone's ever done a song about me.

"Does he mean this in a good or bad way?" I ask.

"He says only that it is interesting to him. Now he comes to look at you."

The fisherman paddles over, breaks off his song, and shouts, "Bon jour, Monsieur Le Blanc!"

"He says, 'Hello, Mr. White Man,'" the old guy adds unnecessarily.

The fisherman and I exchange a few barely comprehensible words of fellowship. We look at each other and smile. When he begins paddling away I ask if I can snap his picture. He says only if I pay him five dollars. In an instant the spell is broken, both of us reduced to stereotypes.

Fascinating as these bucolic encounters are, none put me in contact with the mortal peril I'd come to face up to. This initially has me feeling cheated—surviving the Congolese jungle is supposed to be more of an achievement— but eventually gets me wondering if disappointment isn't going to wind up being the whole point of the experience. As usual, Henri comes to the rescue.

"We have a small problem," he says, kicking off our first day in Boma with his predictable rundown of issues facing Team Congo. "It seems I have made a miscalculation and run out of cash. I need to borrow three hundred dollars. Just until we get back to Kinshasa. There I can visit a bank and repay you."

This is unbelievable. We've been on the road for less than a week in a country where a hundred dollars pays the annual bills for most families. How do you come up three hundred dollars short in that amount of time?

"There are banks in Boma," I say. "I've seen them."

"It is Saturday. They won't be open until Monday."

Henri's request obliges me to confront an obvious fact that I've been hiding from myself since arriving in Kinshasa—somehow I've placed my passage, my faith, my well-being, and most worryingly my four thousand dollars in the hands of a hustler. This isn't a flattering realization for any traveler to own up to, but it's particularly embarrassing for a "professional" who considers himself reasonably independent with well-sharpened instincts for trouble. The fact that I don't even know the day of the week is a frightening indication of how dependent I've become on Team Congo and its chain-smoking, beggar-baiting leader.

Whether I trust or even like Henri any longer is hardly the point. In negotiations, he's meaner than a cornered raccoon, and even in agreeable moments he's the kind of guy who'd buy someone else's kid a drum set for Christmas. But in an outpost like Boma, I need Henri and Team Congo more than they need me. Or my three hundred dollars.

After some cat-and-mouse questioning during which I play the role of prayerful United States and Henri plays evasive, nuclear-armed North Korea, we reach a delicate agreement. I'll advance Henri three hundred dollars on the condition that not only will it be repaid upon our return to Kinshasa, but that a portion of my initial four-thousand-dollar payment will be refunded for the downgrading of my itinerary. Tellingly, the precise amount of "fair refund" is left unspecified—"It will be calculated at the end of our journey."—but we've kept the peace for another day.

As far as sightseeing attractions are concerned, Boma makes Kinshasa look like Venice, but I need some distance from Team Congo. Despite the fact that there's almost nothing of interest to look at, I take off after breakfast. In the center of town is a hollow balboa tree that I'm told famed explorer Henry Morton Stanley once slept inside. This is assuredly a fabrication. For starters, Stanley's supposed entrance and interior carvings are at ground level, as though the tree hasn't grown an inch over the past 140 years.

Nearby, the ruined hulks of an old Mercedes Benz and General Motors LaSalle are presented as the Congo's first automobiles; another obvious fiction given that the cars are clearly from the 1920s and '30s. But so what if they do carry some historic legitimacy? You know your town is as tedious as someone else's dreams when the second stop on the city tour is a pair of decaying vehicles from colonial times.

On the grounds of a secondary school I do find one interesting detail—a faded rendering of Belgian king Leopold II painted above the main entrance. Given that he was responsible for decades of looting, rape, punitive amputations, mass slavery, murder, and other unspeakable terror in the Congo, the Santa-bearded despot seems like a strange figure to welcome children each morning. When I ask a few questions about the extant portrait, it becomes clear that none of the teachers, to say nothing of the students, know nor care much about the fiendish face that adorns the door they pass through each day.

At an abandoned Belgian-built hospital undergoing a desultory form of restoration, I'm shown the room in which a former Congolese president died, and I'm informed that after it's fixed up, the room will become a museum. This means nothing to me, nor, apparently, to the Congolese. The old leader's broken bed frame is shoved into a corner. Next to it, tilted on its side, his death mattress is spotted black with mold. Torn curtains lie in a heap on the floor and pieces of broken concrete cover gaping holes in the floor of the entryway like a game trap.

In late afternoon, Team Congo and I reunite for drinks at the hotel. The day apart has done us all good. Even the normally dour Gilles is chatty. Around sunset, Henri and I walk to an outdoor nightclub—plastic tables and chairs in the dirt enclosed by a low, concrete retaining wall— where four large speakers pump loud, rhythmic music. After a couple more Primus beers, my mood is so improved that I barely care that the presumably destitute Henri is spending his (my) money on pricey drinks to go with the most expensive dishes on the menu.

"The only women you see here are prostitutes and girl-friends of married men," he tells me while ordering a round of whisky shots with beer backs for four women and two men he's befriended at the table next to ours.

The dance floor eventually gets crowded, mostly with guys, but the vibe is good. I have about ninety beers as another incredible African sky turns from blue to orange to purple to black. The music gets louder and more insistent. I soldier through broken conversations with drunken strangers. It feels great to be part of the local scene, and Henri is in a companionable mood, but at some point we split up and I walk around town for an hour looking for another bar.

Absolutely nothing is open, so I weave back to the hotel where a wedding reception has the lobby and bar packed with a couple hundred guests. Half in the bag already, I order a couple bottles of water to take back to my room, but the reception has soaked both the bar and restaurant of everything except beer and whisky. I stagger around the party trying to cadge a bottle of water off one of the tables. Even without a gallon or two of beer dehydrating you, it's never wise to be caught short of drinking water in Africa.

For once, however, the exalted Caucasian visitor routine isn't playing. Nobody wants me here. Hard glares let me know this is a closed party. Everyone is impeccably dressed. The women, in particular, look fantastic in their colorful dresses and big hairdos. By comparison, my dirty pants and T-shirt make me look like a Calcutta rag picker.

D. B. is outside guarding the car, but he's no help—the hotel is out of water and there's nowhere else to get any at this time of night. I offer a security guard five dollars to score me a bottle. You know you're screwed when putting up a week's wage for a bottle of water gets you shunned.

Back in the room I slur a fast prayer of thanks when I remember the two cans of Fanta stashed in my bag. I brush my teeth in luscious orange syrup, then finish off the can. I set the other one on the floor next to the bed for when I wake up in the middle of the morning dying of thirst and my heart racing like a chain saw.

I hit the mattress like Chinese leftovers—sad, withered, congealed. Making matters worse is that the hotel in Boma is by far the worst we've checked into. It's impossible to escape the damp in the Congo, but this hotel seems designed to trap it. Mildew coats every surface—walls, curtains, sheets, pillows. A fog of moldy air hangs over your sleep like breath from a cancerous dinosaur.

For three hours I lie dead in bed until a series of abdominal cramps jab me into consciousness, twisting my innards and sending me reeling around the pitch-black room wondering where I am, half angry, half stupid. I figure this is dehydration setting in—nothing that can't be gutted out till morning—but soon begin fearing worse. A sickly sweet brew of Fanta and beer creeps like pond scum across my tongue. My mouth fills with foamy saliva. With vibrant clarity I recall last night's chewy meat and several other meals that have yet to pass through me.

A moment of relief arrives with a splendiferous, sputtering fart that sustains itself for so long—revving up and gaining momentum like an outboard motor lurching up to step speed—that I get a little freaked out. But its glory is ephemeral. Minutes later I'm teetering atop the porcelain donut splattering butt glop into the toilet bowl with such velocity that I can feel flecks of it rebounding off the water back up at my ass cheeks.* (Perhaps the greatest ever description of Third World incontinence is William Sutcliffe's memorable bit from the painfully funny *Are You Experienced?* about travel in India: "The second I had squatted, I heard a strange sound of rushing water coming from behind me. 'What's that?' I fleetingly wondered, 'Who could be running a bath at this time of night?' Then I realized that it was me.")

Between the second and third voiding episodes, I reach for the light switch. After flipping it up and down forty or fifty times I realize the electricity in the hotel is off for the night. This forces me off the john and into the room to root around in the dark for the battery-powered camper's headlamp, which, even though I'm no longer on safari, I keep handy for just such emergencies.

Wrapped like hand cuffs around my ankles, my pants nearly trip me. No wonder so many kids run around pantsless here! I whip off every stitch of clothing. Completely

---

* I report on this reality without apology. I am not crass; bridal registries are crass.

nude, except for the headlamp and its blood-constricting elastic headband, I pitch back toward the toilet like a one-legged coal miner, stubbing my toe on the bathroom threshold on the way in.

The sink doesn't work (huge surprise there), but there is water in the toilet tank. Each time I think I'm finished purging I remove the ceramic lid and use some to wash up. I rinse my face with little handfuls, so overcome with cottonmouth that I allow incidental splashes to pass through my lips and cool my burning throat. In normal circumstances I'd sooner chug antifreeze than let Congolese tap water defile me, but at this point I'm forced to make nice with the local bacteria. A degrading tableau, I admit, running the sluices at both ends and freshening up with toilet water, but in situations like this you cling to whatever comfort you can find. Now seems as good a time as any, by the way, to note that of all the advice I collected before coming to Africa, "Bring your own toilet paper!" ranks at the top of the good-call list.

Having exhausted the attractions of Boma and unable to face the hotel staff with my usual éclat in the wake of the ostentatious all-night ralphing, I rise at noon and, after two emasculating, sit-down hangover pisses that go on forever, begin lobbying Team Congo for a change of plans.

"Boma is awful," I say. "Let's get back out into the countryside."

"But we have only just arrived after a long journey," D. B. complains.

"The toilet in my room may no longer be in service," I inform him.

Still at a political disadvantage over the three hundred dollars, Henri is forced to offer a compromise.

"Zongo," he says behind a floating pillow of cigarette smoke. "We will visit Zongo."

It's surprising how quickly you can clear out of a hotel after debasing yourself in front of a wedding reception and entire staff. Within an hour we're packed and back on the red dirt tracks that pass for roads in rural Congo. Brick and mud huts with grass roofs soon give way to radiant grasslands and rolling hills covered with emerald jungle. Alive again with something approaching cheer— my emotions on this trip are about as reliable as the Italian government—I appraise the loose dirt road, lean toward Henri, and say, "Great ride, but if it rains before we head back we're fucked."

"The rain will not hamper our progress," he says. "What we worry about are other vehicles. Large trucks can become stuck in the mud. The road here is wide enough for only two small vehicles. If a truck becomes frozen in mud, there are few places to go around. Traffic in both directions will stop, sometimes for several days."

I see his point. In most places the track is no more than fifteen feet across. Both sides are lined with thick jungle. But we see only one other vehicle all afternoon, a Red Cross Land Rover driven by a white man presumably on his way back to town from a final supply run to a remote village before the heavy rains strike.

The afternoon is broken up with a superfluous stop at the goddamn Inga Dam, a detour Henri insists on making despite it by now having become a thorn in my side. "I have obtained the permit to visit the dam, and it must be used so as not to incur suspicion," Henri explains.

Personally speaking, as long as the electricity works I couldn't give a shit about dams. Modern marvels, fine, but nodding appreciatively at acres of poured concrete gets tiresome in about two minutes. It's all hydro everywhere I've lived, and I never missed a field trip to marvel at the great turbines that have obliterated native salmon runs so that we can power up Guitar Hero and microwave popcorn in our heated homes that burn more lights than a surgical theater.

Try hard enough, though, and you can make a shit sandwich taste good. Once inside I force myself into a peppy mood, mostly for the benefit of David, the chubby Inga tour leader, who seems thrilled for his first excuse in months to get away from the guys in the welcome shack with the AK-47s propped against the desk.

The tour is OK, but it makes me tense when volunteer cultural ambassadors ask if there are any questions and not one of the deadbeats in the crowd (in this case, Team Congo) has one. So I lob David a couple easy ones. I'm going to forget whatever he tells me about integrated pump units and underground aquifer afterbays, but because I know from experience the slow death that comes from being in front of an audience that gives you nothing in return, I'm sensitive to the needs of guides. This is standard operating procedure for me, making up questions to let tour proctors know that we're still with them in the back of the bus, still engaged in the product. At times, though, it can be an incredible emotional burden being the kind of traveler who goes to Africa and ends up paying more attention to the self-esteem of local service-industry minions than to the pride of lions feasting on a bloated elephant carcass or a massive torrent of water rushing through French-built turbines sunk a hundred feet below the surface of the earth.

Despite my reservations, it is arresting to see the massive Inga I and Inga II facilities in the midst of forbidding wilderness. The two dams, spanning just a small corner of the mighty Congo River, supply power to the majority of the DRC. If completed, the planned Inga III and Inga IV dams are expected to send electricity all the way to Egypt and South Africa. How ironic that Conrad's highway into the heart of darkness now creates light for the entire Congo and could soon illuminate the Dark Continent from top to bottom, perhaps drawing the country a bit closer to burying the dreary sobriquet hung upon it by the old master cynic.

Zongo Falls saves the trip. Not counting Kinshasa destitution, it's the most spectacular natural attraction in the Congo. After a short, sweaty march through twisting, suffocating jungle, we reach the falls, an expanse of sheer rock face more impressive for its width than its height. It's only a seventy-five-foot drop, but from the churning death pool below, explosions of water send mushrooms of mist hundreds of feet into the air.

For several minutes, Henri, Gilles, D. B., and I stand in awe of the falls' power. These are my kind of nature lovers, able to revere the wild in respectful silence rather than feeling compelled to offer beer-commercial hoots and hollers. At Zongo Falls, I feel closer to Team Congo than at any point in the trip.

Taciturn Gilles surprises me by drifting into the brush to pick a bunch of blue and yellow flowers. He arranges the blossoms against a miniature fern, then snaps a picture with his Nokia cell phone. He shows me a series of close-ups of flowers and plants I hadn't noticed him compiling during our trip.

"It's nice to look at, to remember each place," he says while I flip through the shots.

The Zongo capper is dinner of chicken moamba, the famed national dish cooked in a thick, brick red sauce of palm and peanut oil. It's got a mild, nutty flavor, and for hangover food is every bit the equal of Taco Bell. I horse down two large pieces of chicken and bogart the last of the sauce to go on top of a third plate of rice.

Since our Come to Jesus meeting about the three-hundred-dollar loan, Henri hasn't bothered me with any "There is a small problem" preambles to yet more distressing disclosures, but the moamba puts him back on his game. The latest crisis concerns my flight to Johannesburg, now fewer than forty-eight hours away.

"You have a confirmed ticket to leave Kinshasa, yes?" Henri's face is dark with concern.

"Of course. I bought the ticket months ago." I produce the ticket from the sack of valuables that's been connected to me like an extra organ for the past month.

"I've just spoken with Jacques in Kinshasa. It seems when he called to reconfirm your flight, there was no record of your reservation or ticket purchase."

Fucking Jacques. Nothing positive comes out of any situation involving that guy.

"That's impossible," I say. "I have a confirmation code. I have a seat assignment. I have a receipt. I have a ticket right here. I confirmed all of this in Johannesburg the day I left for Kinshasa."

"Flights out of Kinshasa are not frequent and are always full. It takes no more than fifty dollars to have someone at the airport remove your name from a computer and insert a different one. It happens all the time."

"But this is South African Airways."

"But this is Kinshasa."

"You're saying my reservation has been stolen?"

"I have no idea. But, in any case, we must present you in person very early at the airport to fight it out. We will have to leave Zongo tomorrow."

"But we drove all day to get here."

"And skip the visit to the crafts market on the way home."

I could give fuck all about the crafts market. The real issue is Henri. Even in Zongo, the nearest approximation the Congo has to paradise, the man actively courts trouble. He's like the nightmare boyfriend or girlfriend who's never content, who's always looking for problems and when there are none to be found invents a few just to keep things interesting.

Henri lives for "the daily fight." It gives him the chance to show off, to perform, to prove to the locals, and himself, that he can't be intimidated. Hooray for him, but for me it's a different story. In the Congo, I'm like one of those National Guardsmen who signs on to get dirty in the woods for a couple weekends a year only to find himself hunkered behind a bombed-out rampart in Tikrit dodging sniper fire and screaming for the corpsman to pump thirty cc's of morphine into his downed buddy.

"It appears we will have rain tonight," Henri says, looking blankly into the sky and breaking me out of my dismal reverie to face an equally dismal reality.

The drive back to Kinshasa is long and muddy. Another shitty hotel. More cops to negotiate. But essentially my last two days in the DRC pass like most of the ones before them. I'm not traveling; I'm surviving.

Though I do my best to discourage him, Henri insists on seeing me off at the airport. He arrives in a shirt and tie, indicating his readiness for battle over my nonexistent reservation. He tells me he's been working the phones and that we must wait in the parking lot for some official friend of his who has agreed to come and grease the rails for my departure. Given that Henri has already shown up half an hour late and I'm antsy to get checked in, I rudely blow off the plan.

"I think I've got the hang of this by now," I tell him, swinging a bag over my shoulder. "I'll take my chances by myself."

Henri shrugs as if to say, "There is no God, our lives are short, and none of this matters anyway." We shake hands and say good-bye without emotion. I slide D. B. and Gilles handsome tips, receive warm embraces, and walk into the airport with the weight of the Third World off my shoulders.

Inside, a series of "helpers" bum-rush me between airline, security, and immigration counters. This costs me nearly an hour and fifteen dollars spread between various outstretched hands. The good news is that my reservation is intact (a false alarm from the nincompoop Jacques). But the first security counter is manned by a serious sergeant-at-arms type who instantly flags the visa discrepancy in my passport, then refuses to listen to my feeble French-English-Gibberish explanation of the situation.

After casting me aside and forcing me to fidget on a two-foot-high plastic stool for fifteen minutes, he summons me back to his counter and makes me go over the story again—my November arrival, erroneous September stamp, the money I've coughed up across the DRC as a result. This time he listens and bobs his head intently. When I finish he stares into my eyes and says in perfect English, "Do you swear to me that you are telling the truth?"

"Yes, I swear. The whole truth and nothing but the truth."

The ivory whites of his eyes shine against his purple-black face with a deep, incomprehensible strength. A perpetual loser in staring contests, I sense a challenge—loser stays, winner goes free—and don't so much as breathe or blink for at least ten seconds. Neither does he. Finally he mutters, "You may pass."

No bribe. No handout. The last honest official in Kinshasa? The first one, anyway.

The next counter holds the grail, the immigration stamp I need for departure. This is my second trip to the counter, and one of the two men at the window—a guy I passed two dollars to a few moments earlier—smiles and says, "Kinshasa, many problems, yes?"

"Many problems," I reply amiably, a smiling cohort in on the conspiracy.

This angers the other official who lashes out at me with Doberman rage.

"No! No! No! There is no problem with Kinshasa. It is up to you to check that the date in your passport is correct at the time you receive it! This is your responsibility! This is your problem! You created it! Do not blame Kinshasa!" He beats an emphatic stamp like a bruise into my passport and moves me along, his eyes radiating heat like hot briquettes.

At the next checkpoint I endure a comprehensive patdown that includes full frontal dick grabs—two firm, reassuringly hetero squeezes—followed by a brisk hand knifing up the crack in my ass through my thin safari pants. A few seconds later the guy manning the X-ray scanner grabs my carry-on off the belt, sticks out his palm, and tells me he hasn't eaten in two days.

"But you have a job. Aren't you paid a salary?"

"*Patron*." He smiles weakly. "At least buy me a Coca-Cola."

"Are you kidding?"

He motions across the departure lounge to a kiosk with drinks for sale. "Please, buy me a Coca-Cola. I standing here all day. It is very hot next to the machinery."

"Jesus Christ. Give me my bag and I'll get you a Coke."

He hands over the bag and I walk across the lounge and come back with the Coke. Then I return to the kiosk and spend the last of my Congolese francs on a plate of French fries in which four or five ants are crawling.

After a ninety-minute delay in the baking departure lounge, all 182 passengers on South African Airways Flight 51 are herded to the tarmac for another security search. This requires standing in the midday heat for thirty minutes before being allowed into the even hotter aircraft. A tall, attractive young security agent paws through my bag like she's late for a job interview and can't find her car keys. At the bottom of the bag she finds the scattered remnants of the international goodwill I'd conceived back in the States, each still individually wrapped in colorful paper.

"What is this?" She holds up a little square.

"Starburst," I tell her. "Candy."

She turns the square in her hand.

"Sugar?"

"Yes, sugar. Sweet. Candy."

"It is very good?"

"Delicious."

"You give to me."

"Excuse me?"

"You give to me."

"I'm not allowed to take candy on the plane?"

"You give to me."

"You want my candy?"

"Yes. You give to me."

Her voice occupies a territory between threat, order, and request.

"Go ahead," I say, by now practically laughing at this

absurd finale. "I was going to give them away anyway. Take them all."

She pushes around my camera lenses and safety undies and comes up with a handful, graciously leaving me a couple candies for the road.

"Thank you very much." She smiles at me and pauses as though waiting for a kiss at the end of a first date.

"My pleasure," I say, briefly wondering what she'd do if I actually kissed her before deciding to save it for the ground in South Africa.

Did I feel threatened or physically imperiled during my month in Africa? The rip-off attempt in Matadi was dicey, but overall, no, not really. Aggrieved by the petty demands of public corruption and aggressive beggars? Constantly. Insect bites? Despite my best efforts and gallons of bug dope, I came home with dozens. Malaria? So far none of the brain matter behind my eyes seems to be liquefying, which is how Shanghai Bob once described his experience with the disease. AIDS? Not unless you can get it by dropping beer money on bored prostitutes.

I wasn't attacked by a wild animal, swept away in a flash flood, or killed by monkey feces, though in truth I worried about those things the same way I worry about winning the lottery. Which isn't to imply that it's not unnerving to hear hyenas and hippos in the middle of the night snuffing and grunting within inches of your soft, malleable skull while you lie in your tent as still as a sack of bricks, trying to breath through your eyeballs. Shortly after I returned from safari, a tiger named Tatiana leapt over a fifteen-foot moat and twelve-foot-high wall at the San Francisco Zoo and killed a teenager named Carlos

Sousa Jr. Had I known about this incident at the time I might not have experienced those nocturnal visits with such surreal detachment.

I carried five hundred dollars in cash through the mean streets of downtown Johannesburg without incident. I walked unmolested through Soweto, still a hopeless slum but also a tourist attraction. I got sick once, in Boma, but that was probably my fault.

I read a lot of books and met with a lot of people while prepping for the trip, but what turned out to be the heaviest insight came from Dr. Bahr, who more than most kept his eyes open during his two-year Peace Corps stint in Cape Verde: "Africa is human nature stripped to the raw bones; life at its most basic. You find a lot of human traits out in the open there that we prefer to hide—sex, violence, love, hate, sickness, strength, greed, compassion, sadness, humor. It's all right there, with no pretense, and this is what makes it both attractive and repellant to Westerners."

Most of Africa wasn't repellant, just maddening, like trying to put together a bike or figure out a board game with an incomplete set of instructions. The worst joke, or maybe just the historic inevitability, was that, not counting bribes, nearly every injustice I suffered in Africa came at the hands of white people. The ceaseless nattering of the Europeans in the presence of safari animals wrecked what should have been numerous special moments. Henri made off not just with my money, but my trust. For those keeping track of account deficits, I got my three-hundred-dollar loan back, but that "fair refund" turned out to be "no refund," and I ended up eating the nine hundred dollars in prepaid airfare for the trip to Mbandaka that never got off the ground, which in part explains the cold comfort of my snub of Henri at the airport.

Did I have fun? Sometimes. Having drinks at outdoor bars with stars shining like little flashlights and drum-heavy music blaring and people dancing was cool. For a history geek who's traipsed through World War II battle-fields around the planet, meeting a local survivor of the Africa campaign was a thrill. Team Congo pulled Zongo Falls out of its ass for a trip-saving finale. I communed with cheetahs on my birthday, though I have trouble ad-mitting the timing was a huge deal given that I'm one of those people who prefers to ignore birthdays; not just mine, yours, too, especially if we're celebrating it with cake and ice cream in the admin conference room on the fifth floor.

What really made the Congo such drudgery was its lack of complexity. There's beauty in simplicity, but in Africa I started to miss things like baseball box scores, unnecessary kitchen gadgets, gin vs. vodka martini de-bates, diehards who file their Morrissey CDs under "S" for The Smiths, coming back from picking up Korean bar-becue and sitting in the driveway listening to the end of a *This American Life* story on the radio about a guy in Seattle who got over his wife's death by wearing a Superman cos-tume in public, and scouring YouTube at 2 a.m. for old Tenpole Tudor videos. I missed hearing about my friends' problems—the problems of architects, land surveyors, real estate appraisers, attorneys, doctors, construction grunts, tax accountants, graphic designers, social workers, bank-ers, defense contractors, salesmen, musicians, soldiers, students, teachers, cube monkeys.

One of the big troubles in the Congo isn't just that there aren't many jobs available; it's that there are almost no *good* jobs available. Aspiring writers can't go to school and return home to work the city beat for the local news-paper because there is no local newspaper. Entrepreneurs can't get businesses off the ground because there's virtu- ally no consumer market for anything beyond necessities. Ex-jocks can't become local golf or tennis pros because there are no local clubs. I don't know for certain but I'd wager the annual income of the average Congolese that there are more bookstores in my hometown than in the entire DRC.

Not that the Congo lacks for intellectualism. Checking into my hotel in Kinshasa on my first day in country, the young clerk who introduced himself as John D. handed me a room key and asked, "Don't you have an English novel?" I understood the words, but not the meaning.

"A novel," he repeated. "An English book. Something to read. Do you have anything at all you can give me?"

The hordes with their hands out are one thing. You want to help them all, but eventually you have to hold out against the sea of futility. When a guy asks you for a book, however, you're thrilled for the opportunity to give, as well as the chance to pass along evidence of your impeccable literary taste.

I handed John D. my half-read paperback of Saul Bellow's *Dangling Man*. If I really needed to finish it, I knew I could walk to a store ten minutes from my house back home and find a copy.

"It is good?" he asked, brightening like a sunrise.

"So far."

Lest I paint too charming a picture of John D., it should be noted that after I turned over this freebie he hounded me like an Egyptian fishmonger for more handouts every time he saw me. I suspect now that he was probably more interested in selling my books than reading them. Such are the ravages of global capitalism.

I never abandoned my quest for the funniest joke in Africa. The best one came at, of all places, Inga Dam. Among the employees there was a middle-aged, beak-nosed French engineer with wine-stained teeth. Alain was working on contract at the dam through 2011. He'd been in Inga for a year already and confided that the place was much better than Zambia, where he'd first come to Africa to live in a local village for three months as a sort of cultural warm-up.

"Eating with them, sleeping with them, to first experience life in Africa exactly as the locals do, not as a privileged foreign engineer," he explained.

Alain lasted seven weeks in Zambia, during which time he lost twenty-two pounds and became exhausted, sick, morose. Returning to France, he checked himself into a rest home for a two-week stay. There he discovered that his best friend from the Zambian village had stolen his credit card, run up a massive bill, and drained most of the euros out of a bank account he'd also stolen the numbers to.

Alain told his story in the cleansing way you'd speak about an awful breakup or terrible hangover suffered years ago. Seeing that he'd more or less picked up the pieces—though he still pronounced the name of the friend who betrayed him like a snake hissing at a rat—I took a shot and asked if he had any good Africa jokes. Amazingly, he had one that sent him into a fit of laughter before he could blurt it out.

"The biggest joke of all in Africa," he said, "is that I actually agreed to come back to this fucking place."

If that punch line loses something in the translation, it's probably because you've never had a grasshopper wing stuck in your throat.

In the weeks following my return I thought a lot about Africa, but the early conclusions were convoluted and disappointing. I'd survived, met a lot of nice people, a few dickheads, and nothing was as life threatening as it might have been. I'm not sure that I found the funniest joke on the continent—I'm still waiting on any shred of humor from my Peace Corps contingent—but people laugh in Africa as much as anywhere else I've been, and I doubt my reputation will suffer for saying so; if down-in-the-dumps Joe Conrad hasn't precisely been forgotten, it's safe to say not many locals are carting his books around.

That said, I didn't have to travel halfway around the planet for a "we all know that people are the same wherever you go" lesson. Those are much more easily obtained at home. All you've got to do is flip on the Disney Channel.

Months afterward, however, other mental images from Africa began resurfacing—derelict public services, stacks of worthless currency, out of control government, and lunatics like Henri who insisted that all of this dysfunction was somehow normal and simply something to get used to. These thoughts nagged me so insistently that over time I began to sense that Africa might have exposed me to some buried dread that would turn out to be much more complicated than the superficial fears I'd originally conceived.

It would take more confrontations with the horsemen of doom to drive these ideas into the open. But even if I didn't yet fully appreciate it, Africa had put me on a heading for a rendezvous with worries far greater than burrowing tapeworms and conclusions far more difficult to reconcile than Henri and Team Congo.

PART II

COUNTRY

India

5

Heretics in the Temple

There's no good time to visit India. I discover this when I begin consulting friends, family, guidebooks, and Web sites, laying plans for my assault on the subcontinent. May? Fatal dust storms. July? The heat will bury you. August? Nothing but rain. October? Even the mosquitoes can't fly through the humidity. December and January, the only good weather months, are ruined by tourist hordes that turn every attraction into a massive rugby scrum. Even in the summer low season the hip-to-hip shuffle through the Taj Mahal is a lot like the cattle call misery of the Louvre. Except at the Taj, you have to leave your shoes at the door and hope nobody steals them while you're inside.

It's not just that there's no good time of year to visit. There isn't even a good year to go. In the words of one inspirational poem I'd later find scrawled on the wall of a derelict palace:

Land of Sorrow
Ocean of Tears
Valley of Death
End of Life

A historic place of misery and half literacy, India is as formidable a dream crusher in the information age as the rousing verse above suggests it's always been. Having survived the privations of eternal Africa with somewhat less pain than expected, I saw now India anew as the bellwether for nearly every global calamity that had ever kept me awake at night. Among them:

Terrorism

Maybe because that "subcontinent" designation implies a retiring, almost deferential piece of land, few people associate India with Islamic fundamentalism. But with 120 million Muslims—12 percent of its population, making India in absolute numbers the second-largest Muslim country in the world—the nation that shares borders with Pakistan and China has become a favorite proving ground for mad bombers. Consider the following highly abbreviated list:

June 2009: Swarms of protestors enraged over the alleged assassination of a political candidate in Mumbai ransack six railway stations in the state of Bihar, setting fire to trains and stations.

November 2008: Coordinated attacks against ten Mumbai sites, including the traveler favorite Taj Mahal hotel, kill at least 170 and injure at least 230.

May 2008: Nine synchronized bombs kill 63 and injure 216 in Jaipur, capital of the state of Rajasthan and, as a pivot in the Golden Triangle, one of India's most popular tourist destinations.

February 2007: Railway bombs on a train bound for the Pakistan border kill 66, injure 13.

March 2006: Blasts in the tourist city of Varanasi kill 21, injure 62.

Yearly attacks stretch well into the last century. The gruesome Hindu-Muslim violence of the Bombay Riots of 1992 and 1993, for example, left more than 900 dead. As *Time* magazine reported: "The bestiality of human mobs was gruesomely exemplified at Bombay last week, when rioting Hindus and Mohammedans stoned and slashed and disemboweled one another until the dead totaled 106 and the wounded over 600, with the seven-day riot still going on."

Oh, wait. That *Time* quote actually describes Bombay's Hindu-Muslim riot of 1929. Anyway, the picture is clear. This is an explosive place.

Climate Change and Degradation

India receives 5 percent less sunlight than it did twenty years ago due to a cloud of airborne particles released by industrial plants that filters the sun year round. The World Health Organization claims that air pollution is responsible for 527,000 deaths in India each year. The country's rivers are toxic dumps. If global warming is going to strike North America with a vengeance, India is the place where we'll get a preview of the horror.

Peak Oil

During one of many summer 2008 price hikes, the cost of gas increased 10 percent overnight. Literally, overnight. The ensuing panic led to alarmist news reports, including one that ended with a clip of the dog-eat-dog desert resource wars from *Mad Max* and a grave prediction from a Kent Brockmanesque anchor that similar Aussie-style barbarism could become a daily feature of Indian life in a matter of months.

Another depressing thing about India—its news media, like its American counterpart, is perpetually in the grip of doomsday prophecy. Gloom and ruin are inescapable in any newspaper or TV news program. Military conflict. Water shortages. Overpopulation. Poverty. Pollution. Yet another humiliating cricket defeat at the hands of the filthy Sri Lankans. If the world is going to hell in a handbasket, it seems inevitable that the handbasket will be made in India—and at a cut-rate cost American producers of handbaskets can never hope to compete with.

On a personal level the forecast is just as horrifying. During pretrip research, I bring up my abiding fear of gastric distress and doctors diagnosing phony appendicitis to an Indian friend who spent most of her life in the mother country. Anita nods and says that although I have little to fear from rotten meat or toxic chemicals, I am nevertheless likely to suffer a spiteful anal purge and vicious streak-of-thunder vomiting while visiting her country.

"The problem is that most people in India don't use toilet paper," Anita explains. "The majority can't afford it. After they go to the bathroom they simply wipe with their hands. Sometimes they don't wash themselves so thoroughly."

"When you say 'most people' wipe their asses with their bare hands . . ."

"Yes, this includes those who will prepare your meals. It's particles of excrement, not spoiled or bad food, that will get you sick in India."

With that sprinkling of fecal glitter on its reputation as global financial hobgoblin—poised to swamp the U.S.

economy by thieving every call center job and American motel lease available—India emerged for me as the great nexus of all fears. If Africa was a sump pit of primordial simplicity, India promised to be an overflowing cauldron of contemporary complexity.

In *Flashman in the Great Game*—a fictional account of India under Victorian rule written in 1975 that nonetheless distinguishes itself as a valuable primer for visitors to the country—the brilliant George MacDonald Fraser writes, "Everyone hates India for the first thirty days then loves it forever." Taking chances on neither side, I book my visit for thirty-one days.

Next, I go to work on the one and only Joyce, sitting her down in her favorite chair, urging her to forego the dream of a beach *casita* in Baja for another year, burn her entire allotment of annual leave, and join me for the first half of the trip (discreetly leaving out details of my conversation with Anita). Like that Grizzly Man knob who grandstanded himself into a bruin Happy Meal while getting his girlfriend to anonymously film the final slaughter—in which she became dessert—if I'm going to release myself to the Armageddon of India I want someone around to document the heroic effort without horning in on my glory. If there's one regret I'll carry to my grave, it's not having any photographic evidence of my death-defying passage through the hard-currency black market alleys of Kinshasa.

"Colorful bazaars by day, blazing curry dinners by night," I say, painting a picture of Oriental wonder and putting on some George Harrison.

"Am I going to have to get any shots for this?"

"Depends how current your hepatitis schedule is. And

you might need a tetanus booster. Have you had a typhoid inoculation? There are also about a hundred dollars' worth of medications you'll want to buy."

"For what?"

"Apparently an issue with the vegetables. Flesh-eating bacteria or something. And malaria, of course."

Joyce takes her time, but eventually comes around. "Just keep me away from the tainted lettuce," she finally says, forcing a smile before getting into the spirit of things with a childlike enthusiasm that I fleetingly consider smashing for her own good before it's time to go.

For world wanderers, the debate between the independence and loneliness of traveling solo versus the compromises and companionship of traveling with a partner is unending. A robust Italian couple I encountered some years ago while camping on the beach at Bahía de Concepción in Mexico with my Texan friend John May provided my most memorable example of the eternal dichotomy.

Thrillingly tanned in the way only Speedos, French-cut bikinis, and a carefree approach to skin cancer in the face of an unremitting Mexican sun can get you, Marco and Maria were having the time of their lives, chugging Coronas, frolicking in knee-high surf, and talking in that noisy, extroverted fashion that you do at Italian surprise parties (I imagine). Marco was heavyset. Not fat, but thick in an impressive Sicilian bodyguard kind of way. Balding handsomely, he was gilded with an impressive array of jewelry that quite obviously hadn't been purchased from the band of imitation gem and turquoise salesmen that roamed the beach. Maria was even more stunning, a boobtastic, midthirties Sophia Loren ringer with shimmering black hair, deep mysterious eyes, and radiant skin. Everything Italian you'd ever want, minus the marinara sauce.

Marco, Maria, John May, and I stood in our swimsuits talking and drinking beer for thirty or forty minutes—Marco had come over to borrow our bottle opener—watching the sunset and throwing sticks into the ocean for a friendly dog who'd wandered by to check us out. When the sky turned dark, Marco invited us to join them for dinner at a restaurant a few miles up the road.

The fiesta vibe continued at dinner—shots of tequila, a jug of sangria, heartfelt toasts to international friendship. About an hour into the party, Maria—ten drinks in and still as poised as the guy on the Beefeater label—rose and excused herself. Marco watched her like a doting father all the way to the bathroom, but as soon as the door closed behind her his mood darkened. Stretching both arms across the table, he leaned toward us with searching despair.

"My friends, I am in hell!" he said. "It is torture. This woman, she is drowning me. All day, all night. Every minute, we are together. There is no escape. I am ready to die!"

"But she's gorgeous," I replied. "And you guys seem like you're having a great time."

"It is an act." Marco turned both hands into claws and gestured as though a wild animal were tearing apart his rib cage. "Inside is only death. I cannot escape."

"Is she acting, too?"

"I don't know. Who knows these things? Women!"

Marco stole a furtive glance at the bathroom, then lowered his voice.

"Tell me, where will you be later tonight?"

"Later tonight?"

"There is a disco in town, thirty minutes away. Maybe you will be going there?"

"Uh, actually, we'll probably just head back to our campsite after dinner."

"You have drinks there? You will be drinking?"

"We have some Coronas left in the cooler."

At this point, Maria reappeared across the room. As she shimmied toward us Marco whispered, "OK, I will see you at your camp." But when Maria returned to the table he jumped up to greet her with kisses, and after dinner we never saw either of them again.

Joyce and I arrive in Delhi late at night and check into a guesthouse called Eleven, which is run by an instantly likable, mellow-gold fifty-year-old named Ajay. Fortified with Ajay's boundless supply of tea and bananas, we spend our first two days in country on basic tourist detail.

The biggest Delhi attraction is the Red Fort, a redoubtable Mughal construction of red sandstone and white marble synthesizing elements of Persian, Indian, and European architecture. Completed in 1648 by thousands of typically underpaid workers, the ornamental fortress is studded with turrets and bastions and surrounded by a mile-and-a-half-long wall that rises as high as a hundred feet in some places. The complex is worthy of the considerable hype it receives, though it should be noted that its guidebook-baiting UNESCO endorsement may be less impressive than many travelers realize. UNESCO currently counts 878 world heritage sites, including such biggies as the Cahokia Mounds State Historic Site just outside of St. Louis, an attraction appreciated by Missouri public school field trippers as a chance to get out of grinding classroom tedium for a day, but few others beyond the creative grant petitioners who secured its august international standing.

At the Red Fort, Joyce unexpectedly becomes a side

attraction for Indian tourists, several of whom ask to preserve their memories of the historic spot by having their pictures taken alongside her. "Please, Miss," they say, approaching with giggles and waving cameras at her like delectable snacks.

After a third stranger requests a picture, I catch a startling glimpse of Joyce through a viewfinder and realize that while her pleasing all-American radiance may be a factor, the more probable explanation for her unexpected intercontinental allure is an abundance of clearly visible nipple sweat. The modest khaki, button-up blouse Joyce had pulled from her bag this morning in our air-conditioned room has been transformed by the hundred-degree midday swelter into a clingy sage canvas that makes every drop and, quite frankly, pool of glandular secretion available for randy public assessment. On the world stage, Joyce is no pansy—this is a woman who's hovered over the rankest squat toilets in Southeast Asia and shuffled away without a mark on her pant cuffs—but who wants to greet exotic foreigners with twin chalices of perspiration rimming each breast? Even for an infidel, the look is a bit déclassé.

The fort itself is superb, but the sweaty shirt, unwanted attention, and laxative rumbling of Ajay's tea and bananas puts both of us in an edgy temper that's magnified at our next stop, Chandni Chowk, the snarling, overpopulated hub of Old Delhi underclass shops, cafés, temples, apartments, safe houses, hideouts, and DVD pirating labs. In this nest of pickpockets and preachers, the leering shutterbugs are absorbed into the human cacophony, clearing the way for our first encounter with the inescapable agents of darkness who will be constant companions for the next four weeks—salesmen.

Indian salesmen are the fucking worst. The irrepressible dickheadishness of the country's merchant class stalks you like a disease from the moment you step outside your hotel, forcing you to become the kind of blinkered, "Get the fuck away from me" survival-mode tourist asshole you've always promised yourself you'd never become. Being white in this country puts a target on your back the size of a garlic naan.

Amid the stream of pleas, promises, and come-ons there are flashes of levity—"Sir, wouldn't you be honored to visit the shop where Richard Gere, Paul McCartney, and Wes Anderson have all bought spices?" Mostly, though, the pressure comes from wheeler-dealer jackoffs who throw themselves at you in unrelenting waves, like postmodern cinematic hyperzombies—forever approaching, hooting, hissing, demanding, wheedling, pawing, clawing, badgering, hassling, negotiating, renegotiating, reneging, hectoring, flim-flamming, lurking, following, promising, promoting, emoting, up-charging, lying, prying, spying, conniving, and, worst of all, sometimes actually convincing you to buy crap you've got absolutely no practical use for. All of which makes India by a developing-country mile the most annoying place in the world in which to be a tourist. Of course, I've never been to Egypt. Or Target the day after Thanksgiving.

In India, the torment is amplified because you can't even buy things you want without engaging in a mano-a-mano duel of wits and nerve with some street shark who's far more adept at the game than you. At a train station in Udaipur, a wild-eyed schemer selling magazines follows Joyce and me like a piranha closing on a pair of guppies. From the instant we climb out of the taxi all the way to the platform, he stays with us stride for stride. Through my constant rejection—first polite, then increasingly belligerent—his bludgeoning pitch continues for fifteen nonstop minutes and includes everything from the unimpeachable standards of Indian journalism to the seven hungry mouths he's got to feed at home.

We finally shake the guy when we load into our reserved second-class compartment, only to have him burst through the curtain two minutes later and start laying out his entire stock on a bunk, demanding payment for magazines we damaged by forcing him to chase us through the station. To get rid of him I have to literally push him out of the compartment and off the train—after agreeing to buy a fucking magazine. I know, I'm a chump, but this is the way it happens.

I'm not asking for change. India without its army of sleazy, dishonest, pushy merchants would be as lackluster and "safe" as America's smoke-free bars. I'm just saying, even if they'd actually let you look at the merchandise without crawling into your underwear and telling you it's the wrong size, you can only take so much abuse from a gang of opportunists whose personal sensitivity ranks just below Phnom Penh cathouse touts.

I grew up in a tourist town. You expect a few rip-offs in these places. "This traditional painting is done on genuine camel bone," a vendor tells you. Take it out of the wrapper. Tap in on a table. It's plastic. Fine. But as craftsmen of hustle, the Indians make Henri look like a peanut vendor at a minor league baseball game.

A typical, verbatim exchange:

Me (*entering restaurant*): Is the full menu available?

Waiter: Yes, sir! Please have a seat.

Me (*ten minutes later*): I'll have the tandoori chicken and a garlic naan.

Waiter: So sorry, sir, these items are not available because we are not operating the tandoor oven.

Me: No naan, either?

Waiter: Yes, sir. Because not busy today.

Me: But you told me the full menu was available. That's why I asked.

Waiter: Yes, sir.

Me: Could I at least get that beer?

Waiter: So sorry, sir, because we have no license for beer, sir.

Me: Because you have no license for beer, what?

Waiter: Yes, sir.

Me: Because you have no alcohol license you have no beer?

Waiter: Yes, sir.

Me: But when I sat down you took my order for a beer.

Waiter: Yes, sir. One large Kingfisher beer, sir.

Me: But there's no beer?

Waiter: So sorry, sir. Because we have no license for beer, sir. The beer may come later.

Me: May come later?

Waiter: Yes, sir.

Me: Um, OK, just a mineral water then and the vegetable curry.

Waiter: Yes, sir. I will check on the water.

Even in their celebrated holistic arena, Indians' tenacious sales instinct remains a core attribute. In the Kerala town of Thekkady, I lay down for one of the region's famed ayurvedic massage treatments, a blizzard of oils, herbs, and "vein straightening" considered medicinal when submitted to in large, agonizing doses. On the advice of a reliable contact, I'd sought out a venerated local specialist, an organic, gray-bearded guru with several martial arts degrees and thirty years of experience rubbing people down before twisting them around like an antler. Ten minutes into the session, with bamboo flutes, burbling water, barking dogs, and fighting children in the background, the visionary master launched the up-sell.

"Best ayurvedic program is seven-day course," he said while wrenching my shoulder into a position best known to orthopedic surgeons and NFL linebackers on the disabled list. "You do seven-day course you are new man."

"I'm leaving Thekkady the day after tomorrow."

"Perfect! Two-day course is even better. You come back tomorrow. Eleven o'clock, first appointment of morning is best. I give special price."

The shocking low point came after the massage when the guru climbed naked into the shower with me to wash my back and me having no small difficulty convincing him to leave.* I stumbled away reeking of cumin and lemon furniture polish—an all-natural potion, the guru assured me, though I'm certain Dow Chemicals was involved—with no further commitments, financial or otherwise. Even nude and soapy, you have to remain resilient in the face of the Indo hard sell.

The most instructive retail lesson comes in a dingy textiles shop in Delhi—everything from elephant-embroidered eye pillows to elephant-embroidered shoulder bags—where Joyce and I watch a middle-aged French couple in matching faux-leopard-skin outfits attempt to drive a hard

---

* People ask all the time if I make this shit up and the answer is no.

bargain with the equally intense owner, a tall, skinny guy with bloodshot eyes and a mouthful of canine teeth. The French want ten elephant-embroidered baskets for thirty euros, exactly one-third the asking price. They really don't want to budge from their "We're volume buyers; you will meet our price" position, but with Broadway exasperation the French woman finally slams a fifty-euro note on the counter and huffs, "Last offer. You take fifty euros; we take all the baskets."

The French woman appears to believe that fifty euros will feed all of Delhi for a week, but the owner still wants his ninety euros, and the couple eventually storms off in a cloud of disgust. As the climax of this petty drama is being reached, a gaunt, unshaven Brit, the same form of postcolonial ghost you see all over Asia, wanders into the shop with his two cents.

"You're a poor negotiator, Dabi," the Brit reprimands the owner. "Your starting price is too high."

"The price is clearly marked on each item," Dabi replies. "If they don't like my price, don't buy."

"Yes, but your price is five times what it costs anywhere else. It's a rip-off."

"People who are smart enough not to be ripped off should be smart enough to avoid my shop. There is no sense getting angry about it."

A turn off one of Delhi's nondescript, smog-choked thoroughfares leads us into a five-hundred-year-old Islamic neighborhood known as Nizamuddin, a Middle Ages hive of stacked adobe buildings so thoroughly Muslim that Delhi locals regard it as the closest thing to Pakistan this side of a stolen Sidewinder missile. Dark, narrow passageways meander like Faulkner prose deeper and deeper

into one of those teeming backwaters that either repels or
seduces the Western visitor. Fortunately, I'm easily en-
tranced by Eastern exotica even if, as is the case here, I have
to step over puddles of urine to get to it.

Every block is a wonder: Five men squat around a
stone oven sunk into the ground, slapping slabs of
stretched dough against the smooth rock. Frothy white
liquid steams in open vats—it looks like dirty bathwater
but apparently is some kind of beverage. An open window exposes a roomful of men in prayer kneeling on
mats. A line of goats lounge on a flight of crumbling stairs
ascending to a faded blue door. Women walk by covered
head to foot in black robes without even a slit for their
eyes. Old geezers in skullcaps, ZZ Top beards, and flowing white robes argue, laugh, and fling good-natured Arab
curses at their friends, the bastard sons of milkless whores
every last one of them.

I buy a cell phone at a street stall for thirty dollars.
Easy transaction. Just as in the Congo, my experience in
India confirms how jacked up American phone plans
are—ten dollars of minutes will end up lasting me two
weeks, eight or nine calls to the States included.

After eating two oily curries from a local legend called
Karim's, Joyce and I trip the Islam fantastic until well
past dark. Like the catacombs of Paris, Nizamuddin is a
hidden universe within the recesses of an utterly different city, the kind of hostage-hiding alien maze your
mother would shit bricks to see you in. (Relatively few
American moms appreciate the thrill of getting lost among
Muslims.) I'd be lying if I said that "crowded market . . .
homemade bomb . . . twelve killed . . . forty-four injured"
didn't ticker through my head like an AP bulletin from
some distant hellhole. Except that this time I happen to
be in the heart of it, shoulder to shoulder with Joyce,

brushing against people who may or may not begrudge our nationality.

While the idea of projectile-nail bombs and mangled faces does give the thoughtful traveler pause, my mind is more occupied in places like this by how little interest most Americans seem to have in them. More U.S. servicemen have died in battle in Asia than any other continent, yet we still understand so little about it. Nizamuddin will turn out to be one of my favorite stops in India, though I doubt that saying so will inspire anybody I know to book a ticket. Still, if you find yourself in Delhi without dinner plans—Karim's.

Whatever upbeat traits can be attributed to Islam—generosity, hospitality, innumerable recipes for fresh goat shanks—they coexist in India alongside the combustible touchiness you sometimes see harnessed for flag burnings, Great Satan protests, and ever-popular rock-throwing parties. At the gates of Jama Masjid, the largest mosque in India—built by five thousand laborers in the 1650s, the Muslim megachurch can brainwash twenty-five thousand followers at a time—Joyce and I get a harsh toke of the testy manners that must drive the hard-working folks at the Visit Islam publicity office absolutely bonkers.

Admission to the enormous mosque is free even for infidels, but as soon as I remove my shoes at the entrance a pair of rough-looking teenage boys collapse on me like Punjabi horse thieves and begin grabbing at my trusty Jansport. (If this pack survives my danger year abroad, I'm going to have it bronzed and displayed on a pedestal at the entry of my home.)

"You have camera! You have camera!" The guys gets

so close that I can smell their donkey breath as they shout bits of afternoon curry into my face.

"Yes," I say. "I have a camera. What about it?"

"Two hundred rupee! Now! Camera charge! You pay two hundred rupee! Give to me!"

India is filled with grifters, scam artists, bullies, and fakes of all kinds. If cadging money from stupid foreigners is an art form, avoiding scams quickly becomes an artful dodge for tourists.

"No, no," I say, smiling and pulling my bag from their grip. "Admission is free."

I try to continue through the gate, but the boys circle around and block the way. A small crowd coagulates behind us.

"Camera charge two hundred rupee! Give to me now!"

Two hundred rupees is about five U.S. dollars. Not worth getting kneed in the balls over, but the guys extorting the ad lib fee are dressed in the same rags as everyone else, nothing at all that suggests officialdom. Even in Kinshasa the shakedown artists appeared to carry some sort of administrative credential, such as an automatic weapon.

Charging ahead like Thomas the Apostle, Joyce has disappeared from view. But it's obvious we're together, and a random psycho breaks from the crowd and chases her down like a Border collie, escorting her back to the gate where a sizable crowd is now lowing for action.

With the tide moving against us, I grab Joyce's arm and say, "Fuck it. It's a nice building, but what do we give a shit about this place? I'm not giving these assholes two rupees let alone two hundred." If we really want to see the giant worship hall of some bat-shit religion we can go to Eighty-second Avenue back home and watch the

Pentecostals—they meet every weekend in a converted multiplex movie theater.

Joyce and I slink away from the sneering mob as more Arab oaths—"May the fleas of a thousand Jewish camels infest your sister's crotch!" and so forth—mock our departure. Taking all of two minutes, the episode nonetheless erases the agreeable vibe of Muslim amity we'd taken away from Nizamuddin; this even after we find out that, despite no signage, visitor kiosk, or indication of any kind, there really does turn out to be a two-hundred rupee fee on the books for taking a camera inside Jama Masjid.

Which is fine. God knows I've paid thousands of dollars in trumped-up tourist fees across the planet without complaint or physical altercation. Had someone merely spoken to us like normal human beings and explained the situation, I would have coughed up two hundred lousy rupees faster than you can say, "As Allah wills it." Instead, within seconds of a minor infraction, Joyce and I were surrounded as though our Blackhawk helicopter had just crashed-landed at the Gate of Mecca.

At Jama Masjid, it's not the bogus camera charge I resent—I actually believe in the gringo tax in poor countries—but the foaming hostility that has become such a stereotypical part of the Islamic posture toward the West. And anyone who wants to deny this in the name of the great pacifist religion is either a liar or has never been drummed out of a mosque by teenage dirt-ball believers hoping to squeeze an easy five spot from unsuspecting visitors.

What a bunch. A few years ago I recall watching news footage of the Pope in Turkey, a trip taken on the heels of a speech the raccoon-faced pontiff had delivered in which he noted the historic violence of the Muslim faith. Peace-loving fundamentalists, of course, don't much care for reminders of all the beheadings, jihads, and IED explosions carried out in their name over the centuries. The predictable angry mob that greeted the Apostolic See in Turkey included a seventy-year-old woman in a black robe who'd turned out to huck a few rocks, rattle her wrinkly fist, and belt out toothless profanities in the direction of the CNN cameras.

Now, I'm as appalled as the next CCD alum that the Catholics chose a pope who not only looks like an aging Nazi, but who actually *is* an aging Nazi (well, former). I get that forgiveness and revelation are part of the package but shouldn't that "Hitler Youth" line on a résumé disqualify you from at least *some* jobs? Still, it's hard not to contemplate a society that produces rock-throwing old women who can't handle someone's vaguely offensive historic remark without thinking, "What a massive head trip has been done on this part of the world."

Fifteen- and sixteen-year-old boys venting hormonal rage by whipping pieces of cinder blocks at tanks I sort of get. But seventy-year-old women? Over one crummy comment? These people literally haven't moved past the sticks and stones stage of playground interaction.

It's easy to see why Muslims come off so uptight. In a good year, your basic Christian attempts to observe ten commandments. Only one or two if they're "born again" or some other form of "nondenominational" KKKristian.*

* The contemporary followers of disenfranchised slave state segregationists who were forced underground after the mainstream triumph of the Civil Rights movement of the 1960s, then reemerged in Southern churches in the 1970s peddling an updated brand of the same old seditious hate, often as stridently anti-intellectual members of the Republican Party and always in the name of a hijacked Christianity, are called "KKKristians."**
** By me, anyway.

By contrast, Muslims, theoretically at least, are required to observe as many as 2,793 Islamic Laws, some with so many variations and addendums that the World Federation of Khoja Shia Ithna-Asheri Muslim Communities maintains a heavy-going Web site to keep everybody up to speed.

Islamic regulations can range from the self-evident Law 2645, subsection xviii—"When eating a fruit, one should first wash it before eating"—to the mildly helpful Law 57, which points out, "It is obligatory to conceal one's private parts from insane persons." All in all, not much to argue with there.

Things get trickier when the guidelines turn to such matters as the relationship between sex and fasting. Law 1593, for example, is pretty clear-cut: "Sexual intercourse invalidates the fast, even if the penetration is as little as the tip of the male organ, and even if there has been no ejaculation." A few lines later, however, Law 1595 attempts to sneak in some leeway by speaking to doubts about whether "penetration was up to the point of circumcision or not." Roughly twice as many Islamic laws govern masturbation as intercourse, including a personal favorite, Law 1600: "If a person who is observing fast wakes up from sleep while ejaculation is taking place it is not obligatory on him to stop it." On-the-record proof that Muslim clerics aren't complete sticks in the mud about everything.

I know religious talk puts lots of people in the mood for a long afternoon nap, but even if I wasn't in India in part to confront the bleeding Mohammedan heart, the topic is virtually impossible to ignore in a country dominated by religion in a way that America didn't approach even back in the day when almost half its population was wearing square hats and buckled shoes, sniffing out witches, and voting for Sarah Palin. Given my habit of lobbing Molotov cocktails at organized religion, it's probably prudent at this point to clarify my own position on affairs of the unknown.

First of all I'm no atheist, though plenty of my close friends seem to be. This is because while I do believe in the spiritual order of the universe—and one pretty much in line with the hard-to-shake Christian principles I grew up with—I also consider myself a rational and pragmatic person. As such, I realize that anyone who's being intellectually honest with themselves has to concede that on the God vs. No God question, pretty much all of the logical points fall on the side where the atheists are busy giving hand jobs to Christopher Hitchens. And by the way, how'd you like to have your long-running ax to grind against the perverted ruling order finally articulated so well by such an unlikable war pig, a guy who actually believes that Mother Teresa deserves bashing as much as George W. Bush deserves fellating?

This doesn't mean that atheists are necessarily correct. The spectrum of human understanding would be woefully incomplete without a consideration of the spiritual complexity of the universe. The problem that religious people get into is trying to apply their ethereal beliefs to the real world. This is why atheism is a good and probably necessary invention and why we might be better off in this country if we just once gave a shot to an atheist government. Or at least one honest enough to stop lying about its lack of faith and genuflecting before mouthbreathing KKKristians, who believe that God hid fossils under eons of sedimentation to test our faith and that the Dark Ages pathology of Leviticus actually has practical application in a world in which guys like Ray Kurzweil are preparing for the great singularity when we'll all dispose of our imperfect organic bodies in favor of silicon containers housing innumerable copies of our brains in sturdy metal cages.

I grew up Catholic and as a kid considered Catholicism as natural as breathing. Like the rest of the flock, I believed that while other religions were fine and probably had their place, none of them were ultimately very important in the grand scheme of things. As the original and central font of Christianity, Catholics were essentially the Yankees of the religious world—tolerant to the point of understanding that other teams had to exist and have their fans, but also never in doubt at the end of the day that without our organization the rest of the league might as well not exist. The hierarchy of rivals was self-evident. The Muslims were the Red Sox (violent, bitter, dangerous underdogs). The Jews the Dodgers (Brooklyn, Koufax, the showbiz move to LA). The Protestants the Giants (second-rate breakaway squad with delusions of grandeur). The Baptists the Cubs (also-rans clinging to tradition while mired in heartland futility). All those murky copycat denominations—Presbyterians, Methodists, Seventh-day Adventists—the equally irrelevant Texas Rangers, Arizona Diamondbacks, and Colorado Rockies of the world.

For the first couple decades of my life, this worldview served me well. I emerged as apparently one of the five or six people raised in the church not left emotionally scarred by the experience. On the contrary, despite a significantly broadened adult outlook, I retain positive feelings about my Catholic upbringing—confessional booths, the excruciating childhood boredom of Friday mass, and 2007 Notre Dame football team notwithstanding. I was never fondled by a priest. The nuns who oversaw the early years of my formal education were as skillful, patient, and dedicated as any teachers I ever had. I've long maintained that my first three years of Catholic education were as valuable to me as the following thirteen years of public school combined.

The entire discussion of which might have been avoided had those tense dicks at Jama Masjid just said something like, "Hey, bro, there's actually an extra charge to bring your camera inside the mosque," and let it go at that.

From the devout fire into the fanatic frying pan, our last stop in Delhi is the house-turned-museum where Indira Gandhi, daughter of independent India's first prime minister, Jawaharlal Nehru, lived and, tragically, was killed in 1984. The big attraction is a glass case displaying the sari the prime minister was wearing at the time of her assassination. Bullet holes are still visible in the cloth. Visitors crowd around the case three and four deep to have a look.

A path behind the house on which Gandhi took her final footsteps on earth is marked by a series of crystal panels embedded in the ground. The panels are meant to invoke a tranquil river, but given that many of them are cracked, broken, or missing, the tribute looks more like a static security obstacle outside a gated Florida retirement community. The walk culminates with a large glass sheet at the spot where the controversial leader was felled. In an act of supreme treachery—even for this part of the world— she was gunned down by her own Sikh bodyguards.

It's sobering stuff, and I might be more moved had I not seen the same thing, or something very much like it, so recently. The parallels between Gandhi and Delhi and Kabila and Kinshasa are impossible to miss. A leader offed by trusted bodyguards. The succession of a son to power (Rajiv Gandhi became India's prime minister upon his mother's death and was himself assassinated in 1991). Crypts, blood, dynastic families, and shabby memorials erected to the whole catastrophe. The seamless continuation of nationalized corruption. Think about this stuff long enough and the entire sorry procession of history starts looking the same, whether you're in Asia, Africa, Europe, or Crawford, Texas.

After the Gandhi downer, Joyce and I take a cab to the train station, where we discover that civil discord is still the third rail of Indian society. While we've been staring down angry mosque teens and touring the slain prime minister's home, an ethnic group called the Gujjars has spent the day protesting what they feel is a lack of deserved government recognition by ripping up railroad tracks across Rajasthan. As a result, our overnight train to Jaisalmer has been cancelled.

It's doubtful that train service will resume within the week. Worse, because we booked through a travel agent in Mumbai, the harried ticket manager at the Delhi train station—whose window it takes me fifteen minutes of crowd surfing to reach—is unable to make any changes to our tickets. After my third helpless-foreigner plea for mercy, he looks at me sympathetically, indicates the screaming mob pressing against his window, and very politely says, "Sir, your train is cancelled indefinitely. Your situation is beyond help. You must now go away."

We slog back to the guesthouse. It takes ninety minutes to ford Delhi in rush-hour traffic. Ajay gives us our old room back, then sits down to review our options, which look about as promising as a new Rob Schneider movie.

"You could go to Bikaner instead," Ajay suggests.

Ajay is trying to be helpful, but substituting Bikaner for Jaisalmer is like trading Sierra Mist for 7-Up. The ancient caravan city of Jaisalmer, an architectural marvel hidden deep within the great Thar Desert, is one of the national treasures that had convinced Joyce to swap her Mexican poolside vacation for the rigors of India. Neither of us is ready to abandon it.

"There is one more option," Ajay says, spinning a dusty paper Rolodex. "If you are willing to pay for a car and driver, you can perhaps reach Jaisalmer by tomorrow night."

Joyce shrugs. I know what she's thinking. With no airport in Jaisalmer, the Gujjars raging, and our destination at least two days away by bus, we can't be picky. If we want to see Jaisalmer, we're pretty much forced into a classic mode of India tourist transport we'd been hoping to avoid: the private driver. We take our time, but eventually come around.

"You supply the driver; we'll supply the cash," I hear myself saying, getting into the spirit of things with a forced enthusiasm that Ajay doesn't bother smashing before once again it's time to go.

6

. . .

The Unyielding Indian Workforce

Indian merchants are the fucking worst? I stand corrected. Forget salesmen. For that matter, forget terrorists, railroad saboteurs, halfhearted butt wipers, uninhibited massage gurus, belligerent mosque grifters, Ramadan fast breakers, flag burners, presidential assassins, filth, disease, open sewers, child beggars, and the cheese-ball torment of Indian pop music. The single biggest impediment to the traveler's appreciation of India, the primary and most available reason to mistakenly dismiss the whole damn country as just another blighted Third World shit heap, are Indian drivers.

I'm not criticizing the subcontinental wheelman's actual driving skills, which are either terrifying or masterful depending on your appreciation of county fair thrill rides and the hayfoot savants who operate them. The real horror of India's suicide army of "professional" drivers— which includes the operators of everything from bullet-proof SUVs to discarded lawn mowers retrofitted with sidecars into which families of five can and will be crammed—is their unwavering commitment to approaching every job as an opportunity to work a scam.

Here, for example, is a one-act play inspired by actual events in Delhi:

Walking Rupee Sign (aka Tourist, aka Me): How much to Kahn market?

Cabbie: Yes! Kahn market! I take you! Get in!

Walking Rupee Sign (WRS): How much to Kahn market?

Cabbie: As you like!

Third World taxi advice is always to settle on a fare before getting inside the vehicle. Since most Indian drivers regard agreed-upon prices as mere starting points thirty seconds into any ride, however, this stratagem is basically futile here.

WRS: How about ten rupees?

Cabbie: Sir! No ten rupees! Eighty rupees!

WRS: I paid twenty rupees for the same trip two days ago.

Cabbie: OK, sixty rupees. Get in.

WRS: Forty rupees is too much.

Cabbie: OK, fifty rupees!

WRS agrees to fifty rupees, knowing actual fare for Indians is ten rupees. Thirty seconds into journey, Cabbie turns to WRS.

Cabbie: Sir, Kahn market prices are too high. I take you to better market.

WRS: I don't want to go to another market. I want to go to Kahn market.

Cabbie: Sir, five minutes, just have a look. I can get you

good price on anything you like. Kahn market is terrible place, filled with thieves.

WRS: Just take me to Kahn market.

Cabbie: OK, sir, no problem. It is eighty rupees to Kahn market.

Curtain falls as Kahn market passes unacknowledged by Cabbie.

Since most drivers are recent transplants to the cities in which they work, navigation is also a challenge. Owing to the fact that the layout of streets in large Indian cities roughly resembles the pattern you get by throwing a pot of cooked spaghetti on the floor, taxi and autorickshaw drivers often drop passengers miles from their actual destinations. Because Indians are also fond of assigning the name of the same patron or deity to ten or fifteen different streets and buildings, cab journeys usually cannot be completed without repeated stops for consultations with guys hanging out on street corners, who always wave to the north, south, east, and west while delivering extended narrative histories of the neighborhood before finally pointing the driver in the wrong direction.

The fact that I can get from my house in the Pacific Northwest to my brother's house in Maryland with no more than nine turns might take a bit of the thrill out of driving in the States, but Western predictability generally trumps being abandoned on an empty street corner by a clueless yokel who gets so frustrated trying to locate an address that he finally gives up and politely asks his passenger to get out of his cab. But to please pay him first. This actually happened to me in Mumbai.

All of this by way of introducing the remarkable Belu, the
swarthy thirty-year-old, ninety-five-pound long-haul driver
Ajay pulls out of his Rolodex for the all-day ride from
Delhi to Jaisalmer. We haven't been in Belu's banged-up
Tata hatchback long enough to escape suburban Delhi before he begins rearranging our plans. Instead of driving
us to Jaisalmer, Belu now insists we make the much shorter
trip to the alleged attraction of Bikaner.

"Sir, we can reach Bikaner easily in one day. It is beautiful place. You like it so very much, I am sure."

"We agreed to Jaisalmer," I say, attempting to project
cooperative-but-no-pushover-foreigner mettle.

"Sir, Jaisalmer no good place. Bikaner very nice."

"We have no interest in Bikaner. Anyway, we're catch-
ing our onward train from Jaisalmer."

"Sir, now no train. Gujjars make trouble. Very bad
people."

"The newspapers say there may be a quick settle-
ment."

"Sir, not with Gujjars. They crazy people."

Keeping Belu on track is like flogging an elderly mule,
but insubordination is hardly the worst of his behavior.
As has already been noted, the gulf between driving standards in the United States and India is wide enough to
plunge a bus filled with schoolchildren into, but Belu is in
a stunt category of his own. Congenitally unable to remain in his own lane, the jittery chauffeur does the bulk
of his driving on the half of the road reserved in every
mind but his own for oncoming traffic—which, over the
course of the day and night we spend as his passengers,
sets up literally thousands of chicken duels with every
bus, truck, jeep, car, motorcycle, autorickshaw, goat, dog,
cow, and camel with the temerity to be traveling in the
opposite lane.

"Jesus, Belu, can you stay in our lane?" Joyce says after we nearly clip a pregnant woman scurrying for her two lives.

"No problem, ma'am. Indian-style driving!"

Crossing the Thar Desert in the dead of summer with the windows of your Tata hatchback rolled down is pretty much like sitting in a rolling pizza oven while someone blasts you in the face with a hair dryer. The only thing worse than making this journey with a Hindu fatalist behind the wheel cranking the *Best of Bollywood Duets* for seventeen straight hours is making this journey with a Hindu fatalist behind the wheel cranking the *Best of Bollywood Duets* for seventeen straight hours while your traveling companion is in the backseat starting her period.* (Strictly speaking, I suppose it could be worse; you could actually be the traveling companion.) At ten in the morning, in triple-digit heat and Joyce ready to stab everyone in the car including herself, I ask Belu to hit the air-conditioning. I figure this should buy Joyce at least another ten or fifteen minutes of sanity.

"Sir, sorry, AC is no working."

"No working?"

"Yes, sir, compressor is broken."

To prove the point, Belu cranks the AC knob and hits us with a cloud of heat. Then he points to the temperature gauge on the dash, which I note with concern is rising faster than my blood pressure.

"If run AC, car is overheating."

"But we specifically agreed to a car with AC. I paid extra for a car with AC."

* Yes, I know, the brilliance of Bollywood, but spend all day in a car where the only CD is the above-mentioned collection of screechy "classics" and I promise the tune you'll be singing when it's over won't be "When the Mango Harvest Comes and the British Twats Are Dead, I'll Ululate For Thee."

"Yes, sir, this car has AC."

"But the AC isn't working."

"AC is fine. It is compressor which is not functioning properly."

"But the compressor is part of the AC."

"Not technically, sir."

After the backbreaking haul across the desert, and with a disquieting mood of treachery descending upon Joyce, dawn rises over Jaisalmer like Christmas morning. By now, it ought to be apparent that I'm not much for traditional travelogue descriptions of charming boutique hotels, sumptuous "dining experiences," and witless prattle about captivating local markets populated by rustic craftspeople who specialize in recycled-plastic folk-art statuary. By any reckoning, however, Jaisalmer is an authentic treasure; relatively unknown, the city deserves a few lines of gushing praise.

Jaisalmer's principal attraction is a gargantuan, triangular sandstone fort, inside of which lies the most interesting part of the old city. Established in 1156 on a rise overlooking the vast inferno of the Thar Desert, the fort owed its wealth and size to a line of powerful Rajput royals who imposed draconian taxes on the passing silk-and-spice camel caravans that once dominated Central Asian commerce. Within its ancient walls is a labyrinth of twisting streets, narrow alleys, and miniature passageways where those interested in instant cultural immersion can spend two or three rewarding days pursuing the exotic among swarms of salesmen and cow pies; the former, as previously discussed, are the unavoidable spawn of capitalist doxies, while the latter creamy calling cards are left by the sacred creatures who roam the city's cobblestone streets with the impunity of princes.

That's as close as I get to a guidebook rave and it's the honest truth, one I'd stick five stars and a "must see" icon next to were I writing a mainstream blurb for the city. But as interesting as Jaisalmer itself—again, fabulous, especially if you stay at the Nepalese-staffed Killa Bhawan hotel—is the wild terrain that surrounds it. After the decline of the caravans in the nineteenth century, Jaisalmer was pretty much left for the vultures and assorted jerkwater rabble who never received word that the twentieth century had dawned. The first paved road to the city wasn't completed until 1958; in a country that the Brits began covering in train tracks in the 1850s, the first rail connection came only in 1968; in nearby Pokaran, the Indian government tested its first nuclear device in 1974. So, an outpost with little to attract the jet set but much to offer the seeker of out-of-the-way thrills.

Today, only the occasional flybys of Indian Air Force Mirage and Sukhoi fighters patrolling the border zone between India and Pakistan, just thirty miles away, disturbs the bleak silence of the Thar. Armed camps belonging to both nuclear nations dot the desert, making this one of the most heavily fortified and potentially lethal standoffs this side of the 38th parallel—troop deployments fluctuate, but as many as a million total soldiers have been massed along the border at various times over the past decade. According to writer Suketu Mehta, Mahatma Gandhi feared that India's fractious separation from Great Britain would lead to "the most savage independence movement in world history," owing largely to the centuries of animal hatred between Hindus and Muslims.

Although Indo-Pak relations have stabilized in recent years, the old enemies don't exactly get together to laugh over photos of themselves in the bathtub together as kids. Travel between them remains restricted—a barbed wire fence runs across the border near Jaisalmer—and half a century of animosity is openly acknowledged. In Jaisalmer, Joyce and I run into four gregarious young men in civilian clothes who have recently joined the Indian Army. When Joyce asks what their jobs in the service will be, the tallest one smiles like a Pathan warlord and says: "Two words: Attack Pakistan!"

He's clearly joking and his buddies crack up. But a minute later when I ask where the group is stationed, the tall one levels his gaze at me again and repeats: "Two words: Attack Pakistan!"

Just some overaggressive boy soldiers convincing one another of their bravado? No doubt. But what military isn't full of this sort of posturing, all the way up to the four-star gunslingers with their hands on the budgets and buttons?

The classic tourist excursion in Jaisalmer is a camel trek into the surrounding desert. After taking an Indian-made Mahindra jeep into the countryside, I hire a crusty old camel jockey—a ten-year-old boy named Lala whose rough hands, cracked lips, and eyes like glazed ceramic make him more at home in the desert than a lizard. Lala comes from one of the sandblasted villages—round, one-room houses built from flagstone, mud, and cow dung—where locals herd goats, grow a few meager crops, and pay even less attention to the condition of their yards than my next-door neighbors back home who leave their Christmas lights on their house all year.

In the December-January high season, sunset camel tours are a big enough business that the Frommer's guidebook goes out of its way to bitch about all the damn tourists you have to put up with on the ride. In the off-season, however, the scattered dunes pretty much belong to me and Lala and a group of Indian tourists large enough to require nine camels. The afternoon high temperature is variously quoted as 112, 113, and, 114 degrees.* Not coincidentally, these are the three principal reasons Joyce has elected to remain horizontal below a ceiling fan back at the hotel while I ride doubles atop a reeking desert beast with a ten-year-old who relentlessly coaxes our ship of the desert onward by whacking its haunches with a long cord. Lala would have come in handy in the Tata with Belu.

If you've never done it, riding a camel is like sitting atop a washing machine that's churning with an uneven load. Each more or less fluid roll is followed by a jarring dip as the ungainly creature makes its way through the eternal wasteland at a dawdling pace that suggests it believes a dromedary slaughterhouse awaits around the next pile of tumbleweeds. As for the views, the Thar is mostly flat and looks a lot like West Texas, only with fewer water towers and Hindu fundamentalists in place of the football fanatics, which is actually more of an even trade than you might imagine.

With the sunset making a pastel mural of the sky, the ride is pleasant and, in a way, so is the highly competent Lala's mute, cowboylike company. The action doesn't really pick up until after we return to the parking lot.

"The sand will soon come!" Joshi my jeep driver is in a state. He points into the distance, where it looks as if someone has taken a black marking pen and drawn a thin line at the point where sky meets land. I see no cause for alarm in this but Joshi is frantic, and soon enough I un-

* No one knows for sure where the expression "hotter than dick" comes from, but my money is on Rajasthan, a state where the heat is commonly described as "crippling," "Satanic," and "ball wilting." In winter. The whole time I'm here, my scrotum feels like a head of rinsed romaine lettuce.

derstand why. Before I've even taken a farewell photo of Lala, the barely perceptible black line has swollen into a dark cloud stretching across twenty miles of horizon and roiling a thousand feet into the air.

"Hurry! We must get to the jeep!"

Joshi sprints to the Mahindra. In the near distance the sandstorm is gathering steam like a CGI effect from a bad Brendan Fraser movie, thundering across the desert, threatening to block the only route back to town. We jump in the jeep and peel out. Joshi taps the brim of my baseball cap.

"Take it off or the wind will take it off for you!" He has to scream to be heard over the whining engine and howling, hot wind baking our faces.

"Can we make it to town before it hits us?" I shout.

The storm still looks like it's a few miles away, but this is apparently a stupid question. Joshi smiles. He's about sixty. His teeth are dark yellow. Two are missing from the lower deck.

"When the sand comes, close your eyes and turn your head away from the wind!" he yells, squinting and watching the road from a chancy angle.

Joshi hasn't even finished shouting when an explosive gust whips a sepia grit over the road. A scorching wind engulfs the jeep, nearly pushing us into the soft shoulder. Fine-grain pepper shot begins scouring my face. It doesn't hurt—it's like being pelted with discarded beard bristle—but being swallowed by the cloud is like being inside a closet after somebody shuts the door.

Curtains of sand billow through our headlights. Dense drifts accumulate along the road, forcing us to slalom and swerve over invisible asphalt. When a large truck flies by it's like being passed by a semi in a rainstorm on the interstate. Its rear tires launch a sheet of sand that splashes across our windshield, blinding us for a terrifying instant before Joshi hits the wipers and the truck careens ahead.

The jeep has no roof, and Joshi eventually has to pull over to clean sand out of his eyes. I jump out and run into the desert to experience the full tornado of sand.

"Sir, you are fine?" Joshi has chased me into the desert. I spit out a mouthful of sand and nod. For no reason, we begin laughing hysterically. This causes us to inhale a few gallons of sand and subsequently spend the next thirty minutes coughing like rheumatic seals.

"Now in the desert the wind will blow for a month," Joshi tells me. "This will bring the monsoon from the south. We are waiting."

At the hotel that evening, I pick up a newspaper. The text is all Hindi, but the front-page photo shows a boy in Mumbai floating in a flooded street. Behind him a cow plashes through chest-high water. In the north of the country, Rajasthan remains as dry as Baptist happy hour, but the sandstorm means relief is on the way.

Jaisalmer proves to be a tough place to leave and not just because Joyce and I like it so much. The morning we check out, I find Belu loitering in front of the hotel. This is a surprise given that when we'd arrived in the city three days earlier, I'd promptly fired him for reckless driving, general petulance, and air-conditioning malfeasance.

"Belu, what are you doing here?" I ask.

"I will drive you to Udaipur as planned." Belu says this the way Steve Buscemi says, "I'm not going to debate you, Jerry. I'm not going to sit here and debate," in *Fargo*.

"You're supposed to be back in Delhi."

"Sir, get in the car. I will take you to Udaipur." Belu reaches for my bag, and a minor struggle for control ensues.

I'm no grudge holder and insofar as petty disputes are concerned, a three-day cooling-off period is pretty much like soaking me in a vat of Palmolive. Much as I dislike him, I also feel sorry for Belu. If his driving is any indication, the guy's entire life has to be a disaster. Unfortunately for us both, extraneous circumstances are at work.

"Belu, normally I'd be happy to ride to Udaipur with you. But at this point, doing so would require divorcing my wife. Now that the Gujjars have stopped rioting, we're going to resume our itinerary by train."

"Sir, please get in the car."

Getting rid of Belu is like breaking up with a psycho girlfriend. Apparently, he's been lurking in the shadows for our entire Jaisalmer visit. If it turned out that he'd been disguised as a guide on the camel trek, I wouldn't be surprised.

"Sir, as my employer in India, you are considered my big brother," Belu says, shifting from bossing to pleading. "It is your obligation to take care of me."

"Belu, I'm sorry, but a team of camels couldn't drag us into your car. And by 'us' I specifically mean 'Joyce.'"

After half an hour of negotiation, Belu finally allows me to fire him for a second time. Adding salt to the wound, we don't even let him drive us to the station, flagging down a cab off the street instead. From the train, I call Ajay to tell him what's happened.

"I'm sorry things didn't work out with Belu," I say in the hedging way of the habitual apologizer. "Seriously, I think the guy was sort of insane. I feel badly about leaving him out here, but we just couldn't carry on with him behind the wheel."

"You must get off of this guilt trip and stop apologizing," Ajay demands. "You are the aggrieved party here. This man has besmirched the good name of the driving profession. Not to mention my own. Now please get on with your travels and think of this sorry excuse for a man no more."

I hang up feeling better. India's caste system comes in for a lot of criticism, but it must be noted that there's nothing quite like upper-crust sensibility and boarding-school English to help you leave the social troglodytes in your wake.

Over the following weeks Joyce and I cover enough ground to, if not entirely forget about Belu, at least keep the possibility of his return at bay. Our next stop is the "lake city" of Udaipur. Touted in guidebooks and on Web sites as "the Venice of India," Udaipur will be touted in *this* book as an example of why not to trust travel writers. "The most disappointing schlep on the subcontinent" would be a better slogan for this dried-up organ.

Rather than a glittering tourist jewel, the "most romantic city in India" turns out to be a two-bit claustrophobic dump overflowing with the usual brigade of death-or-glory merchants pushing spoon rings, watercolor prints, and a few million other trinkets nobody wants. Teeming with the usual multitudes, all of whom appear content to pass the time of day clogging the sidewalks and streets, Udaipur calls to mind the immortal words of *The Simpsons'* Apu contemplating the possibility of having children: "Well, perhaps it is time. I have noticed that America is dangerously underpopulated."

In Jaipur—where those nine synchronized bombs killed sixty-three—our guesthouse is clean and comfortable and run by a woman who radiates more warmth than a tray of breakfast muffins. The other resident Indians, however, prove it's not just the underclass that's ready to jump all over you in India.

After dinner I get into a political discussion with a local magazine journalist and a retired Indian professor of economics. The journalist, a tubby, smiley guy with round spectacles named Rama, clings violently to the notion that the CIA's covert omnipotence is the cause of every problem in the world, as well as a controlling force behind everyone in the Middle East from Afghan poppy farmers to twelve-year-old Palestinian terrorists. His stridency puts me in the awkward position of once again defending a government whose actions I'm normally happy to bash like a piñata.

"The whole world is united in its hatred of the United States," Rama giddily informs me.

"Just wait until China is running the world," I say.

"China isn't taking any shit from you Americans anymore," Rama says.

I ask him what he means by this, and he refers to America's alleged accidental bombing of the Chinese embassy in Belgrade in 1999.

"Even if that was intentional, which no one knows for sure, how did the Chinese respond?" I ask him.

"They sent a firm message letting you guys know that you're not the only ones on the block."

"A firm message. That's your definition of 'not taking any shit'?"

"The Chinese have missiles in space aimed at the United States." Rama jabs the air, his pudgy fingers representing nuclear warheads raining terror on America.

"Belgrade was ten years ago," I say. "Now China needs the United States as much as the United States needs China. Without America's unprotected markets, China's economic miracle can't continue. India's, either, for that matter. Nuclear annihilation makes no sense for anyone other than rogue terrorists. Even North Korea doesn't want it."

"America is a country whose ruin is awaited by the world and will be cheered by millions."

Punit, the retired university professor, blathers in the same vein. I acknowledge a number of his anti-America points as being at least partially valid, then ask him, "If you were in charge, how would you fix the situation in the Middle East and Iraq?"

"The Americans still haven't learned their lesson," he replies. "They've fought another Vietnam in Iraq."

"Fine, but forget America for a minute. What should happen now? How can problems in the Middle East best be resolved from an Indian point of view?"

"The U.S. created Bin Laden. It supported him. It propped up Musharraf in Pakistan. It intentionally foments violence among the Palestinians."

"Granted. But are Pakistan and Palestine and Saudi Arabia so weak that they bear no responsibility for what happens in their own countries?"

"Look up your facts. U.S. money supports all of this terrorism. Bush started it."

"Get a few more beers in me and I might join you in a chorus of 'Bush the Great Satan.' But you can't be serious suggesting that Islamic terrorism doesn't predate Bush."

"The problem with you Americans is that you need to be taught your lessons."

I suppose confirmation that the United States isn't the only country with a sizable population of dumbshit zealots immune to political nuance should be comforting, but arguing with idiots is as frustrating in India as it is in Indiana. Rama and Punit are like mirror images of Rush Limbaugh and Sean Hannity. The politics are reversed, but the same insatiable hatred blinds the pursuit of rational perspective. After talking with these two supposed intellectuals, I know as little about India's regional ambitions as I did before I met them.

The sacred city of Varanasi on the Ganges River had been the biggest source of my pretrip worries. Its filth is legendary among world travelers—back home, India-travel veterans had advised Joyce and me to pack pairs of "Varanasi shoes," throwaways that would become so dung-encrusted in the befouled streets that they could simply be tossed when we left town. The nurse at the travel clinic had involuntarily flinched when she saw Varanasi on my itinerary. With no further consultation, she scribbled "Imodium" and an antibiotic called "Azithromycin" on her notepad.

On the day we arrive, the local paper runs a front-page story reporting that two young men have been arrested trying to sneak twenty-four hundred detonators into Varanasi. There's also an op-ed piece about the American and British governments' recent travel advisories urging their citizens to avoid large sections of India. As I've previously noted, these exaggerated State Department advisories are most often written in the hysterical hand of ass-covering government bureaucrats issuing blanket pronouncements that will allow them to say, "I told you so" in response to any calamitous act of God, man, or Muslim. But they also give offense to foreign nationals around the world, and the aforementioned op-ed writer is understandably annoyed that these official warnings undermine the upbeat image India wishes to project to travelers and investors. He writes a nice piece, but somewhat working against his argument is a story on the same page bearing the headline, "Smash and Grab: Gurkhas and Gujjars are united by the language of violence."

Despite the Gurkhas, Gujjars, and twenty-four hundred detonators, nothing explodes during our stay. For sheer fright value, Varanasi proves anticlimactic. It's no more dirty, crowded, or overwhelming than any other large Indian city.

Not that it's disappointing. Perhaps more than any other city on the planet, Varanasi reveals a fresh jaw-dropper around every corner: a naked child in a doorway; a steaming cow flop in front of a diamond shop; a tumble-down shelter serving as a home for ten; a lungful of woody incense; an explosion of gold, red, purple, and indigo fabric; a bearded mystic crawling on his knees; the pentatonic notes of a sitar raga; a limbless beggar; a shrine devoted to a monkey deity; an apartment entryway over-flowing with bangles and flash, yet another self-contained universe of beliefs and superstitions and misery and coping. Every year, thousands of Westerners come to Varanasi in search of personal enlightenment, but the place is such a chaotic mess that the only way you could find yourself here is by accident. I may not ever return but if I do it'll be with extra memory for my camera, not an extra pair of shoes.

It turns out the only thing to be afraid of in Varanasi is the water. Described by the *Economist* as "a cloudy brown soup of excrement and industrial effluent," the slow-moving Ganges River is the one attraction that lives up to the hyperbole.

The product of factory sludge, raw sewage, and thirty

thousand human corpses disposed of in its waters every year, the Ganges at Varanasi is a gusher of modern sins. According to world health standards quoted in that *Economist* story, 500 fecal coliform bacteria per 100 milliliters of water is considered safe; in the Ganges near Varanasi, 1.5 million fecal coliform bacteria have been measured. This being India, the toxic count naturally does nothing to discourage sixty thousand Hindu devotees from performing ablutions in the chocolatey Ganges cesspool each day. Submerged in the noxious mix, they lather, swim, play, and even guzzle with devotional relish. Shockingly, dysentery, polio, typhoid, and other waterborne ailments are common along the river.

The question most often asked by foreigners in Varanasi is: If the Ganges is so sacred, why do Indians treat it like a toilet? I put the matter to almost every local I meet, but the only reasonable explanation comes from an attractive, well-dressed woman named Neelima, a video production manager from Delhi working in Varanasi as part of a documentary crew.

"The river, like Hinduism, is all-inclusive," Neelima tells me. "Just because it's religious doesn't mean other things are excluded from it. In the Ganges, the entire cycle of life and death is celebrated. In the Hindu view, everything in the world is connected to religion. Even pollution. Why are these people drinking this water? Because it's from the Ganga Mother who encompasses all life and excludes nothing, good or bad."

If she doesn't convince me to go for a spiritually replenishing backstroke in Mother Ganga, I do appreciate Neelima's insight. But I still worry about the butt coffee drifting down the river on its way to its sacred destiny mingling with the water that will be used to rinse the vegetables in the restaurant where Joyce and I will be crossing our fingers and eating lentils and spinach curry tonight.

For the visitor, going to Varanasi and not floating down the Ganges and visiting the ghats (large sets of concrete stairs that allow pilgrims easy access to the river) is like going to Amsterdam and not smoking hash. Like going to Oktoberfest in Munich and not stepping in someone's vomit. Like going to Salt Lake City and not visiting Temple Square. So, on a rainy, slate gray morning, Joyce and I do like hundreds of thousands before us and hire a private rowboat for a tour.

The most well known of Varanasi's hundred or so ghats is Manikarnika Ghat, a cremation site where Hindu corpses are burned around the clock, every day of the year, sending fountains of white smoke flying into the air. It feels awkward to be a visitor in a place reserved for the intimate acts of strangers—like accidentally stepping into your friend's parents' bedroom when you were a kid—but I hop out of the boat as soon as we get to Manikarnika. Just off the dock, I walk past part of an arm sticking out of a bed of peacefully crackling embers, its skeletal fingers clawing at the air. (Even in death with the outstretched hand!) I move closer to the arm, and my eyes begin picking out other parts of the body. Scapula. Ribs. Pelvis. The Ganges isn't particularly sacred to me, but it's hard not to be moved when you stumble upon a group of mourners chanting around a human skull, its empty eye sockets carefully pointed toward the river and sunless dawn.

After I walk past my fill of skeleton parts, I'm asked for a donation. The wood used to burn the bodies is expensive, and families who haul their dead here usually need help with costs. I hand over ten dollars' worth of rupees.

The man who has taken it upon himself to guide me through the ghat—you don't ask for these hangers on in India, they simply appear and refuse to go away—begins chiding me for being such a tightwad. Twenty dollars is the standard offering, he tells me.

"Twenty dollars guarantees your good karma," he says with a smile that isn't all that different from those of the guys being burned.

"Really? Twenty dollars for good karma? Who calculated that? What if I visit an orphanage? Or a mosque? Still twenty dollars? Or is it a sliding scale?" I know my smart-mouthing is a little unseemly given the surroundings, but this guy is a real barracuda and I can't resist a stupid argument with anyone claiming to represent God's accounting department.

"Good sir, ten dollars is nothing."

"Then give it back if you don't want it."

Travelers incite the scorn of Indian beggars more often than you'd think. Give a kid five rupees and she'll practically spit on your shoes while telling you that five rupees isn't good enough for a Nepalese whore. Give ten and you'll be badgered for twenty. Give twenty and you'll be called a Jew for not giving fifty.

The most interesting encounter I had of this type in Africa came in the Congo, where an able-bodied teenager approached me with a look of beseeching hunger on his face. Having just bought a small bag of popcorn, I decided to simply give the kid the bag. Without blinking, he grabbed the bag, shoved it into his back pocket, then stuck his hand back out and gave me the same imploring look. In India, I experience some version of this transaction almost every day.

At Manikarnika Ghat, my volunteer guide continues hounding me for an extra tenner all the way back to the boat. I end up caving and giving him another five. Don't believe a word you hear about the passive embrace of Hinduism—at least not as practiced by the believers who take you to see the charred skulls on the riverbank of the Ganges at dawn.

The only thing more exasperating than the Indian escort you don't want is the Indian escort you can't find. Reservations, scheduled pickups, and phone confirmations are close to meaningless in the Indian service industry. Moreover, the theoretical nature of punctuality in India would embarrass Hawaii.

The worst of our many hard-luck experiences with the native attitude toward professional commitment begins at the train station in the large and typically frenetic city of Jodhpur. Joyce and I arrive at 11 p.m. for an arranged transit to a desert resort in a small town called Rohet Garh. I scour the station for a smiling man carrying a placard bearing my name; alas, no placard, to say nothing of smiling faces, are to be found in Jodhpur. After twenty or thirty unanswered calls to the resort—there's nothing like two dozen unanswered calls and your ride not showing up at an Indian train station late at night to make you wish you were at home watching *The Daily Show* with the electric blanket turned up to eight—we step outside the station to find a battlefield of forty or fifty homeless men settled in for the night, sprawled on the pavement like reenactors simulating a WWI mustard gas attack.

"No taxi this time, sir." One of the stricken forms stirs and debriefs me on the situation. "Now all taxi on strike.

Big trouble here. One taxi driver attacked, so now is no taxi."

The homeless guy turns out to be right. Just this afternoon, a strike has been called after a fatal double stabbing involving rival factions of taxi and autorickshaw drivers. Mere feet from where I stand, two passengers were knifed to death and two others seriously injured in a fit of rage that erupted when an autorickshaw collided with a taxi while both raced for the same fare in front of the station. The upbraided autorickshaw driver called in a few of his colleagues who, unbelievably, ended up attacking the would-be passengers for siding with the taxi driver in the ensuing argument. To protest this latest episode of territorial passion, the cabbies have gone on strike, leaving hapless out-of-towners such as Joyce and me to take our chances on the assistance of assorted knife-wielding (so it seems) rickshaw hard cases. This in lieu of what was supposed to be a comfortable forty-five-minute ride into the outlying desert via one of the SUVs from our high-end resort's gleaming fleet of luxury vehicles.

The desperation among the motley clutch of agro autorickshaw drivers is twice as ferocious as anything we've yet encountered, including Belu and the craziest cousin he could dredge up. The one who gets to me first grabs my arm and begins pulling me to his rickshaw. He's hairy and fat, with a shedding moustache and jowly face, like that mug shot of Khalid Sheikh Mohammed in the white T-shirt with the stretched-out neck and six-day beard of ass hair. I'd sooner trust an injured wolverine. I make an excuse and tear away from his grasp.

Joyce and I scurry through the parking lot with both hands on our luggage. From the uncombed pack, a young guy with a friendly face, narrow limbs, and pussy-tickler moustache emerges. His name is Vinod and he informs me that he is at our service in every way.

"We're going to Rohet Garh," I say.

"On autorickshaw impossible," Vinod says. "Too far. Need taxi."

"But there are no taxis."

"Yes."

Khalid Sheikh Mohammed reappears and begins arguing loudly with Vinod. The conversation is easy to follow. Khalid saw us first. We're his fare. Vinod rejects the accusation of claim jumping. Three or four other drivers bear in to watch the argument, hands fidgeting ominously in their pockets. One has a seeping neck wound. Someone smells of urine. The intensity escalates like a grass fire. Correctly sensing that Joyce and I are about to bolt like startled deer for the relative sanity of the station, Vinod grabs me by the arm.

"Come on, no problem," he says. "I take you Rohet Garh."

Khalid looks ready to disembowel us all, but we follow Vinod across a lot. We turn a corner and walk down an unlit side street.

"My rickshaw," Vinod says.

A collection of discarded motorcycle parts that looks like it's been put together with a hammer and nails leans at half-mast in an oily gutter. After exchanging the kind of looks you share just before clasping hands and jumping off a cliff, Joyce and I pile our bags into the tiny autorickshaw and shove in beside them. Vinod yanks the engine to life with a single pull of the hand-lever starter and speeds away from the scene with the night's top prize. Nearby drivers salute our escape with shouts that do not sound like invitations to dinner parties.

Jodhpur at night, the parts we can see at least, is never going to land on a tourist brochure. On the road out of town, we pass not one but two knockdown fistfights. The first isn't so much a fight as it is a beat down by a large man holding a teenage boy by the wrist, forcing him to his knees and repeatedly pummeling his head while two women sit silently by. The second is a shoving match between two men that devolves into a horrifying gang assault when three other men join the larger of the combatants and wrestle the smaller man to the ground. As we pull away from the glare of streetlights, the outnumbered man curls up in a protective egg as the fearsome foursome wind up and kick him like a football.

As the edge of town dissolves into darkness, Vinod turns and says, "Rohet Garh is long journey. I pick up my friend. He go with us."

"Wait, who, what friend?"

Along with our practical options, Vinod's friendly expression has vanished. We veer off the main road onto a dirt track and begin puttering through a neighborhood maze of one-room residences. I strain to keep track of the turns but it's useless. It's dark, the web is intricate, and all at once I'm struck with the realization that Vinod is a professional thug taking routine precautions to disorient us before stealing our money, hacking off our heads, and discarding our bodies in the desert, where they'll be stripped to the bone by Jerusalem crickets before dawn. Just as I'm deciding exactly what to do about all of this, we arrive at a two-story concrete blockhouse with no lights.

"One minute," Vinod mumbles.

He rushes inside the dark house, leaving us alone in the deserted street. Dogs bark in the distance. Never in my life have I felt more like part of a setup. Getting in this rickshaw is suddenly looking like a worse career move than Philip Bailey joining Phil Collins on "Easy Lover."*

"We should have just gone to one of the hotels in town," I mutter. "Why does he need a friend to come along? Did you ever see a cab driver stop to pick up a buddy?"

"I have no idea what's going on," Joyce croaks.

Her face is a death mask. We could get out and start walking, but I have no idea where we are and we haven't seen a cab for miles.

A squeaky door opens. Footsteps crunch on the dirt and rock. From the darkness, Vinod reappears with a large, virile man beside him.

"My friend," Vinod says, introducing the highly unwanted interloper. "He know the way to Rohet Garh."

The friend is a foot taller than Vinod, with bulging muscles and a walk like those pro athletes who dick-swagger onto the field as though they've got ten inches stuffed uncomfortably into their cups. He tilts his head at us, then says something fast and low in Hindi. Vinod nods with grave appreciation. The two men jam into the front of the autorickshaw. Each hangs half an ass cheek off the driver's seat, and we spin off once more in a flurry of dust.

International travel requires an occasional willingness to cut the deck and place an immense trust in strangers.

---

* This little attempt to lighten the mood falls as flat with Joyce as it's probably falling right now, but I don't care. I was a DJ when this abortion of Earth, Wind & Fire talent was in hot rotation at KTKU-FM, in Juneau, and playing it every two hours for an entire summer pretty much drove me out of the radio business. If the non sequitur desecration of its memory here is the only revenge I'm ever able to exact, that's better than nothing.

I'm generally a confident traveler who accepts the minimal tradeoff between adventure and security. But no matter how much faith I have in the universal decency of mankind, the statistical improbability of accidents, or even comforting game theory assurances of communal cooperation, on the road I always carry a nagging concern that my luck is inevitably going to bottom out somewhere along the way.

Rohet Garh is supposed to be forty-five minutes out of town, but even accounting for the sluggish speed of the autorickshaw, the trip is taking way too long. After bouncing through a series of potholes, we bank hard left onto what can almost be considered a main road. There are few other cars. No lights. No buildings. But there's asphalt with a painted line in the middle and once in a while a semitruck races by, nearly blowing our tiny craft off the road. We travel this way for more than an hour.

In my head I begin turning over the impromptu self-defense lesson from D. B., suddenly thankful for that strange encounter in the Congolese jungle. The Yoda-like instruction of the old bodyguard ("Apply leverage to the joint") floats into my head from the faraway mists of an African night I never imagined I'd miss.

If it was just me in this situation I'd be anxious; not, as I am now, on the edge of panic. You never like your chances in a two-on-one struggle, but Vinod isn't exactly a prime physical specimen and I'm six-three and unapologetically blew past two hundred years ago. In a crazed fluster I could take him out of action, then maybe outrun the larger dude. And even if I didn't manage to elude a homicidal Indian tag team, at least after being raped and skull fucked, I could die with the dignifying knowledge that I hadn't dragged anyone else along to such a completely pointless demise in the Indian desert.

Joyce's presence changes things. I've seen the Rob Zombie movies, and believe me, you don't have to be a fan of torture porn to entertain castration fantasies after midnight in Rajasthan with a pair of accomplices talking low in the front seat and packing Ganesha only knows how many Gurkha knives and homemade detonators. But just after I whisper to Joyce, "If they take us into the desert, go for the eyes, knees, and nuts, then take off running for the road," an oasis of electricity appears in the distance. Moments later, we rumble past a banged-up metal sign emblazoned with the two most optimistic words since "I do": Rohet Garh.

If Hindus had saints, Vinod would be one. When we find the resort locked down for the evening, he begins banging on the heavy front gate and imploring the night staff to wake up. A groggy clerk surfaces. Vinod dresses him down like a drill sergeant. What is the meaning of leaving two foreign cows stranded at the Jodhpur train station, he wants to know. The clerk produces a registry. Vinod demands to personally inspect our rooms before allowing our luggage to be taken away by a sheepish bellboy.

"OK, I think you are home now," Vinod declares as he hands us the key to the room. Then he clambers into the backseat of the autorickshaw and stretches out. His friend slides into the driver's seat.

"I have been driving since five o'clock this morning," Vinod says, his easy smile returning. "Now you and I can both sleep."

I proclaim Vinod and his buddy heroes and drop generous tips on them. Busybody expats in impoverished places are constantly scolding Western rookies for tipping too heavily or overpaying the working class, on the theory that a large, artificial influx of foreign currency will screw up the local economy. But local economies in these places always look pretty screwed up as it is, and I doubt a pair of twenty-dollar bills will wreak that much more havoc on the Jodhpur cabbie clusterfuck. I don't deny being the clod American overpaying once again. But this time, not getting fucked never felt so good. And, anyway, an ignorant traveler can always use some good karma.

7

. . .

Sex, Rain, and 100 Percent Cotton

Though wide swaths of rural India remain enveloped in what native writer Aravind Adiga calls "the Darkness," an alternate universe of educated, highly motivated tech laborers willing to work for little more than tap water and bread crusts have turned the country into the "world's back office." Not long ago India was a place where Red Cross donations, polio vaccinations, and the occasional Bible were dropped off by benevolent Westerners, but now at least part of the country has become infamous as an outsourcing trove for multinational companies, and thus a festering source of paranoia for American workers. As Thomas Friedman notes: "When I was growing up, my parents would tell me, 'Finish your food; people in China and India are starving.' I tell my kids, 'Finish your homework; people in China and India are starving for your job.'"

Notwithstanding the fact that when I was growing up my parents were more worried about me picking up the dog piles in the backyard after dinner than with what kids in China and India were up to, Friedman's point is an important one for both blue- and white-collar Americans. Barack Obama won the presidency in part by promising to stop the flow of American jobs to countries like India. Though his bootlicking disaster of an opponent also helped clinch the deal; in the words of my buddy Shanghai Bob, "Had John McCain not been shot down by the North Vietnamese, he would have spent his life as a high school gym teacher in Flagstaff."

Regardless of the Obama hope train, the economic tide may have already turned against the West. International companies continue flocking to India to build and staff R & D labs. The country is bolstering its position as a world leader in drug discoveries. Its dynamic steel industry is expected to produce a steel surplus by 2012. The government plans to construct forty-three brand-new "IT cities" in the next ten years. That's forty-three cities, out of nowhere, conceived to thwart the hard-charging efforts of financial and technological rivals, all of which are Asian, none of which is American.

The economic news might as well be splattered in blood on the wall, and the U.S. diplomatic corps has assumed an appropriate posture of defense. One Indian handout offering practical advice for U.S.-bound college students offers a heads-up that interviews between Indian visa applicants and American consular officers "are conducted across a bulletproof glass wall." How unlike America the United States has become. One presumes that the German shepherds are kept muzzled, at least for the graduate students.

The most spectacular example of India's audacious rise through the ranks of world economic titans is Mumbai. With fourteen million people, Mumbai is not simply one of the world's largest and most densely populated cities; according to Pulitzer Prize finalist Suketu Mehta, yet another superb Indian writer, it's "the future of urban civilization on the planet. God help us."

One of the first things you notice about Mumbai is that while it is indeed an intestinal collage of organized pandemonium, things somehow manage to function. Traffic moves along. People appear to have business afoot, or at least somewhere to go. You don't see aimless thousands squatting on broken sidewalks. (When Indians squat, something you do see a lot of, it's usually for a common-enough purpose.)

By the time we reach the city, Joyce's employer is as tired of her being in India as she is. As planned, we part ways in the Mumbai airport, Joyce for a few days of hard-earned R & R at home with *Oprah* and a box of Bon Bons before her triumphant return to the cube farm, me to continue my inspection of the threats posed by a country whose people have yet to surreptitiously remove my appendix, contact my family for ransom money, or force me into a midnight desert-highway Dirty Sanchez.

It's lamentable that so many American tech and service jobs have moved overseas, but to me economic strength is still a product of manufacturing. Because I'll need help to get a close-in look at the real motor of Indian financial might, one of the first people I contact in Mumbai is Anurag Chaturvedi, a mustachioed, fifty-five-year-old muckraking journalist—not quite an Indian Geraldo, but it's a reasonable visual image.

After tea at his home with his U.S.-college-bound son—Javed hasn't experienced the bulletproof interview yet, but he's looking forward to it—Anurag drives us to Bhiwandi, a textile city of six hundred thousand just northeast of Mumbai. In the dirt streets and fly-infested alleys of a place known as the "Manchester of India," Anurag and I can barely hear each other speak over the racket of hundreds of old-fashioned power looms churning away inside open warehouses. Massive machines with intricate gears and long, jointed levers that work like the jaws of mechanical dinosaurs, some of the looms were brought to India nearly a century ago by the British. They still spool out bolts of cloth as long as there's electricity in Bhiwandi, which is usually eight to ten hours a day. Walking the streets here is like taking a stroll through the Industrial Revolution.

We have identical chats with several loom workers. They work, they struggle to feed their families, they attach no geopolitical implication to this endeavor. Bored with these repetitive interactions, Anurag directs my attention to rows of dank, earthen-floor shanties crammed amid the factories. Inside these crude shelters, a sizable community of prostitutes spend their afternoons and evenings waiting to service the loom workers and truck drivers who constantly come and go, delivering raw materials and hauling out finished product.

Anurag greets an old woman sitting on a stoop, and we enter a room where five women sit in the dark watching a soap opera on TV. The teenagers are painted like French tarts, but the effect is more like little girls who've gotten into their mothers' makeup bags. The older ones have gone to considerably less effort to gussy up. The house smells like a locker room. There isn't the slightest pretense of *Pretty Woman* "working girl" glamour here.

"Success in India only begets more prostitution," Anurag says grimly. "Very few are sharing in the prosperity of this new economy."

The price for services ranges from one hundred to one thousand rupees (between two and twenty dollars). Girls turn over 20 to 50 percent of this take to a "ladylord" who owns the dismal rooms where they have sex with customers. "Beds" made of soiled rugs or sheets over small concrete platforms sit inside closet-sized rooms. While truckers and yarn spinners get blown for five bucks by nineteen-year-olds, power looms clank and crash away next door, bringing India's economic miracle to Old Navy and Banana Republic shoppers who appreciate the value of affordable clothing. This is how India's industrial boom looks to Anurag, and when you're standing in the middle of it trying to pry two words of conversation out of a lifeless twenty-five-year-old prostitute who looks fifty-five, it's a hard vision to dispute.

Sordid as Bhiwandi is, it's nothing compared to a workers' district we visit in central Mumbai, where donated clothes from around the world arrive by the truckload to be cleaned, pressed, tagged, shoved in plastic bags, and resold in Asian markets. Like other Mumbai ghettos, this one is alive from sunup to sundown with food hawkers, street stalls, kids walking to school, and tens of thousands of others going about their business. During daylight hours you'd never suspect that the neighborhood is also home to four thousand prostitutes and that "specialty" blocks filled with transgender whores, S&M practitioners, and Sri Lankan and Nepalese women are accessible any time of day.

"Men pay on a 'per shot' system," one completely gray forty-year-old ladylord informs me. She sits on a plastic stool in front of a crumbling concrete apartment. The gutter in front of her is backed up with garbage and human shit. Hundreds of flies hover around the woman's head.

The business arrangement is the same as in Bhiwandi,

she explains. A girl picks up a customer, brings him back to the "brothel," pays the ladylord her cut, and gets down to business as soon as possible. A typical girl will bring in four or five customers a night. Ten or fifteen girls regularly use her rooms. The ladylord is a former prostitute herself, and I ask if she feels any guilt or hesitation about her work.

"My only obligation is to give the girls a condom when they come in," she says. "Whether they use them or not, it's no concern of mine."

I ask to look inside. The ladylord asks me to take off my shoes, then calls for a young girl in the back of the house. Without looking at me, the girl leads me through a short dark passageway, past a series of tiny spaces partitioned by cardboard or scrap wood into miniature fuck chambers. I can only pray that the liquid on the floor that's soaking through my socks is water.

At the end of the hallway the girl shifts a large piece of cardboard away from the concrete, revealing a literal hole in the wall. A suffocating cloud of mildew and spunk hits me in the face. It's about 105 degrees—after spending a summer month in a place where guys get sweat stains on their ties, you get pretty good at feeling the difference between 105 and 108. I gasp for air, which feels like it's passing into my lungs through wet cotton balls.

I crouch down and creep through the hole. The room has just enough space for an ancient cot. The mattress on top is black with mold. Not spotted—black. The walls are an evil shade of congealed brown and black. I couldn't get a hard-on in this sex dungeon if Beyoncé was fluffing me with 1986 Susanna Hoffs's tongue.

"Do any of the men have trouble performing in here?" I ask the girl.

"It's OK," she says noncommittally.

Between the pauses in our sizable language barrier, I realize that my netherworld escort assumes I've got more in mind than an academic investigation of the sexual habits of Indian wage workers. This is understandable under the circumstances—serious journalism often doesn't look much different from opportunistic scumbaggery. Just flip through some of Robert Novak's old columns. Or ask Glenn Beck.

With night approaching, I shake hands with Anurag in front of a soup kitchen established for prostitutes and their children. Although he works as a journalist, Anurag is on the board of Apne Aap, a Calcutta-based nonprofit dedicated to rescuing prostitutes and bringing an end to human trafficking. According to Apne Aap and at least one other organization, fifty million girls and women are missing from India's population as a result of systematic sex-based violence.

"Our only requirement for leading you on this tour is to publicize our Web site," Anurag tells me. After a day like this, he hardly needs to ask: apneaap.org.

Despite the horrors of the Indian slum economy, I find little reason in Mumbai to fear India. Touring the filth, misery, poverty, and decay makes you worry more about where Indians will get their next drink of clean water than tech support jobs disappearing in Winston-Salem and Albuquerque.

Of course it isn't Indian workers that Americans should fear. The idea of resenting "Indians" for snarfing jobs from "Americans" strikes me as a drastic misinterpretation of reality in an age when corporations have gone global and workers the world over have become interchangeable. The ruling international corporatocracy has

already burned its flags, erased its borders, and laid to
rest all nation-state loyalties. I put "Indian" and "American" in quotations because corporations no longer recognize allegiance to any nationality, so it makes little sense
to apply those labels to their workers and customers.

You can't blame Indians for taking work when it's of-
fered. Indian streets are filled with healthy, intelligent
young men and women living in conditions that would
shock a 1920s Mississippi sharecropper. Any American in
their position would take the same call center or manufacturing job from a foreign employer and, in fact, many
Americans do. Just ask an autoworker in Ohio or Texas
who's slapping together cars for Honda or Toyota.

There are two Indias. One is wealthy, technologically
fluent, and ferociously expansionist. The other is hopeless. Like the point and eraser of a pencil, the two are in-
extricably connected yet will never meet and are fated to
fulfill utterly different destinies. Westerners are comfortable with the idea of a starving brown horde forever on
the butt end of progress. As it's become sharper, however,
it's the tip of the pencil we've been led to fear.

The idea of a Third World rich/poor dichotomy isn't an
original one, but for those who haven't seen it close up, it
bears explaining that the two Indias often exist within
inches of each other. Show me another place on earth
where outside the door of a newly opened hotel bar that
charges twenty-five dollars for a martini—you'd think you
were in Manhattan, especially with the way they serve it
a notch above lukewarm—six-year-old orphans beg in
front of open sewer flues.

I overpay at a number of these up-market bars in the
company of a pair of local go-getters, Anjan Das, art director of *Rolling Stone*'s India edition, and his girlfriend,
Laura Silverman, a New York magazine refugee working

on several high-profile local launches. With its emerging class of fashion-conscious credit card holders, Mumbai has become a flourishing market for Western publishers— *Vogue, OK!, People, GQ, InStyle,* and many other familiar titles have appeared in recent years—hoping to make up for dead sales at home by scoring accounts with choice Indian advertisers.

"Sales of Western magazines are already far better than expected," Anjan tells me. "People don't actually read the magazines. They just leave them in their apartments or cars so that other people can look at the pictures and say, 'Oh, she's into *Vogue* or *InStyle.'* " So, in addition to everything else, the publishing industry has exported the same art director mentality that's been driving Western editors to apoplexy for centuries.

For three nights, Anjan, Laura, and I hit clubs and restaurants where Indian businessmen power through two-hundred-dollar bottles of Scotch and try to get sexsational Bollywood "item girls" out of their three-hundred-dollar jeans. After the tour with Anurag, it's a relief to find that all is not squalor, and I end up having a great time and many fantastic meals in Mumbai, though the most lasting impression comes on the way back out to the airport, when a handless boy staggers to my cab at a red light and begins pounding on the window inches from my face. I look up to see that the boy's head has been completely burned, so hideously disfigured that it's melted into a permanent Halloween mask. A few patches of skin hang off his face; spectral eyes bulge out of receding sockets; teeth and gums are clenched as though he's already a cadaver— walking, breathing, but otherwise dead. The stumps where his hands should be are covered in a ghastly white secretion, like milk or heavy cream, which smears the

window with long, wretched streaks as he bangs away for
attention.

I reach for my wallet, but the driver leans across the front seat, thumps on the window, and curses the boy with a violent Hindi threat. Ignoring the driver, the boy curls a flap of skin where his lip has once been, cocks his head, and appeals to me with phantom eyes. I roll down the window, but the light turns green. The driver smiles at me. "Forget him," he says, oblivious to the fact that I never will. We speed away, leaving the handless boy to try his luck at the next red light.

What Mumbai is to the überreality of *Slumdog Millionaire*, the coastal state of Kerala reportedly is to serenity, wildlife, and scenery. Home to the subcontinent's largest mountains south of the Himalayas, Kerala is a wonderland of empty beaches, jagged peaks, and sandalwood forests (as well as those vein-straightening ayurvedic massages). Because no tour of India is complete without a visit to this advertised sanctuary of sanity, I catch a flight south for my final week in country.

Though home to elephant, wild bison, and the occasional tiger, Kerala is most famous as the place where ferocious rains and winds first strike India each summer and the annual monsoon season is officially declared by government officials. This occurs with remarkable consistency around June 1, when the southwest monsoon rolls off the Arabian Sea and begins blowing through the country from south to north. By June 10, it has usually hit Mumbai. By mid-June, Calcutta. By July 15, all of India lies beneath a claustrophobic dome of pewter that settles over the country like the lid of a garbage can somebody keeps forgetting to empty. In September, the system begins its six-week retreat across the country and back out to sea. Up in Jaisalmer, Joshi will get a month of rain, but during its near half-year cycle, the monsoon will never completely leave the southwestern coast. When you think fog, you think San Francisco. When you think suicide, you think Ithaca. When you think monsoon, you think Kerala.

Traditionally, the most important time of year for Indians, monsoon season evokes lyrical images of ceaseless showers that bring rebirth to the country. When my Jet Airways Boeing 737 touches down in the midsize port city of Cochin, however, the skies are about as threatening as a "time out" warning to an eight-year-old Ritalin addict. In fact, the rain gods in India operate a lot like annoying children playing with a light switch—on then off then on then off then on then off with maddening unpredictability. As one adage says, the rain falls on one horn of the buffalo but not the other.

Because it's such a historically integral part of Indian society, there are actually a number of adages covering monsoon activity, but nobody mentions a single one as I travel toward my sodden destiny in Kerala. Instead, every Indian I meet wants to know why the hell I'm going to Kerala in June.

"It will rain every day." "You will not be able to tolerate the heat." "June is the absolute worst time of all in India, and a perfect hell in Kerala."

From pussyfied Americans accustomed to the precision deployment of elite local TV "stormtracker" weather teams every time it threatens to sprinkle, I might understand. But I thought Indians were supposed to love the monsoon. Ages-old music such as the "Raga Malhar" has woven the season into the national mythology. Rain-themed movies such as 1949's *Barsaat* are classics, and extended rain dances are beloved Bollywood cliché.* Bookies in Mumbai take bets on monthly rainfall. The country's entire ecological and psychological cycle is said to revolve around a weather system that at its climax covers one-third of the planet and is widely regarded as one of the most important natural phenomena in the world.

Varanasi and most of the rest of India had been a tree hugger's nightmare, but in monsoon country I'd expected to find a more finely developed appreciation of the natural world. So where was the joy? Where was the love? Where was anyone in the entire country who had a good word to say about the importance of the rainy season? If I was going to find out, apparently I was going to be ignoring the advice of a lot of people in the process.

Separate the meteorological reality from the rejuvinating-the-soul romance and the monsoon takes on a dramatically different form. Indian farmers may still await the annual deluge, but motorists hate it and it's motorists who are driving India (literally, figuratively) in its manic aspirational push to keep up with China's manic aspirational push to overtake the United States' position of global economic primacy. In both emerging countries, cars are the most important way of keeping score, occupying a position alongside houses at the top of the consumer-status pyramid.

Cars in India, however, are as much burden as blessing. The monsoon brings commutes to legendary standstills across the country.

* Few people on earth deserve more pity than Indian women seeking able dance partners. Indian men have innumerable assets—intelligence, humor, superhuman tolerance for discomfort—but there's something so profoundly doofy about male Bollywood dancers that it makes the white man overbite boogie look positively African by comparison.

"And we come to the same story . . . which is repeated every year," bitches a typical *Times of India* article. "The story of the monsoon showers playing havoc on the city roads, and the harried commuters praying for relief and cursing the authorities all the while." The conclusion is simple and sad: what was once poetry has become a monumental pain in the ass.

Cars are important to this discussion because more than anything the country's thriving auto industry illustrates the fundamental theme of contemporary India, one that bears an ominous message for the rest of the world: it is no longer a primarily rural nation. As Suketu Mehta writes in his quintessential *Maximum City: Bombay Lost and Found*: "Fifty years ago, if you wanted to see where the action was in India, you went to the villages. They contributed 71 percent of the net domestic product in 1950. Today, you go to the cities, which now account for 60 percent of net domestic product."

Unlike old-time fishermen and farmers who rested and threw festivals when the rains came, the work of the modern state doesn't stop for shitty weather. True, hundreds of millions of Indians live in rural areas, and from Darjeeling to Thiruvananthapuram, you'll hear rhapsodic Indian cornpone about how the "cry of frogs and dribbling of water from the leaves" (per my favorite jizz-pumping tourist brochure) make the monsoon the delight of all.

Most of the reasons the monsoon was crucial to Indian society in the first place, however, have become obsolete. Seasonal rains were once the foundation of survival in a country that still has comparatively little assured irrigation, but advances in food storage and preservation have all but eliminated starvation. With improved transportation and communications, remote villages are no longer isolated by annual flooding. The famed wet-sari dances—

for years the only legitimate T & A repressed Indians were allowed to enjoy—have been rendered quaint by the high heels and microminiskirts of the "Bombabes" who are bringing skank fashion and hip-hop sexuality to every corner of the country.

Even children, the most uninhibited and adoring celebrants of the season, are ignoring the monsoon. As one newspaper editorialized, "These days people stay indoors and play video-game consoles. The young are indeed at home, or within the plush environs of hotels and malls. No splashing around in puddles or romancing in the rain for them."

Given that no one likes an outsider who's been in their country all of three weeks lecturing them about their culture, I assume that many locals won't appreciate my notion that the modern state has for all intents and purposes blown past the monsoon. From train platforms to spice shops, I spring my monsoon-is-obsolete thesis on every Indian who will talk to me, yet, astonishingly, not one rejects the idea outright. Many offer waffling resistance— "Oh, you must be careful not to make generalities," and so on—but nobody seems all that offended by my outlandish challenge to the national identity. After road testing it on an array of dumbfounded bystanders, I'm confident my monsoon theory is ready for the ultimate shakedown.

The plan in Kerala is to head into the countryside and, not unlike Linus holding out for the arrival of the Great Pumpkin, find the most sincere place to await the rain. After some inconclusive research on the effects of global warming on the monsoon—disappointing, given that I'd really hoped to drive home my thesis with some shattering evidence rooted in the most fashionable of planetary anxieties—I choose Munnar, a pretty mountain town in the Western Ghats coastal range, four hours inland from Cochin. In addition to being impossibly beautiful, the slopes of the Western Ghats are some of the wettest in the world. The Keralan coast will receive a very respectable seventy-nine inches of monsoon rain, but in a good year the coastal hills will get more than two hundred.

To get to Munnar I hire Baiju, a thirty-five-year-old nature guide who, after submitting to my now highly circumspect driver screening process, insists that his only real deficiency is height.

"Too short for the Indian Army," he says in a way that suggests a life of target practice and drilling at dawn would have been the one for him. "The Indian Army's minimum height requirement for permanent commissions is 157.5 centimeters."

That's about five-two. Baiju missed the cut by 2 centimeters.

It's taken nearly a month but I think I've finally pulled an honest man out of India's bottomless roster of corner-cutting drivers. The barrel-chested, thickly bearded Baiju is exemplary, and not just for being a straightforward type who speaks good English. His 2004 Ambassador sedan is clean and in the kind of shape my engineer grandfather kept his Caprice Classic. Like Team Congo, Baiju knows the times to be quiet and let the scenery speak for itself. And as an amateur photographer, he's savvy to light and angles and stopping points whenever I call out for passing photo ops.

Shouldered by massive rock towers reaching seven and eight thousand feet, the jungle road from Cochin to Munnar is as scenic as any this side of the Hana Highway. The lower slopes of the Western Ghats are covered with tea plantations, manicured rectangles of fluorescent green tea hedges bonsai'd into tens of thousands of near-uniform plots. As we gain elevation, the fragrance of cinnamon, cardamom, coriander, cumin, vanilla, pepper, ginger, garlic, and clove pours through the open windows—Kerala grows half your spice caddy—along with smoke from small cooking fires.

"What do you like to eat?" Baiju asks. "Turn your head anywhere in Kerala and you will find it growing."

At a photo viewpoint we get out of the car to expose ourselves to a light drizzle and assess a promising mass of dark clouds on the horizon. Across the parking lot, four guys in their late thirties leaning unsteadily on the hood of an SUV are roaring at one another and drinking like shipwreck survivors. Drunk is drunk in any culture, but this gang is rolling like a whiskey bottle down a set of stadium stairs.

"Hello! What is your country?" The ballsiest of the crew lurches toward me with an insane grin and the apparent idea of planting a wet-bearded welcome on my lips. I turn my head just in time to receive a sandpaper slurp that starts on my cheek and slides down my neck.

Baiju and I have stumbled onto an Indian version of the weekend roader. Buddies out to drink in the monsoon. Or just drink. I get the sense that the main event, like a trip to the AutoZone Liberty Bowl, is more or less an excuse to get out of town, and it turns out I'm right.

"We are four from Cochin," one of the more coherent guys tells me while thrusting a filthy glass into my hand. "This is our annual trip to the mountains. No wives and children. Now toast the monsoon."

Normally, I'm pretty sociable in these situations, but drunks on twisting mountain roads need no encouragement, especially when they're passing around a bottle of something called White Mischief. This turns out to be a popular Indian vodka, and it must be the real deal because it's not even happy hour and these guys are already acting like the Soviet Army at the Elbe River in 1945. I consent to a courtesy snort and make a note to confer the nickname "White Mischief" upon my mercurial nephew, Kyle, before Baiju and I manage to pry ourselves free and push on to Munnar without further social entanglement.

Nothing lets you know it's raining bulls and buffaloes like a sheet-metal roof outside your hotel window. The Indians say the monsoon is the best weather for sleeping, but like the rain on my second night in Munnar, I'm up and down all night. Mostly this is from excitement—the monsoon, finally—though spend a month on Indian mattresses and you'll see why they had to invent yoga here.

"It's raining bulls and buffaloes!" Baiju greets me in the morning. "Now you are happy."

In Cochin, Baiju had been a rock of courtesy and professionalism—all "Yes, sir" and "Let me carry that, sir" and "Do not purchase tea in that shop; it is known to be operated by a criminal element, sir." Now that he's gotten comfortable around me, his more local tendencies have begun to flower.

It turns out that Baiju is even more rabid for award-winning monsoon photos than I am. In the car approaching a street corner so flooded that it's got its own whitecaps, he points to an old woman making her way up the side of the road with a sack of vegetables.

"Get your camera ready!" Baiju punches the gas and rocks the steering wheel. "Watch the spray when we pass her!"

Baiju downshifts the white Ambassador and veers for

the woman like a cheetah closing on a gimpy zebra in open grassland.

"No, hey, Baiju, that's not necessary. I don't think we should . . ."

"You not like? It's no problem! She won't mind!"

"No! I not like!"

"Great picture!"

We plow into the minilake and a wall of brown water—backed-up sewers are a big problem during the monsoon—explodes ten feet in the air. I click a few shots through the window. Who doesn't love a sheet of water suspended in midair? The old lady disappears behind the wall. Baiju speeds on, blood in his throat, crazy for more prey.

As the morning progresses and fat drops of rain pop like firecrackers across the hood of the car, we come upon some more serious monsoon casualties. Twenty feet below a two-lane mountain road, four guys are trying to push a Kawasaki motorcycle up a steep, muddy embankment. Moments earlier, a jeep barreling into a curve in the wrong lane—a move that's apparently as common in Kerala as it is in Rajasthan—had forced a potential head-on collision.

"I braked suddenly and the bike slid from under me," the Kawasaki driver tells me, still half in shock. "I was saved by the bushes. My bike tumbled down the hill."

Kerala is known throughout India for the "trail of blood" unleashed by windy roads, slippery mastic asphalt, and what even the Transport Department ungraciously considers a breed of "inept motorists," drivers so bad they make the ones in Washington State look like DMV instructors by comparison. (That's a little regional dig, but trust me, it's hilarious because it's true.) Despite having roughly 3 percent of India's population, Kerala racks up 10 percent of the nation's traffic accidents. In 2008 it accounted for 3,862 deaths in 37,306 wrecks. That's more than ten traffic fatalities a day in a state not much bigger in area than Maryland.

The Kawasaki is so heavy that the guys below look like they're struggling with an injured cow. Finally, someone arrives with a line of thin cord. One end is tied to the bike, the other thrown up the hill. It lands a yard from my feet.

Southern Indians are notably short and wiry, and since I'm notably tall and overfed, I'm the obvious choice for anchor position on the ad hoc rope gang. With four guys pushing from below and five guys pulling from above, you'd think a motorcycle would be pretty easy to rescue. You'd be wrong. But the organization required to get eight screaming Hindus and Muslims and one gung-ho American to do anything in concert does provide fascinating insight into the prickly business of Indian politics.

Aside from the cheap nylon rope cutting into my wet hands, hauling a lump of steel over roots, logs, trees, bushes, and boulders is sort of fun. With the Kawasaki back on the pavement and profuse thanks received from the biker, Baiju and I return to the car with the self-satisfaction of Good Samaritans. Still in tune with the spirit of my quest for larger-than-life monsoon experiences, though, Baiju loyally manages to summon a dark cloud.

"Had there been a serious injury, we might have gotten better photographs," he grouses as we move down the road.

The big drama comes during a late-afternoon lull in the rain when the ever-alert Baiju spots a group of three elephants—a bull, a female, and a baby drinking at the far edge of a lake, about half a mile from the road. We pull over and gaze with reverential appreciation upon the lumbering dots from behind a barbed-wire fence—the elephants are on a wildlife preserve. It's exciting to see elephants in the wild, but since we're so far away, our conversation goes like this:

"See the young one standing behind the mother?"

"Oh, yes, I see it now."

"That male looks like he could be pretty big."

"Yes. But he also looks quite small from here."

After a few minutes of this scintillating interaction with India's rare charismatic megafauna, an older man wearing a steeply peaked policeman's cap pops out of the nearby woods. This is a local game officer, who, after a brief chat with Baiju, shows us a spot where a cut in the barbed wire fence is hidden in the brush. If we're so interested in the elephants, he says, why don't we climb through the fence and hike down to the edge of the lake while he looks the other way?

Just as in the Congo, Indians in official positions are depressingly shitty stewards of the land. On a visit to the Kerala Forest & Wildlife Department office near Munnar, the head ranger ran me through the wildlife I might encounter in Pampadum Shola National Park. When I asked him about bird species, he said, "Of course, there are many birds."

"Yes, but what kinds?"

"Don't worry, there are many birds. Look up in the sky and you will see them." He snickered at my apparently ridiculous question, then made a crack in the local dialect that got a pretty good laugh out of the office underlings.

The old dude in the cop hat is officially in charge of keeping interlopers out of the elephant habitat, but he suggests again that we slip through the fence. Since I've grown resistant to blatant solicitations to grease official palms, I do what I can to help him maintain the integrity of his position.

"No, we're fine," I say, trying to convey the immense personal satisfaction I derive from respecting the terrain of wild animals. "We're happy to watch from here."

Baiju, however, has no intention of letting an official offer to skirt the law pass him by, especially as it gives him a rare opportunity for close-up wildlife photography. Baiju charges into the brush shouting "Come on, come on!" Not because he's afraid I'll miss out on anything but because he knows my pricey Canon 200 mm zoom lens will bayonet right onto his shitty old EOS body, instantly making him four times the photographer his after-market 50 mm lens keeps him from being.

Feeling guilty about trespassing on protected land but also wanting to get a better view, I follow Baiju through the fence. We sidestep down a slippery hillside covered with tall razor grass. Pellets of rain begin tickling our faces. At the bottom of the hill we get a clear shot of the elephants across the water, barely fifty yards away. I hand Baiju the 200 mm.

"I can see the hairs on his ass! It is fantastic!" Baiju clicks off twenty identical frames. He shakes with delight each time he lines up a trunk in the viewfinder, but with the rain picking up I can't help worrying about my lens. That thing was expensive as hell and it's not like I'm sitting on a trust fund back home myself. I shove my camera under my shirt for protection, but Baiju waves my lens around as though it's made of Gore-Tex.

After snuffling around the lakeshore for a bit, the elephants make an unexpected plunge into the water and begin swimming directly toward us. Judging from the fresh turds, flattened grass, and rapid approach of the great gray dreadnoughts, Baiju and I are standing in the middle of a popular elephant hangout. I mutter something about our possibly illegal and certainly uncool encroachment on pachyderm property, but Baiju stays crouched in the reeds.

While Baiju burns chip memory—he's recently discovered continuous-fire mode—I detect a slight itching near my ankle. I look down through the wet grass at my Teva'd feet and find two slimy, purplish-black streaks, like squiggles of dark snot, writhing on top of my right foot. For a moment, I have no idea what I'm looking at. Then I hear a sudden, guttural scream, as though someone has just had a basketball thrown into his stomach. The scream turns out to be mine.

"Leeches! Baiju, goddamnit, leeches! Let's get the hell out of here!"

The rains have brought the bloodsuckers out in force, and they seem particularly excited for the opportunity to dig into something warm-blooded that's not protected by two inches of elephant hide. I swipe at my feet and shout at the leeches like a gorilla hoping to intimidate a rival.

Holding his ground against the approaching elephant onslaught, still in the thrall of Japanese technology, Baiju is blind to my horror. This is the dumbest part of all because by now it's raining really hard and also getting dark, and even in the best circumstances, you need a 400mm lens, minimum, to get worthwhile wildlife images. Baiju is bracketing for all he's worth, but I know damn well he's getting a bunch of shit shots no one outside of his biweekly Essence of Photography workshop will look at twice.

I haul ass up the elephant track and back to the road. The game officer is still there, standing in the rain next to our car, smiling as though he's expecting a tip. I ignore him and conduct a deeply personal body search, toenails to taint—I think I've gotten all the little vampires but you never know. Baiju pops out of the bushes five minutes behind me, out of breath, out of battery power, and, most alarmingly, out of professional boundaries.

"There were many leeches where I was standing," he says. He peels one off his calf as though picking a spot of lint off a sweater and holds it up for me to examine. "I must ask you the generosity of allowing me to take a hot shower in your hotel room tonight. You may have to call for an extra towel."

For two days after the motorcycle wreck and elephants and leeches, Baiju and I drive through magnificent countryside exposing ourselves to the full power of all-encompassing showers and endangering the lives of more camera lenses. We share the welcoming laughter of strangers huddled for shelter in doorways. We watch umbrellas mauled into useless skeletons of twisted wire, even ripped clean from their owners' hands by unexpected gusts. In obscure villages we stand on the sidelines while delirious boys slip, slide, and howl through mud soccer games. In Alleppey, we laugh at two men who race out of a bus and literally dance a jig amid drops of rain so big they look like a meteor shower. The happiest discovery—because temperatures are in the eighties and nineties, you can stay out in the rain forever and never get cold.

It's all pretty great. Except for one thing. Sure, the rains are exhilarating, but with each inch that falls I feel my arch monsoon theory being washed away in a tide of collective joy. Far from being hostile or even indifferent to the monsoon, the people of Kerala embrace it, clearly drawing from the storms a reaffirming, communal assurance. Nature still matters, at least to some Indians.

At some point the old woman and wall of water return to haunt my sleep. My last night in country becomes such a restless hell that by the time Baiju picks me up on the morning of my flight home, I'm in an uncharacteristically pissy mood.

"Why didn't you tell me?" I complain, as we claw through Cochin traffic.

"Tell you what?"

"That I was wrong. My theory. That India is a capitalist death ship willing to drag the planet down with it, and that deposing the monsoon proves the point. We talked about it for a week. You translated interviews. You told me I was a man blessed with keen insight."

"I believe you have a good theory five days a week. Look out the window. It is Monday again." Baiju motions at the traffic. "The soccer games and dancing you will find only on the weekend. Now the people are going, as they say, back to the real world. It is just another gloomy Monday."

I roll down the window. Dirty rain, diesel exhaust, angry blares of late-for-work car horns roll into the Ambassador. It feels like India again. I recline the seat, close my eyes, and settle in for the rush-hour slog to the airport.

For the schmoes on their way to jobs in threatening IT office parks, predatory call centers, and world-altering auto factories, it most certainly is another gloomy Monday. For me, though, things are looking good. Thanks to Baiju, I have five-sevenths of my theory back. I have some decent, if gore-free, monsoon pictures. And I have a reliable ride back to the real world, from the dull comfort of which I look forward to extending to India a hearty and empathetic: welcome?

PART III

CITY
Mexico City

8

· · ·

Red Fighters, White Tequila, and Cruz Azul

For a guy who once spent an evening held captive by kidnappers—huddled on the floor of a moving cab while a knife-wielding goon draped an arm over his wife in the back seat—David Lida is remarkably sanguine about crime in Mexico City.

"It happened a long time ago," Lida tells me. "I was unlucky. This is a fantastic city."

Lida and I sit in a cantina called Bar Montejo at a heavy wooden table crowded with plates of pork tacos and shot glasses of white tequila. With mariachi trumpeters playing for a rowdy but good-natured bunch of drinkers in the corner and more annatto-roasted pig meat on the way, it's hard to argue with Lida. Mexico City is a fantastic place—for the moment, anyway.

Lida's "express kidnapping" took place in 1996 during a wave of similar abductions, which he writes about in his gritty yet affectionate city profile, *First Stop in the New World: Mexico City, the Capital of the 21st Century.* After a night out in the fashionable Colonia Roma neighborhood, Lida and his wife flagged down a cab. They got in and found nothing amiss until the driver turned down an un-lit side street and hesitated at a stop sign. Two men bar-reled out of the darkness and into the car, brandishing a knife and pushing Lida to the floor. The larger one cozied up to Lida's wife "so that if anyone looks inside we don't raise suspicions—we'll appear to be sweethearts." Promis-ing no violence in return for cooperation, they immedi-ately confiscated wallets, watches, wedding rings, and jackets.

What they were really after was Lida's ATM card. In typical "express kidnappings," culprits demand a bank card and PIN, then withdraw the maximum amount al-lowed before releasing their victims, who are sometimes held twelve, twenty-four, or more hours, through several ATM availability cycles. Lida and his wife were freed af-ter two hours. Neither was harmed, let alone raped, which had been known to happen. As Lida writes of the mid-nineties crime wave in the capital, "Taxi kidnappings had become widespread. Anything but cooperation was a bad idea." One friend of his was "tattooed pretty badly" for resisting. Another had his ear sliced open when he tried to escape.

I'm a sucker for screamer headlines, and I tell Lida that if I'd been writing his book, I'd have never had the self-control to wait until page 176 to introduce the kidnap-ping. I'd have been quivering on the floor of that cab on page 1. Not only that. I'd have slapped it on the cover, outlined a novel, pitched a screenplay, written two Spike TV specials, and booked a guest shot on Larry King be-fore even turning on the computer.

"It's funny you say that because originally I'd had it as the first chapter of the book," Lida tells me. "But I wanted to demystify the crime problem here and I decided that starting with an abduction might give people the wrong impression of Mexico City."

I tell Lida I can see how this might be a concern.

Like most *chilangos* (the term for residents of Mexico City, though it's used across Mexico as shorthand for rude, abrasive, arrogant louts), Lida loves his city. His superlative book reflects the matchless complexity of the largest metropolitan area in North America and the unofficial economic and cultural capital of the entire Latin world. From music and business to buying dildos and the Good Friday tradition of dragging a splintered cross through the streets pretending to be Jesus on his way to Calvary, nothing escapes his celebratory view.

"If it's so safe, why aren't more Americans interested in Mexico City?" I ask. "It's just a few hours flight from Houston. I came direct from LA and there weren't more than ten or fifteen gringos on the plane."

"Propaganda works." Lida shrugs. "Mexico City is the poster child for contemporary urban chaos, with a terrible reputation for crime, poverty, pollution, overpopulation, social injustice. As a member of the media I grow weary of the myopic tendency to blame the media for every societal problem. But in the case of Mexico City, the toxic affect of the U.S. media on its reputation has significant validity."

"But doesn't getting 'express kidnapped' have validity, too? You're the first person I've ever met who's actually been kidnapped. By someone other than their stepdad, I mean."

Lida is calm when he talks about the kidnapping ordeal, but I notice the tequila has been going down a little faster since we got on the subject. He repeats for the third time in the single hour I've known him that as long as I'm not out at two in the morning looking for smack in the barrio, nothing bad is going to happen to me in Mexico City.

This sounds reasonable. After all, the nineties are ancient history, and, the tocsin sounders of the American press aside, everyone I meet tells me Mexico City has cleaned up its act. I might as well be as worried about mad cow disease or a Lindy Hop outbreak as an express kidnapping.

"For as long as I've been here, this city has been associated with crime, and that's not fair," Lida says. "I can't possibly make a list of all the good things that have happened to me in Mexico City. The kidnapping and getting my camera stolen are the only bad things that have ever happened to me here."

"When was your camera stolen?

"Last week."

"Last week?"

"In a bar in the Centro Histórico. But don't worry, you'll be fine."

"Last week?"

"Yes. But it was mostly my fault. I wasn't paying attention."

Oh. OK then. As long as it was the victim's fault, I shouldn't have any problems.

Given its reputation for all-purpose hazard, for many, travel to Mexico City has become the equivalent of the old Seinfeld joke about scuba diving: "Another great activity where your main goal is to not die." For the first few days, however, I find Mexico City just as Lida has promised—agreeable locals, historic architecture, and not a masked insurgent in sight.

The city's ridiculous size—seventeen million people

spread over six hundred square miles—promises an enormous hassle. Like Los Angeles or the *Law & Order* franchise, there seems to be no beginning and no end to Mexico City, but the grand plaza known as the Zócalo is a logical orientation point with plenty of breathing room. The extensive subway system, opened in 1969, is faster and cleaner than New York's and quickly banishes my nightmares about navigating this supertropolis of unbroken humanity. Traffic is bad, but rush hour is no worse than in Chicago, Dallas, or Denver and is far better than in any big city I saw in India. None of the cab journeys I chance end in extortion or assault.

Though patches of what is euphemistically called "haze" are occasionally visible hanging over the surrounding mountains, the Chinese-style pollution I'd anticipated is nowhere to be seen. Afternoons are marked by deep blue skies and cotton puff clouds that sail like friendly cartoon characters through beams of sunlight. October is apparently a good weather month here.

The kill-or-be-killed mercantile ethic that imbues the sale of everything from striped blankets to cocaine in Mexican border and beach towns is almost nonexistent in the capital, but a little survival technique I've picked up helps ward off what few unwanted solicitations come my way. Mexicans live in mortal fear of appearing rude, particularly toward foreigners, and do everything they can to avoid using the word "no" in negotiations or business conversations. The polite method of indicating refusal is to respectfully raise the back of the hand and say, "Gracias." I incorporate a little Don Corleone squint and try the move on an overeager shoeshine boy in the Zócalo—it works on him like Kryptonite. Later in the week, a strip bar tout shrinks from the gesture like a vampire trembling before a garlic necklace.

Then there's the food. Though saying so will probably disqualify me from future gigs with *Bon Appétit* and *Cooking Light*, I'll stand behind the opinion that Mexican food ought to be a player in any discussion of great cuisines, right up there with eggy French glop and whatever other country's gastronomy is currently considered world class by overstuffed elites. Find another country that lays out a buffet with so many things on it that you know in advance you're actually going to enjoy eating. Noted for its variety and deliciousness, the Malaysian city of Penang has become an eating-safari destination for rich Singaporeans, who have been known to make the ninety-minute flight each way just for dinner—it surprises me that Mexico City hasn't become a similar junket destination for Americans whose love of the taco is so great that it can now be eaten in pizza form.

On top of all this, Mexicans drink like off-duty cops, boozing it up without apology seven days a week starting in the early afternoon. I've long maintained that there's no such thing as a good drinking town—to misquote Tip O'Neill, "all drinking is local"—but Mexico City might be an exception.

What I mean by this is that inside the walls of a bar every city in the world shrinks to human size and how good a time you have drinking always comes down to the people you're with. In the right company you can have as much fun in a deserted roadside bar in Cardston, Alberta, as you can at the Oak Room in New York or Skybar in LA. Your ass conforms to a barstool the same way in Paris that it does in Medford, Oregon. Once it's in your bloodstream, alcohol behaves in New Orleans exactly the same way it does everywhere else.

Yet Mexico City is an extraordinary guzzling arena, a place where you can depend on the beer being frosty, the music energetic, and the women, if not throw-a-frying-pan-across-the-room-at-you-with-a-passionate-rage-they'll-bring-to-the-bedroom-an-hour-later hot-blooded hot, at least miles more animated than those you find in America's genderless suburban drinking holes. Two weeks pickling my vital organs in a city where you can get buzzed without even trying forces me to reconsider my entire curmudgeonly "no such thing as a good drinking town" gambit. And to recall the parting words of my ex-colleague and provocateur extraordinaire John DeVore, who, as I was preparing to move away from New York City, pulled me aside and said in an avuncular vodka-soaked rattle: "Your alcoholism is going to miss this town."

I once wrote, "No place needs a good PR agency more than Latin America. For a region with so much going in its favor—food, scenery, the most hospitable locals on earth—it has a worse reputation than the Florida Division of Elections." This made me some friends among our neighbors to the south, though not so much with touchy Floridians. Nothing I find in Mexico City changes my mind, particularly about the people.

Spanish colonialism put an undeniable jinx on every indigenous civilization it came in contact with. But while the church and crown's legacy of corruption remains—from Mazatlán to Manila, graft is the mainstay of every country conceived in the wake of the cross—it also left behind a tradition of public grace and manners. Although no longer exactly chivalrous, the hoi polloi of Latin America are still reliably friendly and cordial. Two telling examples stand out from a long list of random kindnesses shown to me in Mexico City.

I walk into a mom and pop pharmacy near Plaza

Garibaldi looking for a sewing kit. I'm told savvy travelers always carry their own, but this is the first time in more than two decades of world travel I've ever needed one. The owner apologizes for his limited stock, then disappears into the back. He returns a moment later with a yard of dark thread dangling from a single needle.

"No kit," he says in English. "Will this do?"

I say it will and break out my wallet.

"No charge," he says, waving off my outstretched hand. "I'm sorry this is all I have."

"It's exactly what I want; let me pay," I say, tactfully not mentioning that all I want the needle for is to gouge a pus-filled boil from the end of my finger.

"It's a gift. Please, put away your money."

Beside him, his smiling wife wraps the needle in paper, improvising a cover for the tip with a tiny piece of Styrofoam so that I won't lance myself when I put it in my pocket.

Next, on my first attempt to purchase a metrobus ticket from a machine, I ask a young couple behind me for help with an automated Spanish command that I don't recognize. With the couple's assistance, I buy a thirty-peso card (about three dollars), good for six rides.

When I swipe the card at the turnstile, however, a buzzer sounds and the gate locks up. A uniformed transit cop informs me that I must put additional credits on the card in order to use it.

"I bought this card ten seconds ago," I say. "There are thirty pesos on it."

I swipe the card two more times and get two more buzzers.

"I'm sorry, señor, no pass," the transit cop says.

Behind me, my new Mexican pals are outraged. Correctly assuming that my rudimentary Spanish is nowhere near equal to the task of talking my way around a dis-agreement with metrobus police, they take up the matter on my behalf.

"This man has paid his fare!" the woman exclaims. "We helped buy the card ourselves. You are a [presumed expletive, not understood] to treat a foreign visitor like swine!"

"He cannot pass through the gate with an invalid ticket. That is the rule."

"Don't be an imbecile," the husband barks. "Look at him. Is this a man who cheats a few pesos for bus fare?"

As usual, I'm dressed to suggest that I'm carrying just enough money to buy a head of cabbage and not much else, so this is an unnecessarily charitable assessment.

"Please don't worry about me," I say to the couple. "It's a bad card. I'll buy another one." I'm no Thurston Howell, but to me it makes more sense to write off three bucks than prolong a standoff with foreign authorities on a bus platform.

"No," says the husband. "We will not leave you to face this incompetence alone."

He says this in Spanish and I can't be completely sure of my translation, but his courtly diction and polite pro-nouns suggest the sort of exactitude you want in your bus station lawyer. The argument ends when the wife swipes her card, passes through the gate, then reaches over the turnstile and swipes her card a second time. The light turns green, and she grabs my arm and pulls me through. As I pass into the Promised Land I glance behind me at the transit cop.

"*Bien*," he says, and shrugs.

On the bus, the couple not only refuses to allow me to repay them for the fare; they actually try to give me thirty pesos out of their own pockets as a refund for the faulty ticket for which they feel personal disgrace and responsibility.

I realize that the more time I spend in the city, the more likely I am to run afoul of local ne'er-do-wells and maybe even become the victim of a petty crime. Possibly worse. If I do, I hope I come out of it with the perspective of a David Lida and don't allow the exceptional to define my perception of the usual, which, so far, has been overwhelmingly positive.

Almost a week into Mexico City and the most apparent danger being the possibility of jumping a pant size—I die a little inside each time I go up a belt notch, and the taco snarfing here is nonstop—the trip clearly needs shaking up. What better place to boost my exposure to the worst a society has to offer, I think, than a professional soccer match?

Fortunately, I've recently met a Canadian gringo named Marty McLennan who has married into a local family. By the rules of Hispanic culture, this automatically makes me nearly as tight as tamales with an affable branch of Lopezes who happen to hold the beloved Mexico City Pumas in the psychotic regard typical of foreign soccer fans. When Marty's wife, Ruth, informs me of a Sunday game at Olympic Stadium against the loathsome barbarians of Cruz Azul, the Pumas' Mexico City–based rivals, I jump at the opportunity to join the family outing.

The day gets off to a promising start. On the bus to the stadium I find myself standing next to a middle-aged Australian. Even though he's wearing a scarf bearing the emblem of the reviled Cruz Azul dirt balls, he seems like a friendly enough guy. Diplomatically subduing my day-old but nonetheless burning Puma loyalty—when it comes to sports fandom, beachfront rentals, and personals ads I'm a big believer in the "come big or stay home" philosophy—I strike up a conversation. A nice thing about Aussies, living in their own country has gotten them used to being accosted by talkative strangers, so they don't mind when random dudes start interviewing them on public buses.

"Bill" has lived in Mexico City for about a year and because he's got a sensitive government job I won't say much about him other than that his Spanish is impeccable and he has a curious amount of knowledge concerning the Mexican and American militaries and the developing political situation in just about every country in Central America. Since I still haven't seen any, I ask him about danger in Mexico City.

"I've only had one instance and it was at the stadium where we're going today," he tells me. "I was pickpocketed there about six months ago."

Finally, something nefarious to report about Mexico City. I knew adding soccer to the mix was a good idea.

"We were coming out of a match, thousands of people all pressed together, herding toward the exit as you do. That's when he got it."

Pickpocket stories always intrigue me, not simply because it's never happened to me, but because I honestly don't think it ever could. Since I usually carry my wallet in my front pocket, I feel immune to this kind of theft. I know the big front bulge makes you look like a wiener, but you get to keep your money.

"That's no guarantee," Bill says. "My wallet was in my front pocket at the time."

"Don't you feel that sort of thing as it's happening? There's no way someone is going to slip their hand in my front pocket without me knowing it."

"I felt it as soon as it happened, but I was surrounded

by a crush of people. I looked around and there were five or six likely suspects. It could have been the guy behind me. Or the woman to my left. Or someone in front reaching behind.

"Anyway, there was nothing I could do. I had my nine-year-old son with me and I was holding his hand. It was either let my wallet go or leave my son alone in a football crowd to chase after a ghost who was already moving in any one of ten directions."

Bill lost two hundred pesos (about twenty dollars) and his credit cards but like any good Aussie he's prepared to up the ante on outrageous tales, even his own.

"I've had transvestites in Bangkok and Rio pickpocket me as well, but they were much less subtle, grabbing at my balls first as a diversionary tactic. I caught out both of them right away."

"So what happened then?"

"The one in Rio made a joke about mistaking the smaller package for the larger one. They laugh and you let them walk away. What else can you do in a situation like that? Beat up a transvestite? Call a cop? Not likely."

The Lopez clan has warned me not to wear a belt to the game. "They'll take it away from you at the entrance," Ruth says, and sure enough, in front of the stadium I pass through two pat downs that check for belts and anything else that might theoretically be turned into a weapon or projectile. The searches are comprehensive and involve lots of touching in the pleats region. If I've got any stowaway leeches left on me from India, these guys will find them.

Security is even heavier inside Olympic Stadium—this is the place where American sprinters Tommie Smith and John Carlos raised their gloved Black Power salutes during "The Star-Spangled Banner" at the 1968 Games, so the history of subversive behavior is thick here. Although supporters of the Cruz Azul child molesters are partitioned from the home crowd by a chain-link fence and a line of police in riot gear, a pair of fans rigged out in Cruz Azul jerseys and caps have found their way into our section. They're with two Puma friends, and I note with relief that rather than causing a riot, the stream of insults hurled among the foursome as well as at the players on the field is regarded by the crowd more as comic relief than fightin' words.

In the cheap seats of the upper deck I'm swiftly introduced to the two most vital words in the Mexican soccer lexicon. The first is *puto*, which means "fag" and is used at one point or another to describe every player on the field, including those on the home team. The second is *puta*, which means "prostitute" or, more loosely, "slut" and is commonly used to abuse the reputations of mothers of opposing players, though also sometimes to challenge the lineage of fellow fans. Five minutes into the glorious Pumas v. scumbag Cruz Azul match, this key terminology is already embedded in my brain by thousands of obnoxicated fans whose voices could cut through sheetrock.

The ongoing vulgarity is a welcome distraction since the game itself is a typical soccer yawner, producing a predictable 0–0 halftime score after a grand total of one shot on goal. As the second half begins, the intensity of the drunken catcalls picks up, providing me an opportunity to add colorful embellishments to my baseline vocabulary.

"*Puuuuuuto!*

"*Puuuuuuta madre!*

"*Pinche puuuuuuto!*

"*Pinche culero!*"

I turn to Marty and his nephews. Roberto is fourteen; Eduardo is thirteen. Both have been taking steady hits off their auntie's beers all afternoon. One of the great things about foreign countries is that you can have straight-faced conversations with buzzed teenagers that might get you put on a watch list back home.

"So, I know *puto* means 'fag,' " I say.

"Or 'faggot,' yes," Marty confirms after consulting the boys.

"So what does *pinche puto* mean?"

"*Pinche* has many uses, but it's like 'fuck' or 'fucking.' "

"So, *pinche puto* is 'fucking faggot'?"

"Yes, that's exactly right. 'Fucking faggot' is what you hear the crowd keep chanting at the players."

"What about *pinche culero?*"

"That's 'fucking asshole.' *Culero* is asshole.' It's a highly offensive term."

"Worse than 'fucking faggot'?"

"Probably not."

Roberto and Eduardo nod in solemn agreement.

"OK, I see. Thank you."

Another common refrain roughly translates as "Your mother fucks like a dog." This phrase is shouted in the same door-knocking cadence we often associate with the old "shave and a haircut, two bits" lyric. I'm told the insult is so well known across Mexico that simply knocking on someone's door with the familiar syncopated rhythm can potentially land you in a fistfight.

Another interesting thing that happens in foreign countries is that you can sit in a stadium for three hours listening to everyone around you bellowing *puto* and *puta madre* as a sort of shout therapy and accept it in a way that you never would at home. Inside U.S. stadiums, shouting "faggot" or "Your mother fucks like a dog" every fifteen seconds would get you escorted out by security, or at least into a nasty altercation with a protective father or self-appointed censor. Though it should be noted that I attend most of my sporting events on the well-behaved West Coast and have never been to an Eagles or Jets game.

Unapologetically mannish Mexican society is as fine with gay slurs as it is with defaming mothers, the most sacred pillar of Mexican culture. As a result, you sit there and grin along with, or at least silently tolerate, fifty thousand loudmouths every time someone's sexuality is slandered. I'm not saying it's right, just that it happens. You go with the flow and tell yourself, "It's OK. I'm having an authentic cultural experience in which it's proper to scream 'faggot' in a public place. How fascinating."

Is there an element of homophobia at work here? Probably. David Lida tells a classic joke: "What's the difference between a straight Mexican and a gay Mexican? Three tequilas."

Brazen soccer vulgarity and a few economic matters aside, however, the merger of the United States and Mexico that some futurists predict will probably be a lot less difficult than most of us imagine. Working-class people here operate very much as they do in the United States. They meets for drinks in bars after work. They catch a show or movie or party on Friday night. They sleep in on Saturday, then clean the house and run errands before dinner. They hang out with the family on Sunday, watch *fútbol* or baseball on TV, maybe even go to a game. They begin the period of existential dread preceding another workweek at approximately 3:47 on Sunday afternoon.

Mexico requires very little in the way of cultural adjustment for an American. I already like Canada and Mexico almost as much as I do the States—moving March

Madness and my favorite craft root beers across either border might tip the balance—so if the grand North American alliance ever comes, I'm not going to sweat it, provided nobody tries to stop me from using my Bible collection for target practice with my .45 Colt Peacemaker. I'm all for progress so long as it doesn't interfere with our most precious schizophrenic rights.

The good humor of the Puma fans lasts only until the *pinche culeros* of Cruz Azul unexpectedly score a goal (all soccer goals are scored unexpectedly) to go ahead 1–0 midway into the second half. The two Cruz Azul boosters in our section celebrate this miracle by whipping off their shirts and performing a tubby, topless salsa around the concrete bleachers, a move that gets them pelted with half a dozen cups of beer thrown by fans in the rows above. Less than a minute later, with the Puma faithful still reeling from the goal and the shirtless guys still mocking them, the Cruz Azul blood farts deliver a deathblow by scoring again with a providential shot that glances off the right post and into the net.

The trauma of an insurmountable 2–0 lead is so devastating that the entire stadium simultaneously swears off the evils of drink forever, flinging their full beer cups into the air like 1920s Prohibitionists at a temperance tent revival. Golden Corona suds fill the skies over the stadium. Hundreds of empty cups are picked up, flattened into little Frisbees, and sailed into the lower decks. A few of these make it all the way onto the field, but most end up clipping the heads and shoulders of inattentive fans. During the literal outpouring of grief, I snap a photo of an adorable five-year-old girl—throughout the game she's been clutching a little stuffed security puma—just seconds before she hucks her dad's half-full beer cup over the rail onto some unseen fellow booster below. While proudly reviewing this award-winning shot in my camera's LCD monitor, I'm struck in the back of the head by an empty Domino's personal-size pizza box.

Next, a sheet of beer sprays the back of my neck and I feel a sharp kick in the middle of my back. I turn around to see one of the shirtless Cruz Azul wankers drunkenly pirouetting to avoid the beer shower, so I figure the kick is accidental and let it go. Normally I wouldn't even think about confronting a shitfaced soccer hooligan—a redundancy, I know, but I'm painting a picture—though I actually consider doing so for a minute before settling back into my wet seat. Accident or not, the guy delivered a hard boot, and I have no doubt that a few thousand enraged hometown fans would eagerly come to the assistance of a Puma brother in the ensuing fracas.

"This really isn't bad," Marty tells me. "Fans used to come to the stadium with plastic Baggies, piss in them, tie them up, then throw them."

"At their own fans?"

"At whoever. It's very upsetting to see their team lose."

This all sounds like an afternoon of great action, but the game ends at 2–0 and other than the flurry of activity following the two scores, the match is as captivating as the liner notes from a Lawrence Welk CD boxed set.

Culturally enlightening though the experience might be, I bring a bit more than the usual red-blooded Yank prejudices to soccer. My problem with the game isn't simply that I find it dick simple, hopelessly repetitive, low-scoring, and devoid of recognizable strategy; nor that I've spent a lifetime irritated by the marketers and TV networks that have tried to force every surefooted nimrod from Kyle Rote Jr. to Freddy Adu on me and the rest of the already sports-sated American public; nor that the primary justification given for all of this social engineering is that since soccer is the most popular game in the rest of the world it should ipso facto be proclaimed a major sport in the United States. (Hands down the number-one absolute dumbest argument in favor of anything, anywhere, at any time. By this logic, we should all be speaking Chinese, living with our parents into our thirties, and getting our peasant girlfriends pregnant at seventeen.)

Beyond these excellent arguments, however, the most empirical reason to abhor soccer is the corrosive influence it has on the sanctified American youth, whose innocence our child-infatuated country is always so quick to defend, even if the freedoms of tax-paying adults are compromised in the process. The ascending profile of the dismal game in the United States can be credited to two overriding principles.

1. Soccer is so easy to play that kids who aren't gifted or gutsy enough to participate in real sports are able to put on glittery shirts and high socks and immediately regard themselves as "athletes," all to the delight of their self-affirmation-craving mommies and failure-phobic teaching professionals.
2. The game's astounding lack of complexity plays into a general trend of adults who are too lazy, busy, or impatient to teach kids games with actual rules and tactics; and of kids too unmotivated to work through the difficulties of any new activity because it's too hard.

Call me reactionary but the diminution of the American juvenile, whose ingenuity and independence have

been traded for Courage the Cowardly Dog pathos and
adult-organized play dates, has left more than minimal
risk and adolescent trauma in its wake. It's led to a dangerous loss of spontaneity, intelligence, and gumption that
follows kids well into adulthood. Perfect example: thanks
to insidiously overdirected activities like youth soccer,
neighborhood baseball games have become distant relics
of childhood civilization, rubbing out such central con-
cepts of the kid sports experience as "ghost runners,"
"pitcher's out," and "right field closed." With these devices,
nine- and ten-year-olds of yore could creatively compen-
sate for having just three or four players to cover an entire
diamond and think their ways through whole games without a single adult inside whiskey-bottle throwing distance.
Similar variants helped small groups of kids cover entire
football fields. Amending the rules of play requires a working knowledge of a sport's many intricate and intellectually satisfying parameters. Meanwhile, soccer's dim bulb
run-kick-walk-Capri Sun routine snares kids and parents
with the obvious and undemanding, hemming them into a
universe of low expectations until well beyond the years
when they should be giving a shit about fake celebs named
Becks and Posh.

Monotonous as the soccer game itself is, the skirmishing
in the stands gets my blood running for action. By now
I've grown confident enough to consider manning up to
some stiffer tourist challenges. Foremost among these is
the infamous barrio of Tepito. Renowned throughout
Mexico as the breeding ground of the toughest boxers in
the country and the acknowledged hub of black-market
activity in a city where as many as 50 percent of residents

live outside the boundaries of the official economy, Tepito is widely considered the essence of Mexico City.

In *First Stop in the New World*, David Lida writes, "The Barrio de Tepito is a seemingly endless labyrinth of alleys encrusted with merchandise . . . contraband, pirated, even some legitimate. Its hidden patios, once residential, now tend to be warehouses that secrete huge caches of goods, drugs and guns." Back at Bar Montejo, I told Lida that I was considering a visit to Tepito, hoping that he'd offer to come along as a guide—it's never a bad idea to have someone who knows what to do in case of kidnapping riding shotgun. So it was a disappointment when he shook his head. Lida won't be joining me for my Tepito sortie. He was willing, however, to offer advice.

"Don't bring a camera or credit cards or anything that it would really hurt you to lose," he said. "If you should get mugged, don't panic. It'll be very professional and over in five minutes."

Before leaving the apartment I'm renting in the comparatively docile Roma Norte neighborhood, I gather my cash, credit cards, ATM card, camera, and sunglasses and jam them into the room safe. Despite the fact that nothing I've seen so far has given me even an instant of hesitation, I take Lida's words of caution seriously.

Then I look at the sunglasses.

Prior to this year, I'd spent a lifetime protecting my eyes from the retina-charring rays of the sun with a revolving collection of convenience-store sunglasses. I prefer ten-dollar shades for many reasons, not the least being my tendency to break, lose, and forget them. Also, I'm cheap about things like polarization so that I can be indulgent about others—impulsive iTunes acquisitions, field-level Mariners tickets, the most expensive bottle of white tequila on the shelf, etc.

Aware of the high-intensity tropical sunlight I'll be exposed to during much of my year of traveling dangerously and also endlessly annoyed at having to walk around with someone in preposterously unfashionable eyewear,* at the beginning of this journey Joyce had generously presented me with a pair of Ray-Ban Flight Extreme sunglasses. Stylish, well-fitting, more protective than a Mongol bodyguard, I'd never owned glasses that minimized glare so mercilessly, let alone came with their own hard case. Just holding them made me nervous. My anxiety was not at all reduced when I finally beat the price out of Joyce: $175. That's the kind of tag Drew Carey flips over on *The Price is Right* that makes you go, "Oh, bullshit, who pays that for a pair of sunglasses?" Which is exactly what I said to Joyce when she told me how much they cost.

I contemplate the Ray-Bans in the safe. Like me, they're survivors. Zambian baboons, Congolese shakedowns, Indian markets, they've seen it all. I've secretly vowed not to let a pair of $175 glasses change me, but now I'm not sure what to do. The Mexican sun is brutal and I've gotten pretty attached to the little guys, but wearing them in Tepito seems like an unnecessary risk. I'm not even chancing the Jansport on this mission.

Still, if the investigative intent of this project is to be respected, diving into Tepito without bearing some mark of the tourist beast will feel like a cop out. I reach into the safe, fix the Ray-Bans at a spry, just-in-from-Cali angle atop my head, stick fifty dollars worth of pesos in my shirt pocket, a U.S. hundred in my pants pocket, and strike out for the blackest of Mexican markets.

---

* You want some CHiPs-era mirror shades? Rodman/Snipes wraparounds? Plaid Pantry BluBlocker knockoffs? Dig under the seat of my car and help yourself.

Tepito begins just north of the Zócalo and Centro Histórico, but the differences are noticeable as soon as you exit the metro. All of the buildings are in worse shape—crumbling, chipped, and faded, with broken windows, strings of balcony laundry, and webs of telephone and electrical wiring that turn the sky into a snarl of industrial profanity. Sidewalks are cracked and broken. Gutters overflow with trash.

An unusual number of young men wear bandages across the bridges of their noses or have red eyes and swollen lips, telltale signs of bar fights or side-street scrapes. Many of these men are either working at or hanging around one of the neighborhood's literally hundreds of automotive part and repair yards. Tepito's streets are filled with old Fords, Chevys, Hondas, and Volkswagens, not one without a rash of visible problems—bashed out taillights, missing bumpers, cardboard windows, wires spilling out of places wires don't normally spill from, blue smoke pouring from under hoods at stoplights.

The Mexican government has a remarkably laissez-faire approach to motor vehicles and the people who operate them. For instance, acquiring a driver's license in Mexico City requires no test of any kind. All it takes to get licensed is proof of residence and forty-three dollars. "No one asked if I knew how to drive," one *chilango* tells me. "They didn't even make me take a vision test." Lack of testing is just one reason why if you see a turn signal in Mexico, your only assumption should be that someone in the front seat of the vehicle is having an epileptic seizure.

Walking through the long blocks of Tepito chop shops appraising Gran Marquis and Galaxies and Dodge Aspens moored behind chain-link fences, I get the sense that a stolen car could arrive here, be completely stripped, and parted out in a few hours.

"Ninety minutes," the English-speaking owner of one of the shops corrects me. "But we don't accept stolen cars."

While not as tightly packed as Chandni Chowk or Nizamuddin in Delhi, Tepito offers just as many singular thrills. I turn off an alley filled with shops selling bridal gowns, bras, lace panties, and freshly butchered shanks of meat—you don't make up this sort of irony—and am stopped in midstride by the sight of a full-size boxing ring set up in the center of the street. Inside the ring, two light heavyweights are flinging leather like heroes in a Hemingway story. A young referee dressed in jeans, white T-shirt, and baseball cap circles them while a crowd of three hundred or so men, women, and children stand by cheering. An announcer on a PA that sounds like it's had a cactus needle dragged across its speakers calls the action with cattle-auction panache.

It's two thirty in the afternoon on a Tuesday. Eighty-five degrees outside. People are fighting in the street. I ask someone what's going on.

"These are amateur fighters from gyms around the city," a man in a Carolina Panthers shirt tells me. "They hold fights once a year here to celebrate the anniversary of this market."

This seems like an odd way to drum up anniversary-specials business, so my first thought is that I've misheard his rapid Spanish. Then again, maybe I haven't. In front of us, a tiny tot wearing a freshly purchased Mexican wrestler's mask is sitting on his father's shoulders and urging on one of the boxers. The combatants wear padded blue or red protective headgear with matching gloves, allowing spectators to shout their support for fighters by calling out their color—*Azul! Rojo!*

The bouts are scheduled for three rounds but one between teenage flyweights ends in the second when the blue fighter opens his stance just in time to receive a lightning uppercut to the testicles. This results in the only knockdown of the afternoon, a slow-motion, limb-by-limb failure of the blue fighter's body that resembles the pancaking of a skyscraper being systematically demolished by explosives.

I assume the debilitating low blow will force a draw or no decision, but apparently shots to the wedding tackle are legal in the streets of Tepito. The red fighter receives a trophy and huzzahs from the crowd as he parades around the ring. The disabled blue fighter crawls out of the ropes with his head down, presumably to continue the process of dry heaving and extracting his gonads in a private alleyway. No trophies are handed out to the losers. No ribbons for second place. No certificates that say, "Thanks for showing up and getting your sack inverted."

Yet this isn't even close to the most surreal fight. That one takes place between two small girls that can't be more than seven or eight years old—the red one in Indian braids, the blue one with a long ponytail—who climb into the ring, roll their heads on tiny necks, shrug birdlike shoulders, beat motivating warm-up blows on their own headgear, open wide to let managers stick plastic guards in their mouths, touch gloves at the center of the ring, then come out throwing haymakers like Rocky Balboa roaring back against Apollo Creed after begging Mickey to cut his eyes.

At first, few punches land and the girls end up pushing and shoving each other into the turnbuckles. The crowd laughs it up and the referee smiles as he breaks the li'l pugilists apart and drags them back to the center of the ring. For the Mexicans it's all unbearably precious, a Norman Rockwell picture slathered in hot sauce.

In the second round, however, the girl in red seizes the upper hand. Having completely figured out her opponent, she begins battering her head with terrifying control and impunity. Not a single body blow, all the action goes upstairs. The blue fighter either hasn't been taught or doesn't remember how to protect herself—or she's just worn out. Throughout the barrage of red gloves, her arms droop at her sides like palm fronds in a hurricane.

The blue girl's ponytail swings wildly as her head is punched from side to side. In a final act of desperation she turns her back on her opponent and tries to escape the ocean of blows by simply running away. The girl in red catches her in the corner and whales away without fear of retribution. At this point the crowd surges forward and begins chanting, *"Roja! Roja! Roja!"*

This is insane. Three hundred people demanding that a pint-sized girl in Indian braids put away her helpless victim—and me without a camera! Fuck David Lida and his paranoid advice. I don't care if my Ray-Bans get ripped right off my face. I can't believe I'm not getting any video of this.

Turned by the crowd's bloodlust, my sympathies now lie entircly with blue ponytail. If only she could slow down the red monster with a miracle shot to the solar plexus. "Go downstairs," I want to shout. "Blast her in the kidney!" I know all of this is wrong, but, like smirking through all the *putos* and *puta madres* at the soccer game, it's impossible not to get caught up in the machismo collective.

Blue ponytail puts on a courageous performance; she simply refuses to go down. But her face is puffing like a biscuit. When the ref finally comes back from his coffee-and-cigarette break and stops the fight, I actually hear a couple of scattered boos from spectators angry at the fight being stopped prematurely.

The bouts continue for another half hour. Like the girl fight, it's almost all head shots, no bodywork at all. The ethic is instant kill. After the last bell, I approach the card table where the ring announcer is putting his things in a black leather briefcase. His name is Marlon and he sports a Founding Fathers mane of coiffed white curls. Sheer confidence. No Just for Men camouflage for this guy.

"I am a ring announcer for professional fights but I offer my services for this event each year," Marlon tells me in English. "It's a good way to see young boxers."

"Very young," I say. "How old were those girls?"

"Rodriguez is twenty years old. She is one of the best amateur females in Mexico."

"No, the really young girls."

"Oh, the *chiquititas*? Both are eight years old. They were very good. Did you enjoy them?"

"It's strange to see people so caught up in a fight between eight-year-old girls."

"In Tepito, if it is a good fight it does not matter; the people will appreciate it."

I've kept Tepito more or less at arm's length all day—circling warily, engaging at favorable moments, but mostly taking stock of the sights from a safe distance: a three-legged dog hopping down a sidewalk with a Pamper in its mouth; a guy passing a small packet to another guy, both looking in opposite directions as though nothing is happening, as though even a gringo passerby couldn't guess what's wrapped in that paper; a dozen more young guys

in wife beaters hanging around a concrete bunker with
Gimnasio Box—Escuela Técnica Deportiva painted in large
black letters on the side.

With the sun dropping below the grimy rooftops, I
wander past a barbershop on Carpinteria Street and recognize an opportunity to mix things up. As in the United
States, old-timey barbershops with red, white, and blue
poles out front and stalwart owners with horn-rimmed
glasses and combs in their shirt pockets are vanishing in
Mexico. Unisex beauty salons dominate the hairscape
here, but the barber on Carpinteria is as old school as an
Archies lunchbox and a paddle across the ass from the
vice principal.

It's generally not a good sign when a business is
empty—this is particularly true of restaurants and
barbershops—nor when prospective patrons have to wake
up the elderly owner by tapping on the side of the chair
he's snoozing in. After the awkward introduction, Fernando shakes himself into consciousness. With elaborate
gestures and roundabout Spanish—I do OK in bars and
hotels but specialized conversation about bangs and layer-
ing remains beyond my linguistic horizon—we arrive at a
shaky agreement as to what each man expects from the
other.

Fernando drags a straight-edge razor up and down
a leather strop attached to the back of the chair like he's
been doing it for fifty years and goes to work around my
ears. I start in with some small talk I imagine is typical of
edifying cultural exchanges such as this one. But Fernando is either the uncommunicative sort or simply dis-
likes foreign dingbats who come into his shop near closing
time expecting to inject their Borat-level language skills
into a delicate professional task.

With a movement that says, "I'm working hard enough

as it is," he bends down, fishes through a cardboard box beneath the counter, and drops a faded magazine into my lap. The inference is clear: Fernando prefers not to discuss work while he's in the middle of it.

The cover of the magazine features a good-looking blonde with an enormous bust corralled into a double-A mesh bikini top. The idea of sitting in a barber chair in Tepito thumbing through vintage Mexican porn while a crabby seventy-year-old cuts my hair strikes me as sort of cool, but it turns out the magazine is just about Mexican entertainment industry figures. No shaved women being cornholed by ethnic midgets, just a bunch of Q & As with ditzy actresses and male models from cologne ads about who they're dating and whether or not they're good friends or bitter enemies with their ex-lovers. The answer to this question is always "good friends," but the magazine asks it often enough that you can't help wondering if something else is going on behind the scenes.

Fernando carries on in silence. Even when he spins me around and holds up a cracked hand mirror to let me survey the back of my head, he says nothing. But when I nod and say, *"Muy bien"*—don't let anyone tell you that ninth-grade Spanish won't come in handy someday—he allows a thin smile. Then he reaches behind a jar on the counter and with a princely nod hands me the sunglasses I'd set down when I'd come in.

"No se olvide," he says. Don't forget.

In spite of the good haircut and Fernando's admirable stewardship of my Ray-Bans, I leave the shop feeling a spiral of depression sucking me down, this one far more worrisome than the brief monsoon-theory setback in Kerala. Mexico City is shaping up as a colossal waste of time on my tour of fear and danger. After a week in town I've got

an alarming situation on my hands: I think I'm falling in
love with this hellhole.

Fortunately, I've already put in a call to the cavalry
back home. Reinforcements are on the way. All I've got to
do is summon back the dread that lured me here and hold
on to it long enough to keep the whole damn operation
from falling apart like an overstuffed taco—at least until
the reservists arrive.

9

. . .

The Electric Shanghai Bob
Margarita Acid Test

In the early 1990s it was my misfortune to spend a year in a bland-as-tofu Japanese suburb called Kojima teaching English as a Second Language to highly unmotivated students at a newly opened branch campus of an American community college. As one might expect of such an academic outpost, the school attracted an eccentric and wildly inconsistent faculty from the global community of wayward ESL instructors willing to sign one-year contracts to live in a place even most Japanese had never heard of. For all concerned—students, teachers, administrators, bemused townsfolk, the school's alleged Yakuza mafia bankrollers—managing the college's rookie season was an intense, strange, troublesome, and impossible-to-forget experience.

I survived thanks largely to a timely discovery of Bombay Sapphire gin and the companionship of a semidashing, heavy drinking, not necessarily warm-blooded American expat known as Shanghai Bob. With a reputation gilded by triumphant stops in various East Asian ports, capitals, and shitholes—China, Indonesia, Thailand,

Philippines—Shanghai Bob arrived in Kojima as a larger-than-life international rogue, rake, and raconteur. With the eternal look of a man in his midthirties, Bob wore sarongs in the evening, consumed brandy by the gallon—some dazzled groupie was always presenting him with a bottle—and whether haggling in waterfront vegetable markets or carousing in hundred-dollar hostess bars, moved with the authoritative White Man in the East bearing reminiscent of more privileged times for white men in the East.

The school's teachers were housed in a shoddy, cherry-tinted apartment complex known to chipper optimists on the faculty as the "pink palace" and to malcontents (whose ranks swelled throughout the year) as the "mauve mausoleum." I lived on the second floor of the mauve mausoleum, two doors down from Shanghai Bob. Between us was a wayward Vietnam-vet-turned-English-teacher with a sweeping intellect and quasi-Victorian manner named Robert Glasser. The following anecdote offers a succinct view of the Shanghai Bob legend and the admiring if awkward position into which it sometimes thrust those of us in his orbit.

You don't normally get intimate views of your coworkers' private lives, but several months after my arrival in Kojima, I was treated to more than a glimpse of Shanghai Bob's turgid after-hours existence in the form of a late-night visit from a local legend named Krazy Keiko. A combustible community floozy in her late twenties with porcelain complexion, anime eyes, and knife-straight hair, her relationship with Shanghai Bob had begun in a yakitori parlor, where she fell quickly under the spell of his urbane magnetism.

Krazy Keiko's good looks, fluent English, and general state of lubrication were mitigated by numerous personal flaws, most of which became evident within five minutes in her hot, wet, clingy presence. She may or may not have had a husband; said husband may or may not have had Yakuza connections; once interested, she attached herself to men like a barnacle to a dock; she was so lacking in conversational discretion that right off the bat you couldn't help but pick up that she was in most regards the female equivalent of a rutting mastodon. In other words, a live wire only men such as Shanghai Bob are equipped to handle.

The evening in question had gotten off to a successful start with Shanghai Bob and Krazy Keiko conjugating verbs in his apartment down the hall and drinking like the day after Hiroshima. These informal personal-enrichment sessions with Krazy Keiko had been going on for a couple months. In the apartment next door, drinking gin and reflecting on our empty lives, Glasser and I were privy to their ecstatic conclusions, devastatingly audible through the tissue-thin Japanese walls. I had inside information, however, that Shanghai Bob was already getting tired of Krazy Keiko. Willing minx that she was, he'd been grousing about dumping her for weeks. Nevertheless, sometime around eleven o' clock, Glasser and I heard Shanghai Bob's front door close and the giddy couple lurch into the night in search of more alcohol.

I had a last drink in Glasser's apartment and went home to bed. Next I knew, stealthy footfalls were heading my way across the tatami mats in my darkened apartment. It was two or three in the morning. I had wakened with a vague awareness that someone had walked through my unlocked front door but didn't gain complete consciousness until I felt, unmistakably, a warm body slither between my sheets.

With the exception of watching the Red Sox come back from 0–3 against the Yankees in the playoffs, I've never

been as startled in my life. I bolted up and hit the lights.
Stretched out on the bed, completely naked, was Krazy
Keiko—a little layer of that baby fat the Japanese like but
otherwise looking as fuckable as a psychotic barnacle can.

"Don't be frightened," she whispered, and once again I
couldn't help being impressed by her English. Goddamn
Shanghai Bob, seducer of wanton beauties *and* A-list ESL
teacher.

"I'm here to do whatever you want," Krazy Keiko clari-
fied needlessly.

Before I could respond, the phone rang. I heard
Glasser's voice bellowing through the wall next door a
microsecond before it came through the receiver.

"Krazy Keiko's in the compound! She's breached the
wire!"

"What the hell's going on?" I was talking into the phone
but looking at Krazy Keiko, who smiled back enigmatically.

"She's been trying to break down Shanghai Bob's door
for the last twenty minutes!" Glasser screamed. "Thank
Christ, I got her out of my apartment. Shanghai Bob refuses to open his door. They've had some kind of quarrel."

I hung up and asked Krazy Keiko to leave. She demanded to know why I wasn't already in the act of ravish-
ing her. I told her this was beside the point. After several
minutes of this sort of chitchat, she disarmed me by beginning to sob. I convinced her to get dressed, move to the
couch, have a cup of tea, and sit still for some big-brother
counsel—once again the whammy of a Christian upbringing leaving me too paralyzed by morality to seize a golden
opportunity. Say what you want about religion, it does a
piss-poor job preparing young men to take advantage of
those precious few occasions in life when insane young
hotties offer themselves up for the taking.

Krazy Keiko regrouped and recounted the night's drama. Essentially, Shanghai Bob was through with her. No surprise there, but I pretended a little for the sake of decorum. I told her that getting back at Shanghai Bob by screwing his friends was certain to have the opposite effect of what she intended, that the sun would rise again in the morning, and that there were other sharks in the sea for her to cruise with. She sipped her tea, subdued a few sniffles, apologized, gathered herself anew, and stood to leave. And then, as unexpectedly as she'd slipped into my apartment, she pounced on me again, pinning my arms to my sides and kissing my neck like a spurned starlet in a 1930s melodrama.

"Don't you want to bone me?" she demanded, adding "daddy" to several more similar entreaties. If you want to find out what kind of culture America exports through Hollywood and hip-hop, pay attention to the idioms that roll off the tongues of town tramps across the planet.

I grabbed Krazy Keiko by the shoulders and shoved her out of the apartment.

"You must be gay!" she shrieked as I shut the front door on her arm. "You have a tiny penis! Fag!"

Krazy Keiko lingered at Glasser's door shouting, "Tiny penis!" before stopping to beat on Shanghai Bob's door and scream, "I hate you!" and "Fag!" thirty or forty times before finally disappearing down the stairs.

We saw Krazy Keiko only fleetingly after that, but I stayed in touch with Bob, crossing paths with him every three or four years to confirm that, if anything, his reputation as global ladyslayer was growing even more widespread. Years later, as a *Maxim* editor poring through thousands of responses to a sex survey conducted by the magazine, I came across a reply from a woman in California who revealed that her boyfriend had nicknamed her genitalia "Vaginasaurus." I immediately fired off an e-mail to Shanghai Bob speculating that Krazy Keiko had finally followed her dream and made it to America. He wrote back: "Which Keiko are you talking about?"

I thus consider it auspicious that as I'm prowling the Mexico City streets for harrowing experiences, Shanghai Bob happens to be in the midst of his biennial return from Asia, visiting family in the Midwest and already bored out of his gourd reacquainting himself with nieces, nephews, and Old Style beer. A few descriptive e-mails promising an endless river of tacos and at least one round of margaritas on the house are enough to lure him across the border. For Shanghai Bob, Mexico offers new turf upon which to lay his mark—vagabond of the East though he might be, the man has never been south of Arizona. For me, his arrival means I can finally stop harassing local writers, families, and strangers for advice, insight, and bored-guy conversation in my grammar-proof Spanish.

Shanghai Bob's reputation as an instant catalyst, a man whose rapscallion energy reliably attracts the socially sensational and morally unrepentant, reaffirms itself within hours of his arrival in Mexico City. At La Guadalupana, one of the city's most atmospheric cantinas, a distinguished-looking older gentleman with his right arm tied up in a blue canvas sling beelines across the bar and introduces himself before we even sit down.

Max is sixty-eight, a self-proclaimed artist who says he's sometimes mistaken for Sean Connery. You can sort of see it. He's tall, tan, and balding in a manly way.

"My friends call me Crazy Max," he says in fluent English, shaking hands with his left mitt while nodding at the sling. "This is a carpel tunnel injury suffered due to excessive painting. I have been unable to work for two months. It's killing me."

Other than to establish himself as a member in good standing of the worldwide fraternity of bar blowhards, at first Crazy Max does little to justify his nickname. Stopping only to swig from the beer we buy him, he rambles at length about his extensive travels as a former photojournalist—Canada, Turkey, Thailand, Egypt, and Israel, where he covered ongoing Arab-Israeli conflicts. Just when Bob and I are sending each other you-ready-to-shake-this-nut signals, Max breaks out his wallet.

"I want to show you something," he says.

Max hands me a small laminated photo of himself wearing a full-on uniform of a Nazi SS officer, complete with swastika armband. I pass the picture to Shanghai Bob who promptly spits up half his Sol beer.

"What do you think?" Max asks, like a proud papa showing off photos of a newborn.

"Max," I say, "you are the first person I have ever met who not only has a picture of himself dressed as a Nazi, and who not only carries that picture around in his wallet, but who actually shows it to people he's known for less than fifteen minutes."

"I was invited to a costume party," Max explains. "There was a prize. I wanted to win."

"Where was the party?" Shanghai Bob asks. "It sure as hell wasn't Tel Aviv."

Max laughs like a choking hyena.

"It was in Mexico City," he says. "Not far from this cantina."

"Where the hell do you even buy something like that?" I ask.

"I had it made. Every bit is custom stitched. Others

came to the party in rubber monster masks or funny hats.
I won first prize."

"Who came in second, Mussolini?" Bob says, earning another hyena chortle and brotherly slap on the back from Max.

I tell Max I don't think he should be showing people pictures of himself dressed as a Nazi.

"Why not? Are you Jewish?"

"No, but you don't have to be Jewish to take the Holocaust seriously."

"Mexicans don't give a shit about the Nazis," he says. "All that happened a long time ago. Most of them don't even know about it."

We get on the subject of U.S.-Mexico relations. Does the border fence bother him?

"I couldn't care less," he says. "That's for wetbacks, not me. But it will come down like the Berlin Wall because America needs cheap manual labor from the Mexicans."

Max insists that Mexicans are the hardest workers in the States, then adds apropos of nothing, "The Negroes are lazy. They would rather sleep than work."

"Why would you say that?" I ask. "Where do you form an opinion like that?"

"I spent time in LA. I saw it with my own eyes. It's a problem in your country. It does no good to deny it."

Now, besides having more ego than an NFL wide receiver, and aside from the der Führer photograph and the unsavory views on race, here's the problem with Crazy Max and plenty of others like him. In person he doesn't come off as that horrible a guy—more like a self-involved, politically outdated old coot. His friends no doubt consider him crazy but probably also entertaining.

I'm not defending him, I'm just saying that having a

beer with him isn't as appalling as you'd think it would be judging from the outrageous statements printed above. As Dr. Bahr's anthropology professor father once told me, "Nice is overrated."

"Nice may be overrated, but you can't come off appearing to stump for a guy like Max," Bob warns during Max's third trip to the john. "And I'll tell you something else. Old Loco Max didn't get that arm injury from painting too much. He got it falling off a barstool."

When Max returns I tell him about my mission in Mexico City and mention the surprisingly easy tour of Tepito.

"Tepito is nothing," he says. "You go south of here to Santo Domingo. That's a place you don't want to go alone."

"What's so bad about Santo Domingo?"

"*Cabrón!*" Max waves a hand and sneers.

"What's *cabrón?*"

"It means 'fuck' or 'shit' or 'motherfuck.' It can also mean 'goat,' but it's usually a word for something nasty."

"I wonder why I didn't hear it at the Pumas game."

"Do you ever go into Santo Domingo?" Bob asks.

"A year ago I went with a friend. We went to a bar. They put out two lines for me on a table. It was my first time to try it. Do you know what I'm talking about?"

"Cocaine?"

"Hell, yes, man! Cocaine!"

Shanghai Bob's ears perk up.

"Could you take us to this bar?" Bob asks.

"Why not?"

"And you say there's cocaine?"

"But now I must go home to my wife," Max says.

With the promise of fairy dust in the air, we make an appointment to rendezvous at La Guadalupana the following afternoon for a guided tour of Santo Domingo. At the appointed time, however, Max doesn't show and doesn't answer his phone. Being stood up by Mad Max is the only outright act of discourtesy I experience in Mexico City, but, to be honest, I'm kind of relieved. We wait around for an hour and end up contenting ourselves with Sol beers and lunch at a stand selling deep-fried *churros rellenos* filled with molten caramel that are almost as addictive as blow, and probably twice as unhealthy.

Having scouted out barrio barbers and she-child pugilists and read through half a dozen Mexico City books before Shanghai Bob's arrival, I now consider myself qualified to lead him on a tour of local attractions. In a few days we hit all the biggies—the pre-Hispanic pyramids at Teotihuacán, the National Museum of Anthropology, Frida Kahlo's "Blue House," the Zócalo, and Centro Histórico. Each is worthwhile and there's little I can add about any of the sights that can't be found in the popular literature, although having Shanghai Bob along does lend fresh perspective. Gazing at the bravura Diego Rivera murals depicting the history of Mexico on the walls of the National Palace, Bob steps back from the images of native women being raped by Spaniards and fat-cat Wall Street bankers counting their pesos and reflects, "Like most leftist art, totally overdone. This guy really had a grudge against the papists, didn't he?"

Not that his commentary reveals a latent devotion. As he darkens the door of a church for the first time in two decades—the Metropolitan Cathedral is a principal tourist attraction—we stumble into a Spanish mass in progress. Bob listens in respectful silence for a moment before whisper-cackling, "As boring as I remember it."

Just as it did me, the food wins Bob over right away.

Two things you're filled with after every street meal in Mexico City: meat and regret. This is because every time you leave a *puesto* (stand) serving the best greasy tacos you've ever eaten, you pass one on the next block that looks even better. That remark about jumping a pant size wasn't a joke. According to a recent report, 75 percent of women, 69 percent of men, and 35 percent of school-age children in Mexico City are overweight.

Sadly, not every meal is perfect. For The Big Dinner—the celebratory binge set aside by friends who haven't seen each other for so long that they conclude the only appropriate response is to feast like blue whales at a sea lion rookery—Bob and I select Hostería de Santo Domingo, a landmark establishment that specializes in a creation unique to Mexico called *chiles en nogada* (and which has nothing to do with Max's Santo Domingo).

Every guidebook to the city praises this "festive" and "hugely popular" restaurant. One goes so far as to proclaim the signature *chiles en nogada* the culinary equivalent of Greek drama, with its hot spices and mild walnut cream sauce battling for preeminence, its chewy pepper and savory stuffing of meat and cactus leaf serving as both emblem of Mexico's riotous mash-up of cultures and symbolic substitution for the human flesh that comprised a sacred part of the national diet before the killjoy Spaniards showed up to outlaw all the primitive fun and replace it with their own weekly make-believe flesh-munching ceremony.

We arrive at nine o'clock, Bob in a tailored suit from Hong Kong and me in my church jeans and the least wrinkled shirt in my closet. A corpselike maître d' greets us at the door and escorts us to a table on the edge of a completely empty dining room. Barren. Deserted. Quiet as the Pope's tomb. The kind of place you know you should leave the second you walk in, but before you can pull your thoughts together you've got a table, menus, drinks, and a commitment.

From the back of the room, a chef pokes his head out of the kitchen to make sure he's not being misled, that there really are customers who want to eat. The wait staff nods at him—see, gringos no less—then returns to eyeing us with shame and despair. Just when things can't get any less promising, an elderly couple emerges from behind what looks like a closet door. The oldsters wheeze across the silent room to a violin (she) and a Technics electric piano (he) that sits on a massive stage. Someone hits a switch and a feeble string of Christmas lights trembles to life behind the piano. The crushing stillness of the restaurant is broken by a keening version of "As Time Goes By," sung out of tune and in Spanish by the old woman as though she's entertaining at a Bulgarian funeral.

It's a ghastly performance. Fiesta Mexico may be right outside the door, but we've stepped into a Soviet Black Sea resort circa 1955. The restaurant clearly had a stroke a few years ago but nobody's bothered to come around and commit it to a home yet.

The much-ballyhooed "riotous blend of *chiles en nogada* flavors" arrives less than two minutes after we order, always a bad sign. The plate is cold. The food is chilled. I find out later that *chiles en nogada* is most often served at room temperature, but you could use this walnut sauce to sooth third degree burns.

Unwilling to concede easily to the failure of The Big Dinner, Bob and I gamely attempt to validate the meal despite the desolate echo and pulmonary rhythms of the geriatrics on stage. True, ice-flecked cream sauces can be off-putting to the untrained palate, but this one has an attention-grabbing way of lingering on the roof of the mouth. The meat is interesting. Mixed beef and alpaca? Pork and ostrich? The filling isn't exactly hot, yet it's warm, sort of, a welcome contrast to the rest of the dish.

I down a hefty gulp of wine. I savor a quarter-forkful. The band shuffles through its songbook in search of another number—it's so quiet you can hear the pages turn. Shanghai Bob sets down his fork and the clang of silver on porcelain reverberates so loudly that the violinist looks up to see what all the hullabaloo is about.

"If I'm going to eat mucus, I prefer it to be hot," Bob says, tossing his napkin onto the table.

"Something wrong?"

"It looks like dog vomit."

Bob whips out his camera and snaps a photo of the atrocity on his plate. The flash reflects across the entire room, startling the old man at the Technics into an off-key note.

I inform Bob that the green pepper, white walnut sauce, and garnish of red pomegranate seeds represent the colors of the Mexican flag, just one reason *chiles en nogada* is revered across the nation. This little chestnut appears in all three of the guidebook descriptions I've read about Hostería de Santo Domingo, and I'm hoping it might enhance Bob's appreciation of the dish.

"A recipe based on the colors of a flag?" he says. "How fucking dumb is that? That makes this abortion worse." As a longtime hotel man, Shanghai Bob is famously testy in the face of inferior F&B standards.

I struggle through a few more bites, trying to prove a point, then drop my fork in defeat. The waiter doesn't ask if we want a box. He just carts the plates away like dead bodies. The staff appears as relieved as we are when we reach for our coats and head outside in search of the nearest taco stand.

I'm certain that Bob and I have witnessed a legend in its death throes, a restaurant that won't possibly be open three months from now. Later, however, several locals assure me that the Hostería de Santo Domingo remains popular with a certain "mature" demographic, that it bristles with activity between its prime time of three and six in the afternoon, and that no matter what uncultured opinion I may have to offer on the matter, this is still the best place in the world to get *chiles en nogada*. I'm happy to take these experts at their word.

The most rewarding attraction by far is Plaza Garibaldi, ground zero of mariachi culture, where dozens of groups converge every night for a massive Mexican-style battle of the bands. Though groups can be found specializing in every type of indigenous music in the country, mariachi dominates Garibaldi with bands of anywhere from three to twelve members playing violins, trumpets, guitars, drums, upright basses, and whatever else comes out of the Mexican kitchen sink.

Music is everywhere in Mexico City, but in Garibaldi it's everywhere all at once. Standing in the middle of the wide, outdoor plaza while four, five, or six bands play simultaneously—partying patrons purchase individual songs for a few bucks a pop—it dawns on me why mariachis sing with such loud, proud voices. It's the only way they can be heard in proving grounds like Garibaldi.

Facing the plaza, Salón Tenampa is the most famous mariachi bar in the country, a musical universe unto itself that's celebrated in such songs as Los Lobos' "Río de Tenampa." Inside, Bob and I quickly down three margaritas. No ice, no froth, not particularly cold. Just lime and tequila. Are these "authentic" margaritas? There's no way of asking over the din of roving musicians banging on guitars, blaring on trumpets, and singing like drunken ranchers at a sheep-shearing festival. Either way, the drinks are going down so fast, we start ordering two at a time.

A quartet dressed in Virgin Mary white—hats, jackets, shirts, belts, pants, even boots, all blinding white—approaches the table and asks if we'd like a song. One of the guys is hauling a full-size harp, the centerpiece instrument of the sweet *sones jarochos* music of Veracruz. Where else can you slam margaritas with Tecate chasers while a guy jams on a harp five inches from your head?

"I don't know any Veracruz songs by name," I tell the guitarist. "You pick."

"La Cucaracha?"

"No, something different. Something from Veracruz."

"La Bamba?"

"For God's sake," Bob says. "We get it; we're gringos. Play something that won't embarrass us."

The band rips through two up-tempo numbers that sound pretty good, though it's hard to tell for sure. Next to us, seven vocalists in gaudy *charro* suits with silver-studded black sombreros are singing for a table of Mexicans, every one of them enjoying the hell out of "La Bamba." Every sound in the bar—the music, laughter, talking, and shouting for more drinks—merges into a muddled roar. This must be what it's like to be an old dude with the batteries running low on his hearing aid. I can barely pick out the harp notes, even though by the end of the song the *harpista* is practically in my lap.

When the band finishes, a spindly character with slack, greasy hair and the wide, owly eyes of a child approaches the table and sets down a crude wooden box the size of a hamster cage. A pair of wires protrude from small holes cut in the side of the box. From the minute we walked in, I've

been watching this guy make the rounds through the bar.
Whatever he's selling, lots of people have been buying.

"Hola!"

"Hola."

"Would you like to play?" he says in Spanish, holding up the wires. Up close, I can see they have thin metal handles, like a pair of rudimentary jumper cables.

"What is this?" I ask.

He places the handles on the table and turns the box around. On the back are a pair of thick, round dials, like knobs from an AM radio control board Wolfman Jack might have worked with. The dials are numbered zero to ten.

"You hold the handles and I turn the knobs," the man explains. "The higher I go, the greater the intensity of electrical current that enters your body."

"Why would I want to do that?" I ask.

"To test how much you can take."

"So, this isn't some kind of therapeutic thing?" I ask, ruling out an earlier guess. "There's no alleged medicinal value at all? Just a pure test of machismo?"

"Yes, just a test. For fun. See that one? Moments ago he made it all the way to nine. He is very strong. His friends were impressed."

"I'll bet."

"It's easy. Why not give it a try?"

"You ever hook that thing up to someone's nuts?"

"Oh, señor, no. Give it a try."

"How much?"

"Ten pesos."

So, less than a dollar to get electrocuted in a Mexican bar.

"You do much business with this?" I ask. "Make a lot of money?"

"Yes, it's very popular."

How exactly one drops into the business of talking guys in bars into getting jolted with an electrical current I don't know, but I like this man's idea of a good time. Even more, I like the fact that what little Spanish Shanghai Bob understands was drowned and left for dead somewhere between the ninth and tenth margarita of the night.

"This guy's contraption looks pretty interesting," I say to Bob. "I'm going to treat you to a piece of authentic Mexican culture."

"It doesn't look safe." Shanghai Bob didn't just roll into town on top of a load of avocadoes.

"It's perfectly safe. I couldn't get everything he said but I think it's a sort of relaxation thing."

Now, it goes without saying that a man doesn't earn a name like Shanghai Bob for being a downy innocent easily conned into barroom scams. But as I "explain" the box, and its owner stands by with the placid trustworthiness of an Amway salesman, I absolutely know that despite the glaze of skepticism in his eyes, this far into the evening a ferocious tequila mallet is hammering away at Bob's better judgment. And that inside his head my margarita accomplice is imploring, "C'mon, big fella, how often are you in Mexico? Take some chances. Live a little. Chuck has a lot of Mexico experience. He knows what he's doing."

Bob looks at me like a baby harp seal and slowly reaches for the handles. I offer a "Good show, old boy" expression and turn to the man at the dials.

"Do your worst," I say, fully expecting a first-round knockout. But the guy isn't just electrician, he's part artist, with a deeply refined appreciation of the dramatic essence of his craft. He moves his fingers over the dials like a ballerina putting on her tights.

Level one passes without incident.

At level two, Shanghai Bob's face acquires a kind of beatific radiance, the countenance of a simple man touched by the innocence of a child or the splendor of a spring meadow.

At level three, he appears mildly stoned.

At level four, the electrocutioner lingers. A creeping confusion in Bob's eyes evolves rapidly into suspicion and alarm.

At level five, Bob's cheeks begin to tremble. His eyelids flutter like a hummingbird's wings in front of a bright red flower the instant before penetration.

At level six, Bob's head snaps back and he howls like a child who's just seen his dog run over. "Holy fucking shit!" he screeches, flinging the scorching handles to the floor. "This guy's trying to kill me!"

The electrocutioner calmly bends over and picks up the handles. Bob sears both of us with a glare of unfiltered contempt.

"What the fuck is inside that box, a car battery?" Bob asks—guessing correctly, as it turns out.

"How high did he make it?" I ask the electrocutioner.

"Almost seven."

"That's pretty good."

"It's typical. See the girl standing at the bar? Last night she reached nine and a half."

This is a dubious claim. The trick, it turns out, is simply hanging on. Once the current becomes strong enough— usually between seven and eight—the arm muscles seize so tightly that it becomes physically impossible to let go. Had Bob's "uncle" instinct not kicked in just before he reached the point of no return, he might still be clinging to those live wires.

———

After a dozen margaritas and the shock-and-awe gim-crackery inside Tenampa, Shanghai Bob is desperate for fresh air. Back in the plaza we buy a couple of Coronas from a guy toting around a Coleman cooler. To drown out the sound of Bob complaining about being electrocuted, I pay for a song from a wandering norteño outfit in match-ing black-and-white fringed leather jackets and hand-tooled cowboy boots.

A small crowd buzzes around to hear our accordionist and two singers barrel through a loud polka. A man carry-ing a four-foot-high stack of cowboy hats in one hand wan-ders by and talks Bob into buying a black one for fifteen bucks. For cardboard covered with felt, the hat doesn't look all that bad.

"I hate cowboy hats," Bob says as he puts it on. We're in that drunken, irrational, freewheeling mood in which temporarily stepping out of character makes perfect stu-pid sense. "Only Mexicans look good in cowboy hats."

The cowboy hat either has magical powers or, in con-cert with Shanghai Bob's own mystical faculties, it ac-quires an explosive synergistic authority. Bob isn't bald, but like Tim McGraw, he undergoes a godlike transfor-mation with the black hat on his head. For the first time I sense the potential for the redoubtable charisma of the expat's expat from the Orient to be fully realized in the Latin world.

Almost as soon as he gets the hat on his head, an ex-ceptionally good-looking, long-haired young Mexican woman in low-cut, pube-teaser jeans and a tight green top leaps out from behind the band and into Shanghai Bob McGraw's arms with a feral take-me-now shriek. At first she appears to be joking, or maybe on the losing end of a dare, but when she straightens up and asks him to dance, Shanghai Bob hands me his beer and makes a few gallant turns around the plaza. As adept at the thankless role of the wingman as anyone, I discreetly feed more money to the band.

As the polkas speed up, so does the interest of the girl in the green top. After three songs and an ever-tightening grip on the girl's waistline, Bob looks over his shoulder and shouts, "Charlie, I'm not sure where this is going, but we might be taking separate cabs home."

I shoot him the old "no problemo" sign and slip another two hundred pesos to the band. While the music plays on, I wander the plaza checking out more bands and buying more dollar Coronas. Thirty minutes later, Bob taps me on the arm. The black magic cowboy hat looks like it's never coming off, but Bob is cruising stag once more.

"What happened to the girl?" I ask.

"Eh, you know," he says. "She wasn't looking for anything seedy.".

They usually aren't, but that's never stopped Shanghai Bob before. Still, he doesn't look disappointed and I let the comment pass. I don't want to think about Shanghai Bob growing too old to be vulgar.

The night in Garibaldi Plaza ends at three thirty on Sunday morning. Although it's always enjoyable to recount drinking binges in Mexico, there's a larger point in my retelling of this one. Neither Bob nor I tend to be belligerent or obnoxious drunks, but on this night we are by any measure two red-faced gringos blasted enough to test a homemade device that sends an electrical surge through the body; to slam room-temperature margaritas without once uttering a complaint; to open our wallets and drop cash like pirates on holiday in full view of anybody who happens to be stalking an area well known for impaired tourists throwing their money around; to listen to five bands at a time and love every one of them; to buy CDs that we'll lose before the night is out from bands whose names we'll never know; to pretend to be pros at the norteño hustle in front of a crowd of hooting strangers while holding on to a twenty-year-old girl and coming God knows how close to a Mexican shotgun wedding. And at the end of it all, not only *not* getting rolled, but reeling off the sidewalk into the middle of the street, flagging down the first cab that comes by, and trusting the driver to get us back to our hotel and apartment in the heart of Mexico City with most of the money in our wallets and all of the virginity in our asses intact at the end of the ride. And having it all go down exactly like that, having it end on a harmonious note that mistrustful worry warts the world over who have never set foot in Mexico City would not possibly believe it could.

Gloom, fascism, and matching unisex outfits are standard futurist predictions for human society, but despite prophecies of doom and evangelical hard-ons for the end of days, some parts of the world are getting better with the march of time. Mexico City appears to be one of them.

"This place is incredible," prezapped Bob had shouted to me over the noise in Tenampa. "Why can't Mexico City live down its reputation? When I told my brother I was coming down here, he asked me to get my life insurance papers in order first."

It's startling how certain themes keep resurfacing during my travels. Bob's remark about Mexico City is almost the same as the one made in *Harper's* about the Congo's inability to live down its gruesome reputation.

Crime isn't the only issue that dogs the capital's name. Despite a widespread negative perception, for example, air quality in Mexico City is much better than it was a decade ago. In the late 1980s, Mexico City began shifting away from its manufacturing base toward a service economy, shedding most of the thirty-five thousand or so outdated factories that once polluted the city. Since the 1990s, all new cars in Mexico have been required to have catalytic converters; annual exhaust tests as well as restrictions on weekend driving in the city have also reduced emissions.

Of course, there are twice as many cars on the road in Mexico City as there were twenty years ago—the same devilment that's at work in India. And there's still smog. But the layer of brown I flew through out of Los Angeles looked no more toxic than the one I flew through coming into Mexico City. And I've seen the sky over Houston look worse than week-old *horchata*.

As for general filth, the city is far cleaner than I expected, light years ahead of India in public sanitation. In two weeks of roaming the city, I see exactly one rodent, a fat, nasty brute scurrying along the sidewalk in Zona Rosa. During any given two-week stretch of the time I lived in Manhattan, I would have seen an average of 27.4 rats.

One of my clearest memories from the near two years I spent in a street-level apartment on First Street in the East Village, by the way, is being serenaded to sleep each night by a concert of rats gnawing and screeching at one another while battling over garbage in the overflowing bins located just outside my door. One day, I complained to my pal Dave Malley, "I love New York, but whenever I end up leaving, the one thing I'm not going to miss is the sound of those rats fighting outside my door." To which longtime New Yorker Dave replied, "Chuck, I've got news for you—those rats aren't fighting."

I'm sure, by the way, that millions of rats live in Mexico City, just as they live among all large human populations. I'm just reporting my experience. One rat. And not a single roach in my fifty-five-dollar-a-night apartment. My good fortune could simply be karmic kickback for those extravagant tips to Vinod and his buddy in Rohet Garh, but insofar as vector control in the Mexican capital is concerned, I have no complaints.

From misplaced fears of carbon inhalation to heroin-war crossfire, the news media rises once again as an easy target of blame. A *New York Times* story, published a few weeks before my arrival, on a menswear shop in Mexico City that specializes in stylish bulletproof suits and other garments for paranoid businessmen and fashion-forward drug lords includes the following paragraph:

"The rash of drug violence, together with a surge in kidnappings for ransom, has shaken everyday Mexicans. Ask a stranger for directions on the street these days, and fear is the first emotion that crosses the person's face. He or she might recover enough to describe how to go this way or that."

Never mind that the bulletproof haberdasher "scoop" is old news—the store has been operating for two years and peddles its wares at Harrods in scary London, as well—the line about jumpy *chilangos* is patently ludicrous. Because it's so radically at odds with my experiences, I ask a number of locals about the notion of a public so frightened of others that they not only pay outlandish markups for bulletproof blazers, but cringe at the approach of strangers. My inquiries are met with universal disgust.

"Preposterous," says the most offended of my interviewees. "This is the opinion of someone who knows nothing about Mexican people."

The hyperbole of ambitious writers looking for a big story is understandable, and not just because competing for space with the *Times*'s other foreign desks is undoubtedly an ulcer-inducing task requiring of the bureau man a certain degree of imagination. It's also reflective of a more basic human emotion. As one local tells me with pride and conviction, "The number of murders in Caracas in one month is equal to the number of murders in Mexico City in one year. Among the most dangerous Latin American cities, Mexico City does not even place in the top fifteen." A nice point for Mexico City, but one that also perpetuates the scourge of Caracas—another place I've managed to escape without suffering anything worse than a mild hangover and regrettable purchase of decorative papier-mâché fruit.

Bob leaves a couple days ahead of me, taking most of the momentum of the trip with him. I spend an afternoon recuperating from his visit and, between bursts of sleep and efforts to rehydrate, nagged by the disembodied voice of Crazy Max telling me, "Tepito is nothing."

Since I can't go home with anything less than absolute certainty that Mexico City isn't the turista death sentence it's made out to be, I spend my last day on a sojourn to the villainous district of Iztapalapa. On the southern edge of the city, Iztapalapa has both the highest population—with as many as a million and a half residents, it's among the most densely populated places in North America—and highest crime rate in the capital, making Max's coke-riddled Santo Domingo a farting lap dog by comparison.

It takes almost an hour to reach Iztapalapa from my apartment in the city center. The first thing I notice when I arrive is the graffiti. A number of crown-of-thorns Jesus murals are drawn on concrete walls in the bold, comic book motif I associate with 1970s subway trains in the Bronx, but the most prominent style is that ubiquitous tagger scribbling that looks like something freshly curled out of a Chihuahua's ass.

The worldwide bane of metropolitan aesthetics runs rampant throughout Mexico City, though to be fair it's not half as jarring here as it is in other places. I've dropped my head in dejection at the sight of tagging while riding a gondola through the canals of Venice and been heartbroken by squiggles in the Rocky Mountains backcountry. No city on earth has been more uglified by this "art form" than Berlin, where I suppose the embrace of tagging as hallowed public expression has at least exacted some form of revenge against Hitler's pristine "Germania" dreams for the city, even if it does make one of the most interesting metropolises in the world one of the most repulsive to look at.

Conditions in Iztapalapa are visibly worse than Tepito. Wandering past houses with address numbers spray painted on the sides of their cinder-block walls, I find windowless buildings and shards of beer bottles on sidewalks where children are playing. The filthiest little white dog I've ever seen comes scrounging for a handout. His curly coat of matted hair is literally the color of diesel exhaust—a dog so dirty he wouldn't even lick his own balls.

Every house or business with something to protect is surrounded by razor wire and salivating Rottweilers, though there are few enough that are so lucky. An estimated 62 percent of *chilangos* live in poverty. Of these, 15 percent are considered "extremely poor," a stat I might not have believed had I not seen Iztapalapa, which seems to go on forever. I spend four hours walking and probably don't see a tenth of the place. As in Tepito, no one bothers me, though one Mexican tells me later, "Everybody left you alone because they saw those sunglasses and assumed you were a drug dealer."

I walk until my arches throb—don't let the kayakers

and rock climbers of the world kid you; being a city tourist takes just as much out of you—finally winding up at sunset on the outer fringe of this outer-fringe neighborhood. From an overpass above the Boulevard Trabajadores Sociales, I look down on six lanes of stalled traffic. Two acres of dirt field abutting the road are overrun by a makeshift slum. Rows of one-room dwellings made of scrap wood and corrugated sheet metal list like boats on rough seas, the houses of the defeated and dispossessed as opposed to the merely poor, a colony of piecemeal shacks whose common walls lean against one another for support against the storm.

Iztapalapa is far enough from the city center to provide a panoramic view of the high mountains that form the natural bowl in which the ancient city was founded. From the elevated vantage point of the overpass, I get my first true sense of Mexico City's vast reach. The air feels thick and dirty here. Factories and warehouses are the only discernible landmarks. Below me, like the tail of a poisonous snake, an endless line of red taillights serpentines away from the hazy outline of the pulsing glob of a city that, from this distance, from this height, from this remove, you couldn't blame anyone for not wanting any part of.

PART IV

CALAMITY
Walt Disney World

10

. . .

To Sneer or Not to Sneer?

It would seem the worst is over. With three monsters met and wrestled to at least a standstill, I know that whatever challenges may await in Central Florida, they won't include twelve-hour flights next to inconsiderate wailing infants, exotic bacteria, civil wars between sworn ethnic enemies, territorial autorickshaw drivers, rampaging narcotics traffickers, or murderous political factions. For one thing, the next major U.S. election is still a ways off.

For what Orlando's Walt Disney World might lack in physical adversity, however, it demands by far the greatest psychological effort of all my supposed hardship destinations. Despite the anxiety I'd felt about Africa, India, and Mexico City, preparations for each of those trips had been infused with the type of nervous excitement that comes before a blind date—while experience might tell you that the whole idea is a setup for disaster, in some corner of your soul an inexhaustible flame of optimism flickers with the understanding that beautiful things often come only after giant leaps of faith. As the departure dates had drawn nearer, I'd been able to channel my dread effectively enough to bury my nose in guidebooks, Web sites, and history texts. Like Sarah Palin cramming for a debate, I'd cheerfully filled the little cashew between my ears with as much information as it would hold on short notice about places I knew almost nothing about.

Nothing like this happens before Disney. No burst of ephemeral curiosity to know all things Magic Kingdom sinks its jaws into my frontal lobe and refuses to let go. No grand philosophical breakthroughs or halfheartedly culled Internet factoids—Walt Disney was an alleged FBI spy in the forties; the story that he was cryogenically frozen is an urban myth—fire my synapses.

The logistical hassle of visiting a "park" roughly the size of Honolulu is crippling enough for the average traveler to contemplate, but it's the cultural dominance of Disney's superficial piffle that has inspired a much wider sense of brand aversion and made me personally reluctant to embrace the putative world treasure known to boosters as The Happiest Place on Earth. Neal Gabler, whose doorstop bio *Walt Disney* is probably the most measured and readable account of the man and his legacy, sums up the case against "Disneyfication" as well as anyone. Disney was "a corporate vulgarian who coarsened the culture through commercialization and simplification," Gabler writes. His company's "faux environments and manipulated experiences would become a metaphor for a whole new consciousness in which . . . the fabricated was preferred over the authentic."

Gabler isn't by a long shot the only voice of dissent upon which the Disney basher can hang his rumpled mouse ears. The ballad "One God" from the outrageously undervalued catalog of The Beautiful South—defiantly British founders Paul Heaton and Dave Rotheray are probably the

best pop songwriters of the last twenty-five years—offers
the following incisive couplets:

> Thick lipstick on a five-year-old girl
> It makes you think it's a plastic world

> The world is turning Disney and there's nothing you can do
> You're trying to walk like giants, but you're wearing
>   Pluto's shoes

Thick lipstick, indeed. I know Britney Spears is an easy and passé reference, but as the machine that created her, Disney doesn't get enough blame for the direct line that can be drawn from the ex-queen of casserole country to the army of twelve-year-old slatterns her image has unleashed on the nation over the past decade. To say nothing of the subsequent celebration of such cultural touchstones as Ashlee Simpson's nose job nor the depressing fact that I can drop the wildly ingenious spelling of her first name without having to bother fact-checking it. Unlike most low-culture critics, by the way, I've actually lived in both a duplex and a trailer and can lay legitimate claim to my patented man-of-the-people routine—but, Christ Almighty, how did Americans let an obsession with chubby white trash make the leap from closing time at Joe's Tap into the mainstream?

The transformation of prepubescent girls into harbor trollops is, of course, an excellent reason to excoriate Disney, and there are plenty more; the most reprehensible from my perspective being the "Make Your Dreams Come True" sloganeering invoked like a profession of faith so ceaselessly across Disney's corporate dominion that its recipients no longer seem able to distinguish between crude salesmanship and old-fashioned greed. If "following your dream" and "reaching for the stars" involves a payoff, financial or otherwise, that's called ambition, not cockeyed optimism. The desire to become a movie star or a millionaire is not a dream. It's an economic aspiration.

Dreams are entirely different and recognized by the fact that 99.99 percent of them are impossible to attain. Becoming invisible. Meeting a mermaid. Winning the lottery. A three-way with Carrie Underwood and Sofia Coppola. (I know, weird, but she seems supercool.) Being a Christian nation and invading a Muslim one, then expecting its grateful citizens to shove flowers in the barrels of your tanks as you roll through the streets of their capital. These are dreams. Things that might make one happy to imagine in the lonely hours of the evening, but delusions that no one with an IQ over eighty should ever believe will actually come true. Though one should always be ready to accept calls from Underwood and Coppola.

As the tourist embodiment of "follow your dreams" perversions, I've long imagined WDW as a gigantic torture chamber of spoiled children and accommodating adults, long distances and obscene parking fees, "real" cartoon characters pestering "kids and kids at heart" for photos, two-hour lines spent bumping shoulders with the endomorphic masses for the privilege of being carted past talking pirate mannequins and faded displays of hooray-for-America sanctimony, strategically placed eating stations pushing reconstituted chicken lumps deep-fried in lard batter—in sum, a forced march through a puerile temple of consumerism dedicated to the epitomic scourge of twenty-first-century American culture: cartoons and comic books.*

* Bad enough to reach my sexually active years in the era of facial piercing, tramp stamps, and fake knockers without also having to live through an age in which Iron Man, Speed Racer, and the Incredible Hulk are momentous collective reference points, discussed and dissected in the pages of *The New Yorker*. And worse, after cannibalizing

Though he didn't start out that way, Walt Disney became, again according to Gabler, "the leading avatar of small-town, flag-waving America." Which leads to another reason I've avoided WDW like a rectal exam. Even though I grew up in small-town, flag-waving America, I've come around to the realization that the recent mouth-breathing stupidity of small-town, flag-waving America has soiled the country's reputation abroad, made possible the plunder of the public treasury for jingoistic corporate wars, and, worst of all, created a career for Ann Coulter. And, no, it doesn't make me un-American to have assiduously avoided setting foot in a fabricated dream patch plopped in the middle of a morally rudderless state of bogus elections with a half-baked citizenry who think absolutely nothing of supporting an idiotic fifty-year embargo of Cuba or taking the Camaro with the slave-days flag decals to the corner market for a pack of smokes without bothering to put their shirts on.

So, Disney.

Impregnable as the mental fortress surrounding my abiding distaste for Walt Disney World has traditionally been, I nevertheless find myself in a bind as my departure nears. On the one hand, Disney is such an easy target to slam that doing so feels like a cliché. What's the point of going someplace for a week if all you're planning to do is sneer at it? Misgivings aside, as a seed-spitting populist, I feel like it's wrong to look down my nose at an institution so warmly embraced by the masses. If that's all this exercise is going to be about, I can stay home and watch *Hannah Montana*.

---

pretty much the entire canon of sixties and seventies comic books, Hollywood still hasn't gotten around to making a Sgt. Rock movie. Note to studios: my treatment is ready!

In addition to the "to sneer or not to sneer" question, there's another issue to be resolved before I depart: to "do" Disney with or without children?

For most people, this dilemma probably seems like no issue at all. For most people, there's no reason to go to WDW *except* children. Walt himself envisioned his parks foremost as places parents and their miscreant spawn could enjoy together. (Because I was one for almost thirty years and because my taxes help pay for their underperforming schools, I'm perfectly entitled to complain about children.)

My position is clouded somewhat by the fact that although I have no children of my own I am orbited by a small and devoted cadre of nieces and nephews. Though each of them might be overjoyed by a WDW vacation under the temporary guardianship of their illustriously loose-with-a-buck uncle, none of them suits my immediate needs.

Already of legal drinking age, Erik and Chuck 2.0 both attended college in Daytona Beach, where they diligently honed career-enhancing beer pong and poker skills— experience that makes them superb company between 9 p.m. and 4 a.m., but unlikely participants in early-bird inspections of princess castles and stomach-churning thrill rides. Fall months mean freshman football for Dylan. Day-care stalwarts Carlitos and June are too young. Jacob is the usual seven-year-old handful. With five-year-old Grace currently in the midst of an appalling tiara and jewel-encrusted-scepter obsession, her duly enlightened mother would fillet me with a kitchen knife were I to push her daughter any further in the direction of Sleeping Beauty and Mulan. White Mischief lobbies like a pharmaceutical rep on Capitol Hill to ride along as my aide-de-camp and Disney guinea pig, but no cynic in the world is as unrepentant as a twelve-year-old hipster, the entire race of which comes equipped with an exquisite knack for detecting fakery. The last thing I need at Disney is his peanut gallery commentary competing with my own snide interior monologue.

Joyce turns the Disney trip down flat, even after I offer to pay for her ticket and throw in a week of doing the dishes with a "no complaining" clause to sweeten the deal. Central Florida is too much to ask, even for a veteran of rodent-infested, long-haul Indian trains and torture museums in medieval European cities (ask her sometime about anal pears). In the end, I'm left to confront Disney in a way I hadn't had the nerve to approach any of my other presumed Waterloos—alone.

Walt Disney World is comprised of four primary theme parks: Epcot, the Magic Kingdom, Disney's Hollywood Studios, and Disney's Animal Kingdom. The enormous grounds also include shopping and restaurant complexes such as Downtown Disney, a sports park, and more than twenty hotels anchored by the de trop Grand Floridian. Over the course of an autumn week—with more than seventeen million visitors a year there's really no slow period at WDW, but the *Zagat* guide assures me this is "the ideal time to visit"—I'll check out most of these areas, giving wide berth only to Disney's two water parks. I enjoy a good pool slide as much as the next perspiring northerner but I already feel creepy enough prowling around the premises as an unaccompanied adult male without getting half-naked next to a strange nine-year-old on the Slush Gusher or exchanging notes with peeing preschoolers on the Downhill Double Dipper while pulling a clingy swimsuit away from my crotch.

Though nothing close to exhaustive—whole books can and have been written exclusively about WDW—the more or less chronological observations that follow represent the eleven defining points in my face-off with the behemoth that's referred to locally as "The Mouse" or, by the less enamored, "The Rat."

Epcot

An acronym for the Experimental Prototype Community of Tomorrow, Walt Disney intended Epcot as the crowning gem in his everlasting legacy. Although the days are long gone when American concerns like GE and Monsanto blazed the scientific trail to the future—thanks to the canny American business practice of outsourcing most of its workforce overseas and government regulations that discourage college enrollment and private innovation, that sort of thing most often happens in other countries now—the Epcot aspect of the Disney experience is supposed to remind children that the future will be crafted in corporate R & D labs and that science is good for them.

The predictable response to this quaint idea is visible on the faces of the miserable minors whose parents insist on hauling them through Every Pouting Child's Obligatory Trial. "Attractions" like The Kodak 'What If' Labs do not answer the question, "What if Kodak management had foreseen the digital camera revolution and also not moved a ton of production jobs to China and Mexico?" Behind the Seeds at Epcot offers scintillating views of such wonders as oversized pumpkins grown in hydroponic trays, which children are required to appreciate before they can get to the rides.

Epcot's primary appeal for adults turns out not to be a glimpse of a glorious future, but a portal in time to America's glorious past. Once inside the timeship, it takes only a moment to deduce the staggering differences between Disney's back-to-the-future chutzpah and the reality of contemporary America. At Epcot, as in the rest of WDW, everything works. Everything is clean. Every employee is cheerful, competent, adequately trained, and intelligent enough to answer spontaneous questions from customers. No wonder the Japanese like Disney so much—it's just like home, except without quite so many Japanese.

Moreover, this reassuring sense of a properly functioning society puts everyone in a civic mood. It's not just the employees—in the sway of the park's old-timey, here-to-please ambience, visitors drop their don't-fuck-with-me Darwinian veneers and become supernaturally affable with one another. I haven't come to be convinced of anything, but my irresistible initial impression of WDW is how agreeable the whole place is. Life is well ordered here. Or, at the very least, well signed.

Contrast this with my arrival at Orlando International Airport the previous night. Following a cross-country flight in a seat that wouldn't recline, with a cabin crew that patrolled the aisles like North Korean border guards, ramming their haunches into the shoulders of aisle passengers without pause or apology, I'd gamely followed a disorienting array of signs that obliquely suggested a route to my car rental company's premier-customer lot. These led me on a circuitous path from the concourse to a parking structure to a locked door to an elevator and back to the concourse.

At twelve thirty in the morning, defeated as a navigator, I staggered to the car company desk inside the terminal to ask directions. I knew before the morose counter agent opened her mouth that she wasn't going to be any help.

"I can't find the express check-in lot," I said.

"Sign's behind you," the agent grunted, barely looking at me.

"Yes, uh, well, I've followed that sign twice and haven't had any luck. It leads to a locked door."

"Take the elevator up to the second floor," she said, reciting the instruction on the sign behind me.

"I've done that. Twice. But you exit the elevator to find a locked door. There's nowhere to go once you're up there except back down here."

Finally, a fellow customer broke the gridlock by stepping forward and explaining, "You have to take the elevator down to B1."

"But the sign . . ."

"I know, the sign says go to the second floor. But after midnight they lock the doors and the only access to the car level is through B1. Take the elevator *down* and you'll find a long concourse that runs beneath the parking structure. At the end you come to a stairwell. Walk up two flights and you'll see the rental cars."

The adventure wasn't over. After a long walk and a short wait at the "valued-customer" desk, I received the keys to a car with garbage left in the back seat and an odor that strongly suggested the lot boys had been blazing up inside twenty minutes earlier. I can't say for certain this actually happened, but having worked after high school as an airport reservation agent for a well-known national car rental company in Juneau, Alaska, I speak to this last accusation with some authority.

I can handle a little adversity on the road, and I understand that people working at the Orlando airport at 12:30 on a Saturday night probably don't have a lot of options in the workplace. We have a failing public education system, and these are the consequences. The reason I didn't blow up or lose my head while being assaulted with a beverage cart or given bovine stares of incomprehension at the rental counter is that I've been through these battles before and, like the marines at Chosin, I know the temperature keeps dropping in this war and the enemy never stops coming. All this to say, in contrast to the world outside its gates, Disney World is already feeling like some kind of dreamscape.

Soarin'

One of the most popular WDW attractions, Soarin' is a motion simulator in which riders are strapped into seats suspended in front of an IMAX screen, then tickled with wind and scent machines to create the illusion of a four-minute "hang glider" tour over California—Yosemite, Napa Valley, Mojave Desert, and so on. The advertisements of Soarin's superrealism are the first things that get me genuinely excited about something at WDW.

The helpful signs outside the Soarin' auditorium report a mere thirty-minute wait—guidebooks warn of ninety-minute torments—so I drop into line as soon as I finish a ho-hum "brave new world" tour of the industrial exhibitions inside Innoventions East and West. Despite the slow shuffle inside, I'm kept distracted by the apparel badinage of fellow visitors. The words "You Wish" are splayed across the ass of the cheek-lifting short shorts on the thirteen-year-old (maybe) girl in front of me. For twenty minutes I follow "You Wish" as we snake through the cattle chutes, passing a pair of women in their twenties whose identical T-shirts bear the message:

In Loving Memory of Jonathan Daniel Davis
· 4/17/72 ♥ 07/03/08

The front of the shirts display the stately legend: CAN-CER BLOWS!

When I eventually reach the ride itself, even the four sets of dangling shoes in front of me and the chatty kids from Georgia in my glider who can't stop arguing about the next ride they want to go on don't dim my assessment of the highly impressive Soarin', which is as close an approximation of the universal dream of independent flight as I've ever encountered. I don't exactly succumb to the belief that I am indeed a carefree golden eagle on holiday while swooping at treetop level over kayakers barreling through redwood forest white water, but of all the attractions at WDW, Soarin' is the one I wish I'd waited in line to do a second or third time.

World Showcase

In Epcot's signature World Showcase, architectural landmarks from countries around the world are re-created in "pavilions" for the extant purpose of housing restaurants and gift shops. The country choices are safe and obvious. Nothing against Mexico, Italy, and China, but who doesn't already have an idea of what they'll find in those pavilions? What about Suriname or Uzbekistan or Burkina Faso? I'd have more of an interest in finding out about those places than chowing on a $7 crepe in fake France. Though it was a damn good crepe.

In the Disney tradition, there are some improvements
over the real thing. I can't complain about the lack of fiduciary authenticity in Norwayland, where you can get a beer for $6.50 as opposed to about $92 in the real country (which, incidentally, is why I hightailed it out of Trondheim after three of the most expensive days of my life). Little Morocco might have the world's only Arab market. not plagued by thieving Arab shopkeepers, which explains how I escaped the place without being dragooned into a single purchase.

Ten foreign countries are represented in the Showcase, eleven if you count the United States, which is foreign to a fair number of visitors. Thinking about the United States in this context offers some useful insight into one of Disney's most important markets: foreigners. Imagine traveling to a country—Denmark, New Zealand, Malaysia, wherever—and stumbling upon a cultural expression as colossal as WDW. You wouldn't approach it simply as a place to take the kids on rides and interact with show-offs in animal costumes. You'd experience the whole conglomeration as a grand, summarizing statement on the national character. Wouldn't you?

I start looking at all the Mexicans and Venezuelans and Taiwanese and Russians wandering around the park and wondering what assumptions they're making about the United States based on WDW's unreal sprawl of swampland acreage. The boorish patriotism that pervades so many attractions. The infantile politics. The outrageous markup on Nemo plush toys stitched together by villagers in Indochina.

As a side note, foreigners—whether paying customers or employees—are referred to as "internationals" in company lingo. Walking by a place called the Candy Cauldron at the Downtown Disney Marketplace, an employee tells me offhandedly, "That's where we put all the internationals. They're miserable slaving over candy all day." Indeed, a young Asian woman with an exploited Cinderella look on her face is stirring fudge in front of a picture window. "Internationals" are also widely disliked by WDW waiters for being notoriously lousy tippers.

I try to get a flavor of limey life at the UK Pavilion with a pint of ale. Across the street, four guys dressed like John, Paul, George, and Ringo breeze through Nehru jacket–era versions of "We Can Work It Out" and "Drive My Car." Incredibly, the two crew-cut guys in their early twenties drinking Bass next to me aren't just actual Brits; they're Brits who look like extras in a Guy Ritchie movie about Manchester bookies. I try to raise a discussion of the implications of the World Pavilion and this peculiar representation of both of our countries, but they've seen crude facsimile before—most notably, at home.

"They have this shit for tourists in London," Ronnie tells me, gesturing at pub surroundings that don't look like anything seen by real British drinkers since Flo was giving Andy Capp what for down at the local after-hours.

Ronnie and Joe are thoughtful enough guys but their interest in geopolitical analysis pretty much starts and stops with "George Bush was a right twat, but he wasn't much worse than the lot we're stuck with." The boys have more immediate concerns. Ronnie and Joe love the Florida weather but mostly they're here for the rides. They give Space Mountain a five out of ten, telling me that for genuine fright you don't come to Disney.

"With all the kids and grandparents around, the thrill rides aren't all that thrilling," Ronnie says, observing that nearby competing amusement parks such as Universal Studios are more inclined toward the idea that petrifying the audience is the prime objective.

"Although the Aerosmith roller coaster [at Disney's Hollywood Studios] gives you a pretty good blastoff to start," Joe adds helpfully.

O Canada!

Anyone who's read my stuff before knows that I love our mighty neighbor to the east (assuming you have an Alaska-centric view of the world). If you haven't been to the Maritime provinces or Montreal or Quebec or Toronto or the Canadian Rockies or British Columbia or the Yukon, you really need to revise your travel wish list. This does not alter the fact that O Canada!—part of the Canada Pavilion, which also includes totem poles and a mini-Butchart Gardens—is the biggest bust in the entire wonderful world of Disney.

Lured by the complete absence of a line—a bigger tell here than an empty dining room on a Friday night in Mexico City, as it turns out—I file in for what turns out to be an eighteen-minute film hosted by Martin Short, the least funny person in Canadian or *Saturday Night Live* history, including Tracy Morgan. O Canada! is a deadly morass of classic Shortian unfunniness meandering through a script torn from the pages of an in-flight magazine "special advertising section" and set to images lifted from a 1970s Great White North filmstrip primer on polar bears and industrial harvesting. The only dream this tired sled dog inspires in me is an intense desire to bail out of the theater early.

I don't forgive Canada for all its sins—poutine, those passive-aggressive "We're not American" flags on the backpacks, and the *Oh What a Feeling: A Vital Collection of Canadian Music* four-disc set commemorating the 25th Juno Awards, featuring the *vital* Anne Murray, Glass Tiger,

Céline Dion, Loverboy, April Wine, Corey Hart, and Dan "Sometimes When We Touch" Hill. But the largest country in North America deserves better than this sad excuse for an attraction. On the subject of shoddy representations of Canada, I get the tip of the hat to the pineapple, but shouldn't the name of the "Hawaiian" pizza reflect the contribution of *both* toppings? Like a "salty dog" or "Cleveland steamer," why isn't this immortal après-softball combo dubbed the "Snowy Luau" or the "Hockey Brah"? There's no end of issues to take up on behalf of Canada.

The American Adventure

Hosted by an amiable pair of animatronic robots representing Ben Franklin and Mark Twain, who banter and rib each other like Trapper John and Hawkeye, this half-hour review of U.S. history is embarrassing for its sixth-grade-textbook exclusion of Indian genocide, atomic bombs, Vietnam, and the naked perfidy of the BCS college bowl system. I'm no liberal scold—I hate that revisionist lefty wingdings have made pinko philosophy a pillar of our once grand education system by systematically shitting on the founding giants who built this country—but, c'mon, facts is facts and propaganda is propaganda. Then again, I suppose cultural mythmaking is a duty of the modern state, and presenting the American story as a bowl of cherries for kids has a certain logic. Patriotic legends might as well be commuted to the young and impressionable. What else is college good for if not to learn that everything your parents believe is a lie?

The problem really isn't the truckloads of crap the American Adventure delivers. When you're pushing Exxon, you don't show pictures of dead seals on the beach covered in oil, and when you're trying to keep the family together, you don't talk about mommy and daddy's counseling-session blowup at the dinner table. What gets me is using Mark Twain to shovel it out (who himself wryly noted in *The Innocents Abroad* that "they picture no French defeats in the battle-galleries of Versailles"), a soul as subversive and discontented and angry about blind patriotism as anyone who didn't live through Watergate, Iran-Contra, Florida 2000, and Ohio 2004 could be. You want to pull one over on the kids, fine. But don't mangle the legacy of the greatest malcontent of letters we've ever had by posthumously getting him to do your dirty work.

The Hall of Presidents

In the Magic Kingdom—for fellow Disney-phobes, this is the park with the castle and perpetual fireworks at the entrance—the Hall of Presidents show is, like the American Adventure, both rousing and awkward. The lineup of forty-three animatronic presidents is impressive, though slightly undermined by the front and center position still maintained by George W. Bush—Barack wasn't ready yet at my viewing. Derisive snickers ripple through the theater when the smirking chimp starts talking about peace and liberty, then makes an allusion to the shockingly bogus "No Child Left Behind" tragedy, reminding all in attendance of his administration's twin calling cards of duplicity and incompetence. For a second, I think the Mexican guy to my right is going to leap from his chair shouting, "Death to Zhorjboosh!" But the cynics maintain a respectful silence—perhaps, like me, impressed that the robotic Bush comes off as a more fluid and natural public speaker than the original.

As with a number of presentations at WDW, the Hall of Presidents begs a question that, months later, still bothers me: Why do people applaud at the end of shows featuring animatronic actors?

Pirates of the Caribbean

Though the popular ride long predates the recent movie franchise, it's impossible not to notice that this undisputed classic has been transformed into a live-action game of "Where's Johnny Depp?" As the snug "Pirates" toboggans float through a faux Carib waterway, the delightfully eccentric actor's likeness in the role of Captain Jack Sparrow pops up around every third bend. Judging from the number of pictures taken in flagrant violation of the "no flash photography" rule, these fleeting cameos represent the high points of the ride for more than a few enthusiastic passengers.

"Pirates" has been a Disney staple since 1967, but I wonder how memorable the current commercial incarnation will be for kids who are already geared up by the movie for most of the imagery on display here, and, more importantly, in the gift shop at the end of the line. Like so much of Disney, the ride seems to be more about affirmation than surprise. Expectations are met. Just as they do at the Museum of Modern Art or casino buffets, people move between stations more or less satisfied, but hardly ebullient.

In spite of all the gainsaying, "Pirates" is nevertheless the most intriguing attraction at WDW for its presentation of a land and lifestyle that, the commercially redeemed Captain Sparrow aside, is so patently un-Disney. Cartoonish or not, what you find here is a dystopian world of debauchery, filth, and vermin; a place where drunks lie

in gutters jeering at passersby, white "wenches" with
heaving bosoms are sold as slave brides, and illiterate
thieves and con men are celebrated as picaresque heroes.
When you consider the purity of everything else Disney
promotes, it's an astonishing departure; although, in light
of the day's keynote speaker in the Hall of Presidents,
perhaps not so inconsistent after all.

Adventureland Enchanted Tiki Room/
Toontown Hall of Fame Tent

The tiki room isn't exactly the living definition of "en-
chanted." I mention it only as tribute to the unhorsed
father standing outside the entrance who delivered to his
wife and daughter the best critique of any attraction I
heard all week: "Don't bother with that one. It's just a
bunch of plastic birds that sing."

This casual dismissal of yet another guidebook starred
attraction points me back to my original question of whose
dreams exactly are being serviced here? I've vowed to approach Disney on its own terms, but whatever dreams are
coming true at WDW, they certainly aren't mine nor
evidently those of the flummoxed parents or weeping children pouring out of Mickey's Toontown Hall of Fame
Tent, where kids can have their photos taken with six-foot-
tall cartoon celebrities whose expressions are frozen in
manic glee. I haven't seen so much abject terror since the
first twenty minutes of *Saving Private Ryan*. Apparently,
schmoozing with grotesque caricatures doesn't come naturally to kids not yet socially conditioned by cocktail parties and meetings with people in HR.

Do today's media-saturated children really dream of
photo ops with top-heavy, silent stuffed animals? Of taking

part in walking parades through the hot park? And if so, how come I see so many eighty-pounders scrunched up in baby strollers?*

Space Mountain/Rock 'n' Roller Coaster Starring Aerosmith

The gimmick of these two mainstay roller coasters is that the bulk of the twisting, turning journey through the middle of the mountain—or the streets of LA, in the case of the latter, on the hilarious conceit that a headlining rock band is worried about arriving at a gig on time—is made in the dark. But not being able to see the asphalt falling away, hundreds of feet below you, actually makes both rides a lot less scary than conventional coasters. Ronnie and Joe's five-out-of-ten scoring feels about right; for an equally appropriate summation, I offer, in its entirety, the second-best review my own writing has ever received: Meh.

The best review, for those keeping score: "This book is so full of shit that the toilet overflows on page one." Who says literary critics are just failed writers?

Africa

No one's ever going to mistake a twenty-minute ride through Floridian "savannah" for the real thing, but on the whole, Disney's Animal Kingdom does a commendable job re-creating the African jeep safari, right down to the nattering twits who, despite explicit directions to re-

* My two favorite stroller observations: One: Seeing any child more than three years old or thirty-five pounds being pushed in a stroller. Two: If you use your baby stroller as a shopping cart at the store . . . for beer . . . while your baby is still in it . . . you might be a redneck.

main quiet and still in the presence of animals, can't help tittering and pointing and shouting and generally making baboons of themselves at the sight of any creature with stripes or the ability to eat grass. In the Animal Kingdom, wildlife is delivered on a platter, with plenty of healthy-looking giraffe, hippopotamus, elephant, lion, and even a massive white rhino making appearances.

During two weeks spent running around southern Africa, my safari group spotted precisely one rhino. For sitting on our asses and being driven in a truck to within thirty yards of the formidable herbivore, we were congratulated repeatedly by Tebo and other guides, who can go years between sightings of the great armored beasts. In Disney "Africa," the rhino encounter is essentially the same as it was in Africa Africa. While guests are assured they're in the midst of a magical moment of interspecies communion, the poor, endangered brute just stands there looking tired and sad, plainly uncomfortable and dimly aware of the staged nature of the interaction. Awesome, but also sort of big and stupid.

The high point of "Africa" is the silverback gorillas. As with the Taj Mahal, you've heard about the grandeur but you still aren't prepared for such a commanding presence. I've seen grizzlies in the wild from pants-pissing range, but even from behind a fence the gorillas' occult glares are every bit as heart-stopping.

During the Kinshasa confinement, Henri, Team Congo, and the bungling moron Jacques had supposedly spent time trying to arrange a gorilla expedition for me in North Kivu. With civil war raging in the great apes region, however, I have my doubts that their behind-the-scenes efforts were overly sincere—nobody seemed all that disappointed to inform me there were no available flights to Kivu. So seeing the gorillas in WDW feels like closing the circle a little bit.

Miley Cyrus

One of my early ideas for spicing up my descent into the Disney simulacrum was to immerse myself completely in the brand, ideology, and demagoguery by spending all available hours outside the physical domain of company property exposing myself to a nonstop stream of Disney Channel programming, back-catalog movies, and cartoon marketing vehicles. However, I only get four minutes and nine seconds into this bit of stunt journalism before realizing that a) I've always hated the obviousness of chary schtickmeisters like Morgan Spurlock and b) I dislike child extroverts even more today than I disliked them in junior high. I don't need a week of exposure to beautiful little full of themselves Keanu Reeves look-alikes flirting nonstop with tightly corseted fourteen-year-old crotch benders ("You Wish!") to know that I'd rather spend a week locked in a room watching *Murder, She Wrote* reruns.

I alluded to Miley Cyrus earlier because as of this writing the tween-teen sprite remains the indisputable face of Disney, a logical but vastly more far-reaching extension of the Britney Effect. As with her troubled predecessor, there have already been disquieting indications that the *Hannah Montana* star will not occupy this high-pressure position much longer—a public flap over a lurid *Vanity Fair* cover shoot; a twenty-year-old boyfriend; a tricky leap into feature films; a dues-paying setback in the Golden Globes Best Song category in which she was nevertheless included in the serious-artist company of Clint Eastwood and Bruce Springsteen. (Easing the collective minds of those fearing an unalterable shift in pop music tectonics, the Boss prevailed with another mumbling slice of Americana about scarecrows and one-legged dogs from the film *The Wrestler* but turned out to have more in common with *Hannah Montana* than his fans would care to acknowledge when he closed his Super Bowl halftime set a few weeks later with the peppy Cyrusean exhortation: "I'm going to Disneyland!")

At the moment, anyway, Cyrus remains the Duchess of Disney* and, thus the target of slurs and vague disdain from people like me who admittedly have never seen her act, sing, or dance and frankly don't need to in order to know that she sucks, that we resent her employer for exploiting the sexuality of a kid young enough to wear lip gloss unironically, and still hold in contempt her horndog father for becoming a huge success on the back of a piece of line-dance twaddle called *Achy Breaky Heart* and a Kentucky waterfall—mullet, if you prefer—that required the sacrifice of at least three muskrats.

Inclined as I am to howl at the prevailing winds of pop culture, however, I occasionally find it necessary to reinforce the self-delusion that I didn't spend four years slogging through journalism school for no good reason. Trashing Disney's reigning strumpet sovereign without so much as an introduction to her body of work seems irresponsible even by my standards. Primed with a resurgent sense of professional integrity, I return to my puce and coral time-share outside the gates of the Kingdom, pound the last five Coors Lights in the fridge, and flop on the couch with the goal of subjecting myself to at least one full half hour—no breaks, not even for pissing—of *Hannah Montana*.

I know that to some I come off as the type who likes to stir the pot simply to get under people's skin, the kind of

* It's a vicious business and by the time you read this Cyrus may well have been forgotten, or at least replaced, by another Disney confection. Hilary Duff, anyone?

person who defends the indefensible and utters the unutterable simply to bolster a contrived reputation for social iconoclasm. This is patently untrue—not counting dead-and-buried flings with Panic! At the Disco and red Chuck Taylor high-tops, I stand by every crackpot belief, trend, and theory I've ever championed. In the wake of my one-man Miley viewing party, my critical integrity is important to emphasize because it takes less than fifteen minutes in front of the TV to turn me into her latest apostle.

Anyone who hasn't seen her program may consider the following claim feckless drivel designed to incite the cultural vanguard, but I mean it when I say: I really like Miley Cyrus. She's got talent. She's got spunk. She can act. Her music isn't exactly to my taste but neither is André Rieu's or Il Divo's and I don't hold that against them or my mother's CD shuffle.

Moreover, I'm impressed with her show. The supporting cast is likable. For a kid's program, it's loaded with humor, clever writing, and decent one-liners. It's a savvy showcase for a young actress in whom I can't help but see—Sacrilege alert!—a young Lucille Ball. Or at the very least the next Jennifer Aniston.

I know. I can't believe this either. I've publicly stood up for Robbie Williams, Dan Quayle, and clove cigarettes in the past, but this is beyond defense. Which is why I subject myself the following evening to round two of the Miley experiment. Ninety straight minutes. Hannah Fucking Montana. This time as sober as a pregnant Mormon.

If anything, the command performance only adds new layers of appreciation to my initial appraisal. The mildly subversive you-can't-tell-me-what-to-do subtext of *Hannah Montana* takes me by surprise. Where I expect to be bored silly by a punch-and-cookies role model of obedience and puppy-love virtue, I find instead an ambitious little materialistic tart with something of a bitchy streak, though an indisputably likable one with a vaudevillian sense of comic timing. Beyond catering to the rock-star fantasy harbored by every American kid since 1956, the running conflict that propels Miley's on-screen persona finally demonstrates to me that Disney really is in touch with the most powerful and universal childhood fantasy of all—to grow up. Right this minute. In this context, the *Vanity Fair* cover, sketchy boyfriend, and hussy-of-the-week wardrobe make perfect sense.

But the most shocking discovery of all? In the role of the protective father, Billy Ray Cyrus comes off pretty damn likable himself. Though to be honest I never really minded *Achy Breaky Heart* all that much.

While my hodgepodge odyssey has warmed me to the possibility of a more peaceful coexistence with The Mouse, I remain troubled by the idea of an all-powerful Disney media machine supplanting the ascending ambitions that once motivated this country with a sleepwalking commercial directive of made-in-China consumer wish fulfillment. To help sort out this gathering emotional conflict, I summon an audience with a man as close to the tightly guarded Disney dream-making combine as you can get without Pentagon-level security clearance.

Martin Millay is a burly, tattooed twenty-six-year-old from Pennsylvania who, if not a Disney lifer, is at least a blissful member of the cult. By his own admission. "Internally, we joke about the brainwashing," Martin confides within minutes of meeting me. "But you want the brainwashing. They train the shit out of you here and you like it."

Martin and I meet at an outdoor table in the Downtown Disney Marketplace just as extravagant fireworks are making their nightly appearance. Over beers, he reviews his Disney career, which he began as a reservation agent in the company's Florida call center. A business major with a knack for public relations and speaking in sound bites, Martin quickly moved out of grunt territory and into the marketing department, where he proved such a keen soldier that he was rewarded with a promotion vaulting him well ahead of all but a handful of peers.

"Inside Disney there's a logistical team called the 'Dream Squad,'" Martin explains. "This is an elite team that delivers prizes and basically solves any problem with guests. As a Dream Squad 'super greeter,' you wander the park with almost ultimate power. If there's a little girl crying and you want to grab a stuffed animal off a shelf and give it to her, you can. You can award a FastPass or gourmet meal to any family you want."

Random gifts handed to bummed-out guests are fine—the FastPasses, for instance, allow customers to skip ahead in lines—but what super greeters live for is the chance to bestow highly coveted prize packages on the unsuspecting. These include complimentary nights in Cinderella Castle and Grand Marshal Tours of every Disney park around the world—including Paris and Tokyo—valued at one hundred thousand dollars.

"I did Cinderella Castle twenty-two times during my time with the Dream Squad," Martin says. "My last week I gave away the Grand Marshal Tour. I felt like I was the one winning the prize. Literally, my knees got weak. The super greeter next to me started crying. I mean, you're literally giving someone one hundred thousand dollars.

"Only about a hundred people a year get to be on the Dream Squad. It's a hugely privileged position. These are the best people Disney has to offer. I took a huge pay cut to be on the squad."

"How much?"

"I was making about forty thousand. As a super greeter, I got nineteen thousand."

"Was it worth it?"

"Up to now, it's been the highlight of my professional life. People freak out. They cry; they faint; they pee themselves—the whole gamut. I got to do things for families in the true spirit of giving."

Martin is such a completely decent guy that it's hard to ask him the asshole questions I've come prepared with. But after a fifteen-minute spiel on the glories of spending a night in Cinderella's bedchamber (sans Cinderella), I slip off the mink gloves.

"I understand that it's better to give than receive," I tell him. "But giving away stuff is Marketing 101 for building a customer base. Every radio station and crack dealer in the country does the same thing."

"You're right. I once gave an eighty-nine-year-old lady a three-hundred-dollar gift while she sat waiting for her family to finish on the Tower of Terror. The business rationale of this is that you know the eighty-nine-year-old ain't coming back, but her family will be coming back forever."

"That sounds more like you're fulfilling Walt Disney's dream than the old lady's."

"The way we approach it, even if guests didn't realize it was their dream, at the end of the day they'll think it was."

"Does the overcommercialization bother you?"

"It can. We could sell anything with Mickey ears on it. We could take a shit and shape it into Mickey Mouse and sell it."

"All the Johnny Depp sightings cheapened Pirates of the Caribbean for me."

"A nine-year-old has no clue that the *Pirates of the Caribbean* movie wasn't the first time it's ever been done. To have anything make sense at Disney, you have to look through a nine-year-old's eyes. That's the target. It's old enough to know and young enough to not be cynical."

"Why does Disney want everybody to be nine forever?"

"The park is just a metaphor for a perfect world. A place where reality can cease to exist for a while."

"The social control freaks me out a little."

"It's very much the way support groups work. Everyone's here for a common purpose, so no one's going to look at you twice for being overly nice or stopping to pick up someone else's trash or wearing mouse ears. . . . You'd be surprised how compliant people get in this environment. Walt was in some cases almost a Marxist—he wanted everyone to be happy, but not to make the choice to be happy."

This last observation is eerily similar to one David Foster Wallace made about the Florida-based cruise ship industry in his landmark travel essay *A Supposedly Fun Thing I'll Never Do Again*: "The promise is not that you can experience great pleasure, but that you *will*. . . . That they'll micromanage every iota of every pleasure-option so that not even the dreadful corrosive action of your adult consciousness and agency and dread can fuck up your fun. . . . you will *have no choice* but to have a good time."

After all the Disney stroking, I assume Martin entertains Eisner-size dreams of company domination. But it turns out he's recently taken a job at the American Cancer Society, staying on with Disney part-time "just to stay involved with the company." Ironically, it was his experience on the Dream Squad that moved him away.

"As a super greeter, the most memorable . . . there

was . . . this sounds . . . there was a woman with stage-four breast cancer. She'd been battling it for three years. The family had decided to stop the treatment, let the Lord take His course.

"She was in the guest-relations office. They were getting a guest-assistance card, which puts her in the FastPass line. After some discussion, she volunteered the information about her condition. I met with the family. They were just these cool people from New York. They didn't ask for anything. The mom and dad were in their midthirties. They had two girls, seven and four. They had an older boy who'd gone to five weeks of baseball stadiums with the mom. The girls wanted to do Disney World.

"We hit it off. I spent a lot of time with them. We all went on the Tower of Terror together, then the Rock 'n' Roller Coaster. That sort of thing. A VIP tour of the park.

"The mom had a charm bracelet. We stopped in a jewelry store to get a charm for the day. She told me, 'I'm collecting charms of every place we go so that when I do pass, my kids will have this.' She grabbed a sorcerer's hat for $10. I went to the counter and picked out a $270 charm and gave it to her and she started bawling. We took the girls to Bibbidi Bobbidi Boutique for extreme princess makeovers. It's $170 per girl. No charge. I can't tell you how good it feels to give that away. They appreciated it so much.

"At the end of the day the mom said to me, 'For three years we have worried about what to do about our kids when I pass. You made it possible for me for one day not to worry.' I just start crying right there. We're both there crying and hugging."

Martin's eyes are puffing up. He's no fake. Neither am I. It's getting a little dusty at this table. Maybe lingering smoke from the fireworks. Either way, my eyes are itching, too.

"I'm still in touch with the family," he says. "They're the main reason I quit Disney and went to work at the American Cancer Society. The mom is now in remission. We have plans to meet up again this summer. Assuming all goes well."

Though it has fewer strip clubs and Gambler's Anonymous chapters, Walt Disney World has a lot in common with Las Vegas, in that both envelop their visitors in an overwhelming cocoon of synthetic control. Like the city of broken dreams and bad TV series, WDW is magnificent for forty-eight to seventy-two hours of sensory overload. Once the initial awe wears off, however, the law of diminishing returns kicks in with a fury. After a near week of Mickey, Miley, and Martin, I'm gasping for a change of scenery.

Orlando is famous for theme parks—there are eight major ones in addition to WDW—so in the interest of giving all of my Florida biases a full airing, I decide to take a day away from the Kingdom for a look at the competition. Universal Studios is by many accounts the most popular attraction in Orlando after WDW, with a reputedly higher caliber of rides than WDW and 444 acres of filming locations. Given that a bitter 1927 licensing feud between Universal and a young artist named Walt Disney led directly to the creation of Mickey Mouse and the Disney empire, it seems like a logical place to start.*

* For eighty years Universal clung to rights to the Disney-drawn Oswald the Lucky Rabbit before finally relinquishing them to the Walt Disney Company in 2006 in exchange for the release of sportscaster Al Michaels from his Disney/ABC contract. The "Do you believe in miracles?" icon calling Sunday Night Football games for NBC Universal is just one of many examples of Old Walt extending his cultural reach from beyond the grave.

The contrast between the two parks is clear from the moment I drive into the Universal lot and immediately get bogged down in traffic that zigzags for fifteen minutes through a dark indoor structure. It's utterly unlike the open, speedy drive through the Disney lot. The sheer size of WDW can paralyze visitors, but ample space for exploding car traffic and park growth was part of Disney's original brilliance. His secretive acquisition of a chunk of Central Florida twice the size of Manhattan—carried off without anybody knowing he was the buyer, most especially the city of St. Louis, which believed his multimillion-dollar enterprise was coming to their city—is a fascinating study of business subterfuge.

At Universal, I get in line at 10:48 a.m. to exchange a prepaid voucher for a park pass. A Hispanic family standing behind me starts in with the "inch ahead in line" game, first creeping up alongside, then sending one of their kids on an aggressive scouting mission a few paces in front of me. Calling on my hard-earned experience with lines in Africa, I maneuver in front of the bandannaed punk to block his baldfaced cut in line before the whole *familia* can pile through the breach.* A few feet away a rail-thin, tattoed blonde sits on the ground breastfeeding an infant while two other children sprawl at her feet on the concrete. By the time I fend off the *familia*, fail to avert my eyes from the sidewalk circus, and reach the ticket window, it's 11:05. Seventeen minutes have elapsed.

* Here's how Africans form lines. 1. Ignore the twenty or thirty people already in line. Proceed immediately to front of line and make loud demands for attention from harried clerk or official dealing with the five or ten other people engaged in step one. 2. Argue strenuously for several minutes before accepting defeat and proceeding to back of line. 3. Stand next to, never directly behind, the small group of people amassed at rear of the "line." 4. Spend next forty-five minutes shoving forward as many places as possible before resuming argument at front of line and threatening physical harm to newcomers engaged in step one.

At Disney, the voucher-to-ticket transaction took all of three minutes, including the wait in line.

After a week in the unremitting arms of Disney, I've begun to form a weird kind of loyalty. This is an unexpected development. Even the competitor's minor failings suggest a critical inferiority and I find myself on the lookout for any little thing to snipe at.

To be fair, from the twelve bucks for parking to the ominous biometrics fingerprint scan at the entrance to the life-size Dora the Explorer and Jimmy Neutron to the cups of frozen lemonade going for the approximate price of Chanel No. 5, the setup and crowd at Universal aren't all that different from WDW. But they're not quite the same, either. The Disney template—rides, shows, emphasis on concessions—has been copied by a number of would-be rivals, with varying degrees of success.

The lamest ride at Universal is Twister . . . Ride It Out, an unbelievable waste of time based on the unbelievable waste-of-time movie from 1996. Other than a few buckets of water and some cheesy "lightning," the dominant feature of this attraction is some ancient behind-the-scenes footage of Bill Paxton and Helen Hunt reliving with typical thespian pomposity the metaphysical experience of pretending to be scientists in a fake storm. That they allowed a woman in a wheelchair entry into the ride should have tipped me off to the actual level of thrill I was going to get inside.

On the other hand, the Spider-Man 3-D ride, with its combination of frenzied motion, 3-D film, and elaborate sets, capped by a virtual four-hundred-foot free fall, rips open my eyeballs to the wild applications of modern thrill-based technology. It's a close call, but Spidey 3-D gets the nod over Soarin' as the best four minutes in Orlando.

The most remarkable of Central Florida's inspired-by-Disney parks has to be the Holy Land Experience, a Biblical theme park operated by the Trinity Broadcasting Network that from the outside looks like a made-over Medieval Times restaurant. After Universal, I repair to this assumed repository of only-in-America surrealism, where an overly friendly young man claiming to be Paul the Apostle greets me at the gate dressed in a flowing robe of ancient Israel. Behind him, an old dude pretending to be Moses stands draped in a bedsheet holding plastic tablets into which are carved the Ten Commandments.

"Paul" wants to know if it's my first time in the park, then opens my guide and map and starts explaining the layout to me, like so many patrician church fucks in my past assuming that I can't read or figure things out for myself. Here again I have to remind myself of my promise to approach each destination on its own terms. This is southern Christianity, after all, so I guess literacy among the flock can't be taken for granted.

Evading Paul's entreaties, I soon find myself alongside a replica of the unfortunate Jonah trapped inside the surprisingly roomy belly of a whale. The story broadcast over well-worn speakers is a familiar one, though in the Holy Land version Jonah is accompanied on his penitential adventure by a wise oyster and goofball octopus sidekick. The latter speaks with a dipshit backwoods drawl, like an outcast from the Country Bear Jamboree. I don't recall either of these figures from the book of Jonah, but I suppose wisecracking invertebrates are no more implausible than a lot of the stuff in the Bible. In fulfillment of the scripture, Jonah escapes the great fish's digestive imperative in time to issue his famous admonition to the citizens of Nineveh to repent and don sackcloth or face an eternal lake of fire. Given that the ruins of Nineveh lie near modern Mosul, Iraq, we now know that Jonah wasn't just bullshitting around.

At the Jerusalem Street Market, I'm approached by Pastor Sandra, a lively, heavyset black woman in her sixties who introduces herself as one of the park's "prayer warriors." I ask what this means. Pastor Sandra explains that her job is to wander the grounds and pray for or with anyone who needs it—sort of the Holy Land equivalent of Martin the super greeter. Only with less access to $270 souvenirs and Bibbidi Bobbidi Judaic makeovers.

We talk a little politics—Barack, Bush, unborn babies— but Pastor Sandra keeps telling me I have to stop worrying about this world and just concern myself with Chuck and God's plan for him. This of course is classic fake-Christian dogma, which grants absolution for willful ignorance and unalloyed egotism—there are no bounds, no rules, just the Almighty and the almighty YOU. For some reason, though, I'm never as put off by evangelizing African Americans as I am by fervent whites. Something about their preaching seems less judgmental; or at least more rooted in actual oppression, which makes the clinging to guns and religion bit a little more understandable. Plus, their church music is way better.

I stick around for the sunset "Crucifixion and Resurrection" show, a gala event that begins with Roman centurions marching onto an outdoor stage, brandishing swords and threatening the audience of believers. It's a nice *Tony n' Tina's* effort, but for Roman thugs about to hammer the King of the Jews to a piece of lumber, it's pretty weak sauce. You see more convincing taunting by perturbed French Huguenots in *Monty Python and the Holy Grail*.

A bedraggled, bloodied Jesus appears at stage left dragging his cross and imploring, "Father, forgive them. They know not what they do." And after some halfhearted beating, "My God! My God! Why have you forsaken me?" With the exception of a sobbing woman in a middle row—fifty-fifty odds she's a plant—the audience doesn't seem particularly moved as the parade makes its infamous way up a mini-Golgotha. Competent dinner-theater pros sing dramatic songs, and the crucifixion is pulled off with more flair than you'd expect given the desultory nature of the rest of the park.

The final test—for me, not Christ—comes just as I'm leaving. I'm within sight of the turnstiles when Paul the Apostle beelines through the dispersing "Crucifixion" crowd to intercept me. Up close, I see he's got the opaque, meth-addict eyes of a lobotomized Eric Roberts. He clasps my hand and gets down to business.

"Do you know if you are going to heaven?" he asks.

I respond to this extremely forward pickup line by saying that it would be nice to think so but that I'm really not sure any of us know the answer to that question. Such low-level cynicism, of course, means nothing to a man who introduces himself to strangers as Paul the Apostle.

"I know for certain that I'm going to heaven," Paul says. "Can I tell you my personal story of salvation?"

Normally I have no patience for these sorts of look-at-me religious exhibitionists, about whom James Clavell was no doubt thinking when he wrote in *Shōgun*, "There's no fanatic like a converted fanatic." But just as it would have been senseless to go to Mexico City and not try the street food, it seems half-assed to venture to the Holy

Land Experience and not sample the complete menu of psychoses. "Fire away," I tell him.

Paul pukes out the familiar convert yawner of a dissolute former existence under the spell of booze, drugs, pornography, loose women, Lynyrd Skynyrd, and every other vice that makes life in Central Florida bearable. Eventually, of course, he hit rock bottom, whereupon God took him by the hand and showed him the Way.

Born-again Christianity is by far the most convincing argument we have attesting to the wicked power of drugs and alcohol. Talk to a few fake-Christian ciphers and it becomes obvious that liquor, coke, and smack are but mere gateways to the hard stuff of megachurch depravity. People with this addiction love nothing so much as their own well-rehearsed saga of decadence—always greatly exaggerated, especially the fucking of loose women these guys *all* make sure you know about—that always leads to their brain-dead salvation. No wonder religious conservatives defended Terry Schiavo's right to vegetate in perpetuity—it's what they're all striving for here on Earth.

I'm bored by addicts and recovery—it was almost impossible for me to make it past the half-hour mark of any episode of *Behind the Music*—and I'm perpetually angry with the hijackers of Christianity, so I have to interrupt Paul.

"Guys like you are the most self-centered conversationalists of all time," I say, as cordially as possible. "You're a fraud who knows nothing of Christian doctrine."

"I never brought up doctrine," Paul whines. "You don't have to go to church or observe a bunch of rules to be a Christian. All you have to do is let God into your heart."

"That's not even close to being true," I say. "There are plenty of rules. It takes a big commitment to be a proper

Christian. There's a code of behavior that has to do with selflessness and charity."

During the entire three and a half hours I've been in the park, not one performer, attraction, or preacher has mentioned anything about traditional Christian values. Not a single word about aiding the poor, comforting the sick, rejecting violence, or embracing personal sacrifice. No one says, "Whatsover you do to the least of my brothers, that you do unto me." Not even peripherally do you hear reference to the humbling Ash Wednesday reminder that from dust we come and to dust we shall return.

What the keepers of the Holy Land Experience do talk about—exclusively, fanatically, without pause—is themselves. Their story. Their relationship with God. That's it. Nothing more. That one thing justifies everything else, as though nothing else is required of the believer beyond a singular devotion to the self and an imagined connection to Greatness.

I disengage from Paul the Apostle by telling him that he's been led astray by dark forces, that there's still time for him to repent, that he's certainly on the path to hell, but that Jesus still loves him and that I'll pray for his soul to be spared damnation. This is more or less the closing argument I've been on the receiving end of in debates with born agains around the world, and after a week of Disney pleasantries, it feels good to turn the tables and vent a little.

Paul and I part with an awkward handshake. I try to give him the traditional priest-greeting-the-congregation two-hand clutch to solidify my old-school church cred, but his hand is a dead fish. Paul does not, as Pastor Sandra and several others have, ask to exchange e-mail addresses.

The night out with Martin and detours to Universal Studios and the Holy Land Experience have been useful in my pursuit of perspective and enlightenment, but I'd already grasped that WDW and its staff are impressive in ways that places employing guys galloping around in the robes of old Judea are not. Although I've got a full day remaining in Orlando, there's really not much ground left to cover. Instead of trudging through Disney's Wide World of Sports Complex or doing princess recon for niece Grace at Cinderella's Happily Ever After Dinner at 1900 Park Fare, I spend my last day in Florida at the condo pool dodging kamikaze dragonflies and reflecting on my Disney experience.

For skeptics, one of the most interesting attractions at WDW is the Hollywood Studios gallery that houses Walt Disney: One Man's Dream. The walk-through exhibit, which culminates with a fifteen-minute film on Disney's life, isn't particularly objective, but it is informative. It's hard not to be impressed by Walt Disney, a man who built an empire without killing anybody, breaking a ton of laws, coercing labor from legions of unpaid coolies, or morally bankrupting himself or his followers. "America's uncle" was only sixty-five when he died. Poll the first fifty people who pass you on the street and their combined accomplishments probably won't come close to Disney's.

I can think of a number of ways to justify my qualified change of heart toward Disney, but the honest explanation is the simplest one—for the most part, I've enjoyed Walt Disney World. The place is organized, much easier to deal with than expected, and entertaining in its own way. In a world increasingly bereft of them, Disney runs a very tight ship. Saying so doesn't amount to an endorsement of the Disney value system, which I still find offputting. Dr. Bahr told me that in Africa I'd find all of humanity's foibles on display without pretense, but he forgot about poor taste, which though rare in Africa is the leitmotif in a lot of Disney. That said, throw a week of vacation, a reasonable budget, and a nine-year-old niece or nephew at me and I'd go back.

I'm not new enough to the travel game to believe that my limited view of Disney can't be refuted or that it necessarily sums up the median experience. And I'm definitely not trying to court "sell out" accusations from fellow flamethrowers. There are plenty of Disney horror stories out there; I know because I hear a number of them, most memorably in the Orlando airport from a mother, father, and fifteen-year-old son on their way home to Philadelphia.

"Twenty-seven dollars for the worst piece of meat I ever ate," grumbles the father.

"An hour and a half to get from the Grand Floridian to the Animal Kingdom," gripes the mother. "And using the Disney transportation system, no less."

"We're never coming back," adds the father.

Buried in his Game Boy, the kid doesn't have an opinion either way.

So much of travel depends on luck. After our first trip to Paris—one of those magical journeys in which the French treated us as though we'd arrived two steps ahead of Leclerc and Patton—Joyce and I sat in an Orly airport departure lounge next to a young American couple who were bitching about the asshole French and vowing never again to set foot in their repulsive, mean-spirited, vile excuse for a republic so long as they drew the sweet oxygen of American liberty. To say that I did not share their view is not to say that I didn't believe them. Just as Fenway Park is Fenway Park, Paris is Paris—the history and crumbling architecture are nice, but it's the crowd around you and the performance of the professionals in the field that will most determine the quality of your experience. All tourist destinations are unreliable because people are unreliable.

Just as I hadn't bothered to involve myself with the couple in Paris, I leave the Philadelphians after a few minutes. They have their Disney issues; I have mine. And however surprisingly palatable the experience has been, the truth is I'm not sorry to be going home. It's an enormous relief to be finished with the year of hellholes, even if, looking down from ten thousand feet as Orlando disappears behind me, I have to admit I'm not exactly Soarin'.

• • •

Epilogue

It's customary upon completion of surveys such as this one for the writer to step back and ask, "What have I learned?" In the wake of an easier and often more enjoyable time than I'd expected in the course of gauntlet tourism, I've come up with a handy checklist answer. This has also proven useful as a reply to queries from friends who want to express an interest in my life but who don't necessarily need to be regaled with long-winded tales of my derring-do:

Africa: Most Memorable
India: Most Exotic
Mexico City: Most Fun
Disney World: Most Congenial

Not a bad scorecard considering the general anxiety I carried into the project.

Larger lessons of travel, of course, take time to synthesize in the mind. Years can sometimes pass before the significance of certain journeys falls into proper perspective. That's a good line for travel writers to lay on the IRS about the two-week trip to Ireland they expensed and didn't write a word about, but it really does work that way. The human mind, deep and inclined to wander off course, doesn't always operate as fast or as linearly as a transoceanic jet.

As it so often does after extended travel, time wound up revealing to me as much about the place I kept coming back to as the places I spent the year confronting. It's supposed to be reassuring to find that people are more or less the same wherever you go, and it was indeed nice to confirm once again that wherever there are people, there's some degree of normalcy. Even in a war-torn bribe factory like the Congo, you can walk down the street and be relatively confident you're going to reach the end of the block without having your intestines extracted by teenagers and used to patch up a roadblock. Or have your Ray-Bans and Jansport stolen. (Both of those items made it home alive, by the way, though regarding intestines, I might as well admit that for six full weeks after returning from Africa I didn't take a normal dump.)

Still, I grew up believing that the United States occupies a special position in the world—the only nation in history founded upon an idea rather than a bellicose gene pool—one whose evolving (operative word) commitment to the common good makes it, if not always the greatest country in the world, at least the best one to come home to. As my catalog of international experiences stacked up against the Bush-Obama-Palin electoral circus and dissolving economic fortunes in the States, however, I began to realize that my travels had become less about surviving horrors abroad and more about facing up to ones at home.

When I lived next door to him in Japan in the 1990s, my friend Glasser used to say something that at the time struck me as the delusional rambling of a muddled Vietnam vet, high on justifiable rage and Shanghai Bob's expensive brandy.

"To the Japanese, the United States looks like a Third World country," Glasser would proclaim in a tone clearly meant to incite young patriots. "Homeless refugees everywhere. Beggars. Police. Garbage on the streets. Institutional incompetence. People dressed like hobos. Cars on the road that by Japanese standards would barely be fit for scrap metal."

Inured to Glasser's cranky booze-yard musings, I always laughed off his insistence that America could be lumped in with the Angolas and Sri Lankas of the world; when I returned to the States at the end of the year with the fresh eyes of an expat, though, I discovered that he hadn't been entirely wrong. In Japan, I'd gotten used to trains and buses that were run on time by friendly, courteous professionals. I'd grown accustomed to convenience stores and fast-food joints and car rental counters staffed—even at two in the morning—by helpful, well-trained employees. I'd learned to expect clean streets, vending machines that worked no matter how old they were, and a general public that dressed as though it was on its way to an important function, not as though it had recently been evicted.

I'm not saying that I'd rather live in Japan or any of the many other countries that operate at a higher day-to-day level of competence than the United States. I wouldn't. No matter what it looks like on the outside, every nation has big problems, and in the midst of America's bedlam, there's energy and vitality you simply don't find in more rigidly maintained societies. Plus, OK, universal health care and the practical pressboard furniture are nice, but who could take a lifetime of Scandinavian cuisine?

Nevertheless, over the past year I was reminded of those testy exchanges with Glasser as nagging recognition grew into grudging acceptance that the unattractive parallels between the United States and more blighted corners of Earth are more than superficial. And it wasn't just me. While I was drawing from the bitter wells of revelation in Africa, Asia, and Latin America, *Harper's Magazine* announced the arrival of "Third World U.S.A." Christopher Hitchens wrote a scathing and not altogether unconvincing story in *Vanity Fair* headlined "America the Banana Republic." A *Los Angeles Times* op-ed piece began, "Hey U.S., welcome to the Third World!" New York City mayor Michael Bloomberg echoed all of the "Third World country" comparisons in a rant about the profligacy of the federal government and ransacked national economy. These weren't simply knee-jerk reactions to the dramatic downturn of investment markets. Many such pronouncements long predated the collapse of the American housing market and banking system, as well as the devolution of the U.S. dollar into the world's leading brand of toilet paper.

If many of the international pitfalls that I'd feared at the start of the year didn't turn out to be all that tricky to negotiate (Henri in the Congo, Belu in India, and O Canada! aside) it's thanks largely to the broad exposure I'd already had to them at home: crumbling infrastructure; religious intolerance; tribal zealotry; epidemic poverty; substandard schools; municipal bankruptcy; crippling national debt; overwhelmed public resources; a government that at least half the population doesn't believe in; foreigners coming in packs to take advantage of an enfeebled currency; military adventurism; a toothless media; vendetta politics; soccer. While the rest of the world has been caterwauling over the insidious influence of American culture—from Pizza Hut to hip-hop to chocolate martinis, with which I regretfully report you can now embarrass yourself in Mexico City—the process has been working even faster in the other direction. If the rest of the world now behaves a lot like the United States, the United States is behaving even more like the rest of the world.*

This doesn't mean the rest of the world is a bad place. Just that the United States is a less special one. That's a loss for everyone.

The begging hordes of India, for example, didn't shock me the way they'd shocked American travelers of the 1950s, '60s, and '70s, who were understandably freaked out by the unfamiliar sight of visible destitution of India. Now you can't walk three blocks or pass a freeway off-ramp in a major American city without being accosted by some unfortunate fellow citizen for a donation. The situation is far worse in India, but the homeless and publicly drug addled are no longer exotic features limited to the more pitiable parts of the world. The same can be said for every other item on the sobering list on the previous page. Passing through this year of bribes, lies, corrupt officialdom, and wearyingly consistent disregard for the public trust, it emerged that the most alarming discovery on the road to some of the world's most dysfunctional places was that they weren't all that different from the place I'd started.

If there were a fundamental principle that once separated America from the rest of the world, I'd nominate institutional integrity. More simply, public honesty. I'm

* Paradoxically, the place that reminded me least of the United States was the one that's supposed to represent the country at its apogee: Walt Disney World.

not suggesting that dishonesty isn't readily found in every civilization, that a Golden Age of American honor ever existed, or that corruption hasn't been with us since Thomas Jefferson was up to his third knuckle in Sally Hemings. Nor am I parading myself as a paragon of virtue. We all lie, to some degree, usually in petty ways, for the sake of discretion or keeping the peace or perhaps on occasion simply because it's the most expedient means available to get what we want.

Still, lying and cheating—perhaps other than to avoid hurting someone's feelings—has never been openly accepted or condoned in the United States, much less celebrated as a "genius" operational tactic (when done with Rovian finesse) from the boardroom to the courtroom. At least, not until recently. While I was in Orlando enduring another sham of a staged political "debate" between the two pathologically dishonest halves of our singular ruling party, Gore Vidal was telling *Hustler* magazine: "Lying has now become a major art form (in America). . . . There is no lie that you can tell that you will ever be called on." Vidal is right, although no one who has stood by and watched eight-plus years of WMD excuses, Swift Boaters, Ken Blackwell, billion-dollar corporate welfare handouts, fudged promises to end wars, and every other manner of fraud be publicly applauded needs to be told this.

Much has been made of the corporate and political scandals that have marked America's passage from democracy to klepto-corporatocracy, and while, again, backroom handshakes between the country's gilded institutions are nothing new, they're being carried out at such rapacious and brazen levels nowadays as to attract the inevitable comparisons to the banana republics and Third World hellholes we once regarded as hopelessly backward. Worse, Americans seem to be reveling in the descent.

Talking about Indian politics, writer Suketu Mehta hit uncomfortably close to the vein when he told me: "For Indian voters it is of utmost importance only that their caste group gets elected; as long as this is accomplished they are willing to accept corruption."

American society is no accident; it didn't evolve by providential decree; its success wasn't inevitable. The protection of two oceans, boundless natural resources, and firebrand leadership didn't hurt, but if geographic barriers, mineral wealth, and religious righteousness were all it took to ensure a great society, the Congo, India, or Mexico could just as easily be running the planet. Americans have historically understood that to create a country in which half the world aspires to live, the first prerequisite is the integrity of its public and private institutions. That's the foundation upon which the country was assembled and its illustrious future once determined.

There's an evolving understanding in the United States that we're squandering our "God-given" natural wealth, that manifest destiny was one thing but mammon is another, and that our gluttonous consumption of resources must be curtailed. What's being overlooked in the rush to save the planet, however, is that we're also pissing away a social gift as great as any people in history have been bequeathed. And that if we don't resist the seduction of the seemingly inevitable road in front of us, it won't matter how much fossil fuel we stop burning, we'll fail to preserve the part of us that mattered most in the first place.

Then again, I never completely bought in to Glasser's pessimism and although I readily admit the American Dream is in significant ways looking more like a nightmare these days, it feels a little early in the game to concede that all is irrevocably lost and that the best we have to look forward to is the dollar turning into the peso. Months after the last stamp has been pounded into my passport, I find my mind returning often to the most harrowing episode of the past year—just nudging out the midnight autorickshaw ride to Rohet Garh—and realizing that even from the diciest of circumstances, it's possible to wring a few drops of optimism.

One evening in Botswana, about a week into my African safari, with the setting sun casting its palette of orange and purple splendor across the Okavango Delta, I decided to take a walk. A hiker by habit, it was odd for me to have been outdoors for a week and not gotten more than a few hundred yards away from the Land Rover.

I was also motivated by a desire to put as much distance between my fellow campers and myself as I could. It wasn't really the Europeans' fault; as I've already noted, while they were a largely anemic lot, they were all also decent, polite people. But I get antsy after extended time in the company of strangers, and I wanted to be alone. I wanted to experience "Africa." I was paying a lot of money for the safari and I felt entitled to a walk, the most natural human impulse outside of breathing, eating, and changing the channel whenever Nancy Grace comes on.

I'm no tenderfoot. I understood that trekking alone into the African wilderness is not like strolling around the block for cigarettes and a newspaper. Bush walks are fraught with implications and, on occasion, grave results. Although nobody had specifically told me not to venture out on my own, on safari, it's more or less understood that the haoles will have sense enough not to wander off at precisely the time of day when big-game animals come out to feed.

After camp chores were done—pit toilet dug, firewood

collected, water boiled—I wandered off for a leak behind my canvas dome tent and kept on going through the scrub brush, down the jeep road, and into the open grassland. Once the camp had receded from view, two thoughts entered my mind. First: I would be incredibly lucky if I were to happen upon a lion. Even though people come to the Moremi Game Reserve from around the world for precisely this purpose, lions are elusive creatures and there's never a guarantee of spotting one. Second: Assuming the improbable occurred and I did happen upon a lion, unarmed and beyond shouting range of our sure-handed, warrior-huntsman African guide Tebo, I'd be scared absolutely shitless.

I walked for thirty minutes with these twin ideas rattling in my head, mostly along a dirt path that veered from the jeep road, then into the untracked veldt. Though I didn't come across anything remarkable—no animal sightings, no marauding guinea worms—the walk was scenic, pleasant, and, best of all, serene. For half an hour I felt unreservedly at peace in Africa.

Then, as I emerged from a grove of sparsely foliated trees with the sun bidding farewell on the horizon behind me, I was stopped cold in my tracks by a magnificent scene. In a clearing thirty yards to my left, eight mature and three adolescent impala stood in a scattered formation nibbling at dry grass and branches.

The South Africans have an amusing term for these ubiquitous animals—JABI, or Just Another Bloody Impala. Elegant though they might be, the gentle, two-toned herbivores are to the African landscape as C-list celebrities are to the Sunset Strip. Upon first sighting, the out-of-towner goes slightly bonkers, admiring the familiar visage, stylish fur, supple physique, and decorative patterns accentuating the crotch and ass. By the twentieth or thirtieth encounter, the initial excitement begins to fade. After the hundredth, any obligation to pull out the camera disappears almost entirely. Soon, the glamorous creatures are passing within ten or fifteen feet without inspiring so much as a second look.

Deep in the bush, however, eleven impala feeding at range close enough to hit with a rock jolts the untethered Westerner into a Neolithic state of awareness. There had been no question in my mind that the Moremi Game Reserve was packed with delicious pickings from the food chain—sightings that very day had included elephant, giraffe, wildebeest, zebra, antelope, baboon, jackal, mongoose, and field mice. But the "theme park" atmosphere fostered by the tightly controlled safari—Walt Disney World really does get a lot of the details right—had lulled me into a false sense of security. Without the Land Rover's diesel chatter and background tourist blather, the impala's snorting and stamping and chewing and twitching were thrillingly audible. In less than a second, Africa had become real for me in a way it had not previously been. These were wild animals. I'd known as much watching wildlife from the safety of the vehicle; alone in a field next to them, I felt it.

Holding myself as still and silent as a frozen lake, I made mental pictures of the agile animals with their shiny coats of chestnut brown and white and the narrow black stripes around their tails and thighs. Alert to my presence, the impala remained mostly still themselves— here an ear flick, there a wary sideways glance—until one or two began munching tentatively again, satisfied that I posed no threat.

For ten minutes I watched the impala graze. Then the spiral-horned buck—a dominant male always leads his impala consorts and progeny—decided he'd had enough of my lurking. Flipping his hind legs behind his head in a breathtaking, gymnastic flash, he vaulted high into the air and vanished into the trees. The rest of the herd followed in a panic.

The flight of the impala signaled a flock of two or three hundred dun-colored birds to abandon hidden positions in the low grass and bolt en masse with a cacophony of squawks and communal flapping of wings that sounded like applause as it drifted into the darkening sky. Within seconds, the entire delta was alive with birds and animals calling out the alarm of an intruder.

Calling out danger. Calling out, of all things, vulnerable me.

Or maybe it wasn't me that spooked the impala. It was at this instant that I first considered the literal possibility of my throat clamped in the jaws of an overpowering predator. Mingling with other easy prey of the delta, I felt for the first time like an integral part of Africa's biological fabric. For those who have never been in the situation, it's strangely exhilarating to regard one's self as absolutely nothing more than a piece of fresh meat.

With the beating of my blood making tom-toms of my ears, I spun around in a furious 360-degree check of the surroundings. No stalking cats. No loitering hyenas. Nothing at all except a rustling wind that conjured a few factoids from Tebo's Land Rover commentary about impala not only having much keener vision and hearing than humans, but also scent glands on their foreheads. And then it occurred to me that dinner entrées in random clearings almost never see their attackers before it's too late, and that I hadn't told my mother I loved her before departing for Africa.

With that nervous inspiration, my not-as-finely-tuned-as-I'd-have-liked survival instinct finally turned me back toward camp. Double-time. Twenty minutes and a gallon of sweat later, with the nighttime sounds of the bush stirring to life around me, I skulked back into camp from the general direction of my tent, hoping to convey the impression to one and all that I'd simply been enjoying a well-deserved nap. Never have I been so relieved to see ruminative Europeans and a campfire.

No one said a word about my absence, so I assumed I'd pulled off my little solo safari undetected—until the following morning when, leaving camp for our daily game drive at the break of dawn, Thilo, the German translator, pointed to the ground from his seat in the front of the Land Rover.

"Human footprints leading away from camp!" the Teutonic Sherlock Holmes shouted in red-hot English. "Who could have made these tracks?"

Icy glares shot round the safari vehicle, as though there was really any question about whose size-eleven REI boot prints were clearly visible marching down the dirt road. A terrible accusatory silence followed. I've never had to face the media after my steroids test came back positive or my bathroom tryst in an international airport had been publicly betrayed by my gay prostitute-lover, but believe me you've never been marked for shame until a truckful of Germans have indicted you with the collective tonnage of their implied Aryan opprobrium.

"I guess it wasn't as windy last night as I thought," I cracked from the back row of the Land Rover in a cavalier fashion I hoped might leave a little wiggle room for plausible denial. When that didn't get any laughs, I went with halfhearted admission. "Those do look a lot like my shoe prints."

"As a reminder to all, it is strictly forbidden to walk alone away from the camp!" Thilo shouted loudly enough to be heard in Dachau.

Tension hung over the safari all day. In the afternoon, I found out why. Far from going unnoticed, my impromptu walkabout the night before had become camp scuttlebutt even before I'd stumbled upon my holy impala communion. I'd been foolish to underestimate Tebo, of course, a man who'd already demonstrated that he was capable of spotting scorpions hiding beneath logs in the pitch dark from twenty paces. He'd detected my absence from camp right away. The subsequent head count he conducted had created quite a stir, especially with Thilo, who'd apparently spent the entire night seething in his tent in anticipation of teaching me a lesson in German scorn.

The most interesting revelation, however, was that in the early morning after my now infamous walk, Tebo had followed my tracks all the way to the clearing where the impala had been. When he returned he told Thilo—who told one of the Germans who relayed the news to the group—that leading back in the direction of camp, my footprints had been shadowed step for step by a set of lion tracks.

It was the Italian couple who confided all of this to me, though only after swearing me to a silence that I've not broken until now. (Thompson Travel Rule Number One: even if they live thousands of miles away, don't take blood oaths with Italians lightly.) Apparently, there had been much unhappy camp discussion about my unauthorized foray into the bush. On the assumption that keeping a lid on conversation would stifle the spread of resentment, Tebo had issued a camp-wide gag order. I was to be allowed to go on believing that all was well, that the entire group wasn't on the verge of lynching my reckless, self-centered, rule-flaunting, dipshit, no-regard-for-consequences American ass.

Thus chastened and sworn to secrecy, I never felt comfortable enough to get confirmation of the story from

Tebo himself. I suppose it's possible that he added the lion-stalking detail for instructive emphasis, but Tebo was the straight-shooting type, and even if the addition of the prowling cat sounds a little theatrical, I have no reason to doubt the story's veracity. Not least because the following day we came across a pride of lions with bloated bellies, sleeping away the morning less than a mile from our camp.

Lion or not, public disgrace or not, the walk remains for me a far more elating than frightening or troubling memory. Yes, bad things were lurking out there, but I would have to have been damned lucky to find them. The numbers on disaster simply don't support paranoia, especially when compared to the exhilaration of exploration.

I'm pretty sure this is why Tebo didn't come after me as soon as he discovered that I'd cut away from the group, even though he could easily have caught up to me and hauled me back to camp. Professional that he was— and I've never met a man I'd feel more comfortable putting in charge of the rifles and hardtack—it's a fair bet that he was as bored with the herd as I was, as disenchanted by the predictability and complacency, and more than a little curious to find out how far a stranger might be willing to travel down a forbidding road with no idea what foreign terror might emerge along the way. Tebo wasn't stupid. But, like me, I'm certain he didn't see the point of being afraid, no matter how unpleasant the outside world might look from beside the illusory comfort of a flickering fire.

Acknowledgments

. . .

Mankind's fear of the unknown or foreign isn't exactly breaking news, but the phenomenon works in a peculiar way for travelers. Some years ago while traveling around the Philippine island of Mindanao—infamous center of Islamic unrest—I found myself repeatedly warned of nearby dangers from friendly, helpful locals.

"Our village is perfectly safe," they would tell me. "But you must not dare go to the village ten kilometers up the road. It is a very bad place. There are many criminals and murderers who will surely make you a target."

A visit the following day to the supposed death village up the road invariably produced the same exchange. "Our village is peaceful," I would be assured. "But the village ten kilometers down the road is filled with thieves, drug dealers, and murderers." I've spoken with travelers around the world who report the same experiences from Kamchatka to Brazil.

Because the elastic balance between trust and paranoia seems fundamental to human affairs, the first acknowledgment here goes to the anonymous hundreds who

ACKNOWLEDGMENTS

inadvertently contributed to this book by showing me both incredible generosity and a little home-fried mistrust during my travels.

Specific thanks are extended to Judy DeHaas for generously sharing her Africa contacts. Since leaving Africa, not a day has gone by that I haven't thought of the indubitable Tebo and eternal optimist Kap. I'm also grateful to Henri and Team Congo, despite it all.

Ajay Anand, Baiju Kuriakos, Suketu Mehta, Dr. P. V. Joseph, Dr. Akhilesh Gupta, and Patrick and Rani Thompson and kids are sincerely thanked for invaluable help prior to and during travel in India. Without Anjan Das and Laura Silverman, Joyce and I would probably still be sitting in a train station somewhere in Rajasthan wondering how the hell we were going to get to home, and I would have missed the two best people out of the millions in Bombay.

David Lida, Gabriel Chaparro Estrada, and the dauntless Shanghai Bob, Blackguard of the Orient, Man of Indiscreet Solutions, were invaluable in Mexico City. Roberto Orellana provided much-appreciated on-call Spanish translations. Marty McLennan and Ruth Mandujano deserve special recognition for everything from helping me choose the correct mole with chicken enchiladas to escorting me to soccer games to negotiating my scalped ticket (for face value, no less) to a sold-out Lila Downs concert.

Disney I did pretty much on my own, though Jon Wilde's insider contact was indispensable and that puce and coral time-share was obtained through the typically boundless generosity of my mother and Uncle Jim.

The line in the Africa section about two rats fucking in a wool sock was borrowed from, of all sources, Japanese baseball enigma Ichiro Suzuki. I don't know if it originated with him, but he's the one I first saw it attributed to. The always funny Sean Cunningham inadvertently directed me to the Apu quote on America's dangerous underpopulation. Thanks to smirkingchimp.com for that timeless Bush moniker, and to Jeff Foxworthy for my attempt at a "You might be a redneck" joke in the Disney chapter.

Continuing gratitude to the U.S. Department of Homeland Security and Citizenship and Immigration Services for steadfastly refusing to explain or resolve the red flag on my passport that gets me searched, questioned, detained, and nearly missing connecting flights every goddamn time I reenter the country.

I paid for all services and products received during travel for this book—specific references to restaurants, hotels, and other commercial establishments were included simply because I thought they enlivened the copy or deserved to be mentioned.

Thanks to Allan Lazo for ongoing Website aid.

The steady-handed support of my agent Joëlle Delbourgo made this book possible. Without Sarah Knight's enthusiasm and unfailing professionalism, it would never have gotten past page 1.

The keen eye and stalwart sensibility of Lindsay Ross saved me from myself on numerous occasions and made this a far better book than it ever would have been without her. Jason Liebman's Web and tech expertise have been invaluable. The support of Dan Farley, Marjorie Braman, Maggie Richards, Nicole Dewey, Theresa Giacopos, Ashley Pattison, Rita Quintas, Lisa Fyfe, Kelly Too, Christine Kopprasch, and everyone at Henry Holt has been consistently gratifying—if only the entire world operated with such consistently high standards.

Thanks and love as always to Mom, Mike, Carlene, and Amy.

ACKNOWLEDGMENTS

The one and only Joyce sacrificed a beach cabana for a tour of Thar Desert villages at the height of a punishing Indian summer. She nevertheless claims to have no regrets about hitching her wagon to mine. Needless to say, neither do I.

. . .

About the Author

CHUCK THOMPSON, the author of *Smile When You're Lying*, is a former features editor for *Maxim* and was the first editor in chief of *Travelocity* magazine. His writing and photography have appeared in *The Atlantic*, *Esquire*, *Outside*, *Men's Journal*, *National Geographic Adventure*, *Playboy*, *Spy*, *Escape*, *WWE Magazine*, MTV's *The Jenny McCarthy Show*, and the *Los Angeles Times*. He has traveled on assignment in more than fifty countries and is the author of two guidebooks, *The 25 Best World War II Sites: European Theater* and *Pacific Theater*. He's played in a variety of professional musical groups and worked as an ESL instructor, radio DJ, deckhand, and assistant sergeant at arms in the Alaska House of Representatives. He grew up in Juneau, Alaska, and lives in the Pacific Northwest.